D1132772

Web Operations: Keeping the Data on Time

Edited by John Allspaw and Jesse Robbins

O'REILLY®

Beijing · Cambridge · Farnham · Köln · Sebastopol · Tokyo

Web Operations: Keeping the Data on Time
Edited by John Allspaw and Jesse Robbins

Editor: Mike Loukides

Production Editor: Loranah Dimant

Copyeditor: Audrey Doyle

Production Services: Newgen, Inc.

Indexer: Jay Marchand

Cover Designer: Karen Montgomery

Interior Designer: Ron Bilodeau

Illustrator: Robert Romano

Printing History:

June 2010:   First Edition.

ISBN: 978-1-449-37744-1

[LSI]   [2011-05-27]

The contributors to this book have donated their payments to the 826 Foundation.

CONTENTS

Foreword

IT'S BEEN OVER A DECADE SINCE THE FIRST WEBSITES REACHED REAL SCALE.
We were there then, in those early days, watching our sites growing faster than anyone had seen before or knew how to manage. It was up to us figure out how to keep everything running, to make things happen, to get things done.

While everyone else was at the launch party, we were deep in the bowels of the datacenter racking and stacking the last servers. Then we sat at our desks late into the night, our faces lit with the glow of logfiles and graphs streaming by.

Our experiences were universal: Our software crashed or couldn't scale. The databases crashed and data was corrupted, while every server, disk, and switch failed in ways the manufacturer absolutely, positively said it wouldn't. Hackers attacked—first for fun and then for profit. And just when we got things working again, a new feature would be pushed out, traffic would spike, and everything would break all over again.

In the early days, we used what we could find because we had no budget. Then we grew from mismatched, scavenged machines hidden in closets to megawatt-scale datacenters spanning the globe filled with the cheapest machines we could find.

As we got to scale, we had to deal with the real world and its many dangers. Our datacenters caught fire, flooded, or were ripped apart by hurricanes. Our power failed. Generators didn't kick in—or started and then ran out of fuel—or were taken down when someone hit the Emergency Power Off. Cooling failed. Sprinklers leaked. Fiber was cut by backhoes and squirrels and strange creatures crawling along the seafloor.

Man, machine, and Mother Nature challenged us in every way imaginable and then surprised us in ways we never expected.

We worked from the instant our pagers woke us up or when a friend innocently inquired, "Is the site down?" or when the CEO called scared and furious. We were always the first ones to know it was down and the last to leave when it was back up again.

Always.

Every day we got a little smarter, a little wiser, and learned a few more tricks. The scripts we wrote a decade ago have matured into tools and languages of their own, and whole industries have emerged around what we do. The knowledge, experiences, tools, and processes are growing into an art we call Web Operations.

We say that Web Operations is an art, not a science, for a reason. There are no standards, certifications, or formal schooling (at least not yet). What we do takes a long time to learn and longer to master, and everyone at every skill level must find his or her own style. There's no "right way," only what works (for now) and a commitment to doing it even better next time.

The Web is changing the way we live and touches every person alive. As more and more people depend on the Web, they depend on us.

Web Operations is work that matters.

—Jesse Robbins

The contributors to this book have donated their payments to the 826 Foundation, which helps kids learn to love reading at places like the Superhero Supply Company, the Greenwood Space Travel Supply Company, and the Liberty Street Robot Supply & Repair Shop.

Preface

DESIGNING, BUILDING, AND MAINTAINING A GROWING WEBSITE has unique challenges when it comes to the fields of systems administration and software development. For one, the Web never sleeps. Because websites are globally used, there is no "good" time for changes, upgrades, or maintenance windows, only fewer "bad" times. This also means that outages are guaranteed to affect someone, somewhere using the site, no matter what time it is.

As web applications become an increasing part of our daily lives, they are also becoming more complex. With that complexity comes more parts to build and maintain and, unfortunately, more parts to fail. On top of that, there are requirements for being fast, secure, and always available across the planet. All these things add up to what's become a specialized field of engineering: web operations.

This book was conceived to gather insights into this still-evolving field from web veterans around the industry. Jesse Robbins and I came up with a list of tip-of-iceberg topics and asked these experts for their hard-earned advice and stories from the trenches.

How This Book Is Organized

The chapters in this book are organized as follows:

Chapter 1, *Web Operations: The Career* by Theo Schlossnagle, describes what this field actually encompasses and underscores how the skills needed are gained by experience and less about formal education.

Chapter 2, *How Picnik Uses Cloud Computing: Lessons Learned* by Justin Huff, explains how Picnik.com went about deploying and sustaining its infrastructure on a mix of on-premise hardware and cloud services.

Chapter 3, *Infrastructure and Application Metrics* by Matt Massie and myself, discusses the importance of gathering metrics from both your application and your infrastructure, and considerations on how to gather them.

Chapter 4, *Continuous Deployment* by Eric Ries, gives his take on the advantages of deploying code to production in small batches, frequently.

Chapter 5, *Infrastructure as Code* by Adam Jacob, gives an overview about the theory and approaches for configuration and deployment management.

Chapter 6, *Monitoring* by Patrick Debois, discusses the various considerations when designing a monitoring system.

Chapter 7, *How Complex Systems Fail*, is Dr. Richard Cook's whitepaper on systems failure and the nature of complexity that is often found in web architectures. He also adds some web operations–specific notes to his original paper.

Chapter 8, *Community Management and Web Operations*, is my interview with Heather Champ on the topic of how outages and degradations should be handled on the human side of things.

Chapter 9, *Dealing with Unexpected Traffic Spikes* by Brian Moon, talks about the experiences with huge traffic deluges at Dealnews.com and what they did to mitigate disaster.

Chapter 10, *Dev and Ops Collaboration and Cooperation* by Paul Hammond, lists some of the places where development and operations can come together to enable the business, both technically and culturally.

Chapter 11, *How Your Visitors Feel: User-Facing Metrics* by Alistair Croll and Sean Power, discusses metrics that can be used to illustrate what the real experience of your site is.

Chapter 12, *Relational Database Strategy and Tactics for the Web* by Baron Schwartz, lays out common approaches to database architectures and some pitfalls that come with increasing scale.

Chapter 13, *How to Make Failure Beautiful: The Art and Science of Postmortems* by Jake Loomis, goes into what makes or breaks a good postmortem and root cause analysis process.

Chapter 14, *Storage* by Anoop Nagwani, explores the gamut of approaches and considerations when designing and maintaining storage for a growing web application.

Chapter 15, *Nonrelational Databases* by Eric Florenzano, lists considerations and advantages of using a growing number of "nonrelational" database technologies.

Chapter 16, *Agile Infrastructure* by Andrew Clay Shafer, discusses the human and process sides of operations, and how agile philosophy and methods map (or not) to the operational space.

Chapter 17, *Things That Go Bump in the Night (and How to Sleep Through Them)* by Mike Christian, takes you through the various levels of availability and Business Continuity Planning (BCP) approaches and dangers.

Who This Book Is For

This book is for developers; systems administrators; and database, network, or any other engineer who is tasked with operating a web application. The topics covered here are all applicable to the field of web operations, which is a continually evolving field.

Conventions Used in This Book

The following typographical conventions are used in this book:

Italic

> Indicates new terms, URLs, email addresses, filenames, and file extensions.

`Constant width`

> Used for program listings, as well as within paragraphs to refer to program elements such as variable or function names, databases, data types, environment variables, statements, and keywords.

`Constant width bold`

> Shows commands or other text that should be typed literally by the user.

`Constant width italic`

> Shows text that should be replaced with user-supplied values or by values determined by context.

Using Code Examples

This book is here to help you get your job done. In general, you may use the code in this book in your programs and documentation. You do not need to contact us for permission unless you're reproducing a significant portion of the code. For example, writing a program that uses several chunks of code from this book does not require permission. Selling or distributing a CD-ROM of examples from O'Reilly books does require permission. Answering a question by citing this book and quoting example code does not require permission. Incorporating a significant amount of example code from this book into your product's documentation does require permission.

We appreciate, but do not require, attribution. An attribution usually includes the title, author, publisher, and ISBN. For example: "*Web Operations: Keeping Data On Time*, edited by John Allspaw and Jesse Robbins. Copyright 2010 O'Reilly Media, Inc., 978-1-449-37744-1."

If you feel your use of code examples falls outside fair use or the permission given here, feel free to contact us at *permissions@oreilly.com*.

How to Contact Us

Please address comments and questions concerning this book to the publisher:

O'Reilly Media, Inc.
1005 Gravenstein Highway North
Sebastopol, CA 95472
800-998-9938 (in the United States or Canada)
707-829-0515 (international or local)
707-829-0104 (fax)

We have a web page for this book, where we list errata, examples, and any additional information. You can access this page at:

http://oreilly.com/catalog/9781449377441

To comment or ask technical questions about this book, send email to:

bookquestions@oreilly.com

For more information about our books, conferences, Resource Centers, and the O'Reilly Network, see our website at:

http://oreilly.com

Safari® Books Online

Safari. Safari Books Online is an on-demand digital library that lets you easily search over 7,500 technology and creative reference books and videos to find the answers you need quickly.

With a subscription, you can read any page and watch any video from our library online. Read books on your cell phone and mobile devices. Access new titles before they are available for print, and get exclusive access to manuscripts in development and post feedback for the authors. Copy and paste code samples, organize your favorites, download chapters, bookmark key sections, create notes, print out pages, and benefit from tons of other time-saving features.

O'Reilly Media has uploaded this book to the Safari Books Online service. To have full digital access to this book and others on similar topics from O'Reilly and other publishers, sign up for free at *http://my.safaribooksonline.com*.

Acknowledgments

John Allspaw would like to thank Elizabeth, Sadie, and Jack for being very patient while I worked on this book. I'd also like to thank the contributors for meeting their deadlines on a tight schedule. They all of course have day jobs.

Jesse Robbins would like to thank John Allspaw for doing the majority of the work in creating this book. It would never have happened without him.

## CHAPTER ONE

Web Operations: The Career

Theo Schlossnagle

THE INTERNET IS AN INTERESTING MEDIUM IN WHICH TO WORK. Almost all forms of business are now being conducted on the Internet, and people continue to capitalize on the fact that a global audience is on the other side of the virtual drive-thru window.

The Internet changes so quickly that we rarely have time to cogitate what we're doing and why we're doing it. When it comes to operating the fabric of an online architecture, things move so fast and change so significantly from quarter to quarter that we struggle to stay in the game, let alone ahead of it. This high-stress, overstimulating environment leads to treating the efforts therein as a job without the concept of a career.

What's the difference, you ask? A career is an occupation taken on for a significant portion of one's life, with opportunities for progress. A job is a paid position of regular employment. In other words, a job is just a job.

Although the Internet has been around for more than a single generation at this point, the Web in its current form is still painfully young and is only now breaking past a single generational marker. So, how can you fill a significant portion of your life with a trade that has existed for only a fraction of the time that one typically works in a lifetime? At this point, to have finished a successful career in web operations, you must have been pursuing this art for longer than it has existed. In the end, it is the pursuit that matters. But make no mistake: pursuing a career in web operations makes you a frontiersman.

Why Does Web Operations Have It Tough?

Web operations has no defined career path; there is no widely accepted standard for progress. Titles vary, responsibilities vary, and title escalation happens on vastly different schedules from organization to organization.

Although the term *web operations* isn't awful, I really don't like it. The captains, superstars, or heroes in these roles are multidisciplinary experts; they have a deep understanding of networks, routing, switching, firewalls, load balancing, high availability, disaster recovery, Transmission Control Protocol (TCP) and User Datagram Protocol (UDP) services, NOC management, hardware specifications, several different flavors of Unix, several web server technologies, caching technologies, database technologies, storage infrastructure, cryptography, algorithms, trending, and capacity planning. The issue is: how can we expect to find good candidates who are fluent in all of those technologies? In the traditional enterprise, you have architects who are broad and shallow paired with a multidisciplinary team of experts who are focused and deep. However, the expectation remains that your "web operations" engineer be both broad and deep: fix your gigabit switch, optimize your database, and guide the overall infrastructure design to meet scalability requirements.

Web operations is broad; I would argue almost unacceptably broad. A very skilled engineer must know every commonly deployed technology at a considerable depth. The engineer is responsible for operating a given architecture within the described parameters (usually articulated in a service-level agreement, or SLA). The problem is that architecture is, by its very definition, everything. Everything from datacenter space, power, and cooling up through the application stack and all the way down to the HTML rendering and JavaScript executing in the browser on the other side of the planet. Big job? Yes. Mind-bogglingly so.

Although I emphatically hope the situation changes, as it stands now there is no education that prepares an individual for today's world of operating web infrastructures—neither academic nor vocational. Instead, identifying computer science programs or other academic programs that instill strong analytical skills provides a good starting point, but to be a real candidate in the field of web operations you need three things:

A Strong Background in Computing

Because of the broad required understanding of architectural components, it helps tremendously to understand the ins and outs of the computing systems on which all this stuff runs. Processor architectures, memory systems, storage systems, network switching and routing, why Layer 2 protocols work the way they do, HTTP, database concepts…the list could go on for pages. Having the basics down pat is essential in understanding why and how to architect solutions as well as identify brokenness. It is, after all, the foundation on which we build our intelligence. Moreover, an engineering mindset and a basic understanding of the laws of physics can be a great asset.

In a conversation over beers one day, my friend and compatriot in the field of web operations, Jesse Robbins, told a story of troubleshooting a satellite-phone issue. A new sat-phone installation had just been completed, and there was over a second of "unexpected" latency on the line. This was a long time ago, when these things cost a pretty penny, so there was some serious brooding frustration about quality of service. After hours of troubleshooting and a series of escalations, the technician asked: "Just to be clear, this second of latency is in addition to the expected second of latency, right?" A long pause followed. "What *expected* latency?" asked the client. The technician proceeded to apologize to all the people on the call for their wasted time and then chewed out the client for wasting everyone's time. The *expected* latency is the amount of time it takes to send the signal to the satellite in outer space and back again. And as much as we might try, we have yet to find a way to increase the speed of light.

Although this story seems silly, I frequently see unfettered, unrealistic expectations. Perhaps most common are cross-continent synchronous replication attempts that defy the laws of physics as we understand them today. We should remain focused on being site reliability engineers who strive to practically apply the basics of computer science and physics that we know. To work well within the theoretical bounds, one must understand what those boundaries are and where they lie. This is why some theoretical knowledge of computer science, physics, electrical engineering, and applied math can be truly indispensable.

Operations is all about understanding where theory and practice collide, and devising methodologies to limit the casualties from the explosions that ensue.

Practiced Decisiveness

Although being indecisive is a disadvantage in any field, in web operations there is a near-zero tolerance for it. Like EMTs and ER doctors, you are thrust into situations on a regular basis where good judgment alone isn't enough—you need good judgment *now*. Delaying decisions causes prolonged outages. You must train your brain to apply mental processes continually to the inputs you receive, because the "collect, review, propose" approach will leave you holding all the broken pieces.

In computer science, algorithms can be put into two categories: offline and online. An offline algorithm is a solution to a problem in which the entire input set is required before an output can be determined. In contrast, an online algorithm is a solution that can produce output as the inputs are arriving. Of course, because the algorithm produces output (or solutions) without the entire input set, there is no way to guarantee an optimal output. Unlike an offline algorithm, an online algorithm can always ensure that you have an answer on hand.

Operations decisions must be the product of online algorithms, not offline ones. This isn't to say that offline algorithms have no place in web operations; quite the contrary. One of the most critically important processes in web operations is offline: root-cause analysis (RCA). I'm a huge fan of formalizing the RCA process as much as possible.

The thorough offline (postmortem) analysis of failures, their pathologies, and a review of the decision made "in flight" is the best possible path to improving the online algorithms you and your team use for critical operations decision making.

A Calm Disposition

A calm and controlled thought process is critical. When it is absent, Keystone Kops syndrome prevails and bad situations are made worse. In crazy action movies, when one guy has a breakdown the other grabs him, shakes him, and tells him to pull himself together—you need to make sure you're on the right side of that situation. On one side, you have a happy, healthy career; on the other, you have a job in which you will shoulder an unhealthy amount of stress and most likely burn out.

Because there is no formal education path, the web operations trade, as it stands today, is an informal apprentice model. As the Internet has caused paradigm shifts in business and social interaction, it has offered a level of availability and ubiquity of information that provides a virtualized master–apprentice model. Unfortunately, as one would expect from the Internet, it varies widely in quality from group to group.

In the field of web operations, the goal is simply to make everything run all the time: a simple definition, an impossible prospect. Perhaps the more challenging aspect of being an engineer in this field is the unrealistic expectations held by peers within the organization.

So, how does one pursue a career with all these obstacles?

From Apprentice to Master

When you allow yourself to meditate on a question, the answer most often is simple and rather unoriginal. It turns out that being a master web operations engineer is no different from being a master carpenter or a master teacher. The effort to master any given discipline requires four basic pursuits: knowledge, tools, experience, and discipline.

Knowledge

Knowledge is a uniquely simple subject on the Internet. The Internet acts as a very effective knowledge-retention system. The common answer to many questions, "Let me Google that for you," is an amazingly effective and high-yield answer. Almost everything you want to know (and have no desire to know) about operating web infrastructure is, you guessed it, on the Web.

Limiting yourself to the Web for information is, well, limiting. You are not alone in this adventure, despite the feeling. You have peers, and they need you as much as you need them. User groups (of a startling variety) exist around the globe and are an excellent place to share knowledge.

If you are reading this, you already understand the value of knowledge through books. A healthy bookshelf is something all master web operations engineers have in common. Try to start a book club in your organization, or if your organization is too small, ask around at a local user group.

One unique aspect of the Internet industry is that almost nothing is secret. In fact, very little is even proprietary and, quite uniquely, almost all specifications are free. How does the Internet work? Switching: there is an IEEE specification for that. IP: there is RFC 791 for that. TCP: RFC 793. HTTP: RFC 2616. They are all there for the reading and provide a much deeper foundational base of understanding. These protocols are the rules by which you provide services, and the better you understand them, the more educated your decisions will be. But don't stop there! TCP might be described in RFC 793, but all sorts of TCP details and extensions and "evolution" are described in related RFCs such as 1323, 2001, 2018, and 2581. Perhaps it's also worthwhile to understand where TCP came from: RFC 761.

To revisit the theory and practice conundrum, the RFC for TCP is the theory; the kernel code that implements the TCP stack in each operating system is the practice. The glorious collision of theory and practice are the nuances of interoperability (or interinoperability) of the different TCP implementations, and the explosions are slow download speeds, hung sessions, and frustrated users.

On your path from apprentice to master, it is your job to retain as much information as possible so that the curiously powerful coil of jello between your ears can sort, filter, and correlate all that trivia into a concise and accurate picture used to power decisions: both the long-term critical decisions of architecture design and the momentary critical decisions of fault remediation.

Tools

Tools, in my experience, are one of the most incessantly and emphatically argued topics in computing: vi versus Emacs, Subversion versus Git, Java versus PHP—beginning as arguments from different camps but rapidly evolving into nonsensical religious wars.

The simple truth is that people are successful with these tools despite their pros and cons. Why do people use all these different tools, and why do we keep making more? I think Thomas Carlyle and Benjamin Franklin noted something important about our nature as humans when they said "man is a tool-using animal" and "man is a toolmaking animal," respectively. Because it is in our nature to build and use tools, why must we argue fruitlessly about their merits? Although Thoreau meant something equally poignant, I feel his commentary that "men have become the tools of their tools" is equally accurate in the context of modern vernacular.

The simple truth is articulated best by Emerson: "All the tools and engines on Earth are only extensions of man's limbs and senses." This articulates well the ancient sentiment that a tool does not the master craftsman make. In the context of Internet applications, you can see this in the wide variety of languages, platforms, and technologies that are glued together successfully. It isn't Java or PHP that makes an architecture successful, it is the engineers that design and implement it—the craftsmen.

One truth about engineering is that knowing your tools, regardless of the tools that are used, is a prerequisite to mastering the trade. Your tools must become extensions of your limbs and senses. It should be quite obvious to engineers and nonengineers alike that reading the documentation for a tool during a crisis is not the best use of one's time. Knowing your tools goes above and beyond mere competency; you must know the effects they produce and how they interact with your environment—you must be practiced.

A great tool in any operations engineer's tool chest is a system call tracer. They vary (slightly) from system to system. Solaris has truss, Linux has strace, FreeBSD has ktrace, and Mac OS X had ktrace but displaced that with the less useful dtruss. A system call tracer is a peephole into the interaction between user space and kernel space; in other words, if you aren't computationally bound, this tool tells you what exactly your application is asking for and how long it takes to be satisfied.

DTrace is a uniquely positioned tool available on Solaris, OpenSolaris, FreeBSD, Mac OS X, and a few other platforms. This isn't really a chapter on tools, but DTrace certainly deserves a mention. DTrace is a huge leap forward in system observability and allows the craftsman to understand his system like never before; however, DTrace is an oracle in both its perspicacity and the fact that the quality of its answers is coupled tightly with the quality of the question asked of it. System call tracers, on the other hand, are a proverbial avalanche—easy to induce and challenging to navigate.

Why are we talking about avalanches and oracles? It is an aptly mixed metaphor for the amorphous and heterogeneous architectures that power the Web. Using strace to inspect what your web server is doing can be quite enlightening (and often results in some easily won optimizations the first few times). Looking at the output for the first time when something has gone wrong provides basically no value except to the most skilled engineers; in fact, it can often cost you. The issue is that this is an experiment, and you have no control. When something is "wrong" it would be logical to look at the output from such a tool in an attempt to recognize an unfamiliar pattern. It should be quite clear that if you have failed to use the tool under normal operating conditions, you have no basis for comparison, and all patterns are unfamiliar. In fact, it is often the case that patterns that appear to be correlated to the problem are not, and much time is wasted pursuing red herrings.

Diffusing the tools argument is important. You should strive to choose a tool based on its appropriateness for the problem at hand rather than to indulge your personal preference. An excellent case in point is the absolutely superb release management of the FreeBSD project over its lifetime using what is now considered by most to be a completely antiquated version control system (CVS). Many successful architectures have been built atop the PHP language, which lacks many of the features of common modern languages. On the flip side, many projects fail even when equipped with the most robust and capable tools. The quality of the tool itself is always far less important than the adroitness with which it is wielded. That being said, a master craftsman should always select an appropriate, high-quality tool for the task at hand.

Experience

Experience is one of the most powerful weapons in any situation. It is so important because it means so many things. Experience is, in its very essence, making good judgments, and it is gained by making bad ones. Watching theory and practice collide is both scary and beautiful. The collision inevitably has casualties—lost data, unavailable services, angered users, and lost money—but at the same time its full context and pathology have profound beauty. Assumptions have been challenged (and you have lost) and unexpected outcomes have manifested, and above all else, you have the elusive opportunity to be a pathologist and gain a deeper understanding of a new place in your universe where theory and practice bifurcate.

Experience and knowledge are quite interrelated. Knowledge can be considered the studying of experiences of others. You have the information but have not grasped the deeper meaning that is gained by directly experiencing the causality. That deeper meaning allows you to apply the lesson learned in other situations where your experience-honed insight perceives correlations—an insight that often escapes those with knowledge alone.

Experience is both a noun and a verb: gaining it is as easy (and as hard) as doing it.

The organizational challenge of inexperience

Although gaining experience is as easy as simply "doing," in the case of web operations it is the process of making and surviving bad judgments. The question is: how can an organization that is competing in such an aggressive industry afford to have its staff members make bad judgments? Having and executing on an answer to this question is fundamental to any company that wants to house career-oriented web operations engineers. There are two parts to this answer, a yin and yang if you will.

The first is to make it safe for junior and mid-level engineers to make bad judgments. You accomplish this by limiting liability and injury from individual judgments. The environment (workplace, network, systems, and code) can all survive a bad judgment now and again. You never want to be forced into the position of firing an individual because of a single instance of bad judgment (although I realize this cannot be entirely prevented, it is a good goal). The larger the mistake, the more profound the opportunity to extract deep and lasting value from the lesson. This leads us to the second part of the answer.

Never allow the same bad judgment twice. Mistakes happen. Bad judgments will occur as a matter of fact. Not learning from one's mistakes is inexcusable. Although exceptions always exist, you should expect and promote a culture of zero tolerance for repetitious bad judgment.

The concept of "senior operations"

One thing that has bothered me for quite some time and continues to bother me is job applications from junior operations engineers for senior positions. Their presumption is that knowledge dictates hierarchical position within a team; just as in other disciplines, this is flat-out wrong. The single biggest characteristic of a senior engineer is consistent and solid good judgment. This obviously requires exposure to situations where judgment is required and is simple math: the rate of difficult situations requiring judgment multiplied by tenure. It is possible to be on a "fast track" by landing an operations position in which disasters strike at every possible moment. It is also possible to spend 10 years in a position with no challenging decisions and, as a result, accumulate no valuable experience.

Generation X (and even more so, Generation Y) are cultures of immediate gratification. I've worked with a staggering number of engineers who expect their "career path" to take them to the highest ranks of the engineering group inside five years just because they are smart. This is simply impossible in the staggering numbers I've witnessed. Not everyone can be senior. If, after five years, you are senior, are you at the peak of your game? After five more years will you not have accrued more invaluable experience? What then: "super engineer"? What about five years later: "super-duper engineer"? I blame the youth of our discipline for this affliction. The truth is that very few engineers have been in the field of web operations for 15 years. Given the dynamics of our industry, many elected to move on to managerial positions or risk an entrepreneurial run at things.

I have some advice for individuals entering this field with little experience: be patient. However, this adage is typically paradoxical, as your patience very well may run out before you comprehend it.

Discipline

Discipline, in my opinion, is the single biggest disaster in our industry. Web operations has an atrocious track record when it comes to structure, process, and discipline. As a part of my job, I do a lot of assessments. I go into companies and review their organizational structure, operational practices, and overall architecture to identify when and where they will break down as business operations scale up.

Can you guess what I see more often than not? I see lazy cowboys and gunslingers; it's the Wild, Wild West. Laziness is often touted as a desired quality in a programmer. In the Perl community, where this became part of the mantra, the meaning was tongue-in-cheek (further exemplified by the use of the word *hubris* in the same mantra). What is meant is that by doing things as correctly and efficiently as possible you end up doing as little work as possible to solve a particular problem—this is actually quite far from laziness. Unfortunately, others in the programming and operations fields have taken actual laziness as a point of pride to which I say, "not in my house."

Discipline is controlled behavior resulting from training, study, and practice. In my experience, a lack of discipline is the most common ingredient left out of a web operations team and results in inconsistency and nonperformance.

Discipline is not something that can be taught via a book; it is something that must be learned through practice. Each task you undertake should be approached from the perspective of a resident. Treating your position and responsibilities as long term and approaching problems to develop solutions that you will be satisfied with five years down the road is a good basis for the practice that results in discipline.

I find it ironic that software engineering (a closely related field) has a rather good track record of discipline. I conjecture that the underlying reason for a lack of discipline within the field of web operations is the lack of a career path itself. Although it may seem like a chicken-and-egg problem, I have overwhelming confidence that we are close to rewarding our field with an understood career path.

It is important for engineers who work in the field now to participate in sculpting what a career in operations looks like. The Web is here to stay, and services thereon are becoming increasingly critical. Web operations "the career" is inevitable. By participating, you can help to ensure that the aspect of your job that seduced you in the first place carries through into your career.

Conclusion

The field of web operations is exciting. The career of a site reliability engineer is fascinating. In a single day, we can oversee datacenter cabinet installs, review a SAN fiber fabric, troubleshoot an 802.11ad link aggregation problem, tune the number of allowed firewall states in front of the web architecture, review anomalistic database performance and track it back to an unexpected rebuild on a storage array, identify a slow database query and apply some friendly pressure to engineering to "fix it *now*," recompile PHP due to a C compiler bug, roll out an urgent security update across several hundred machines, combine JavaScript files to reduce HTTP requests per user session, explain to management why attempting a sub-one-minute cross-continent failover design isn't a "good idea" on the budget they're offering, and develop a deployment plan to switch an architecture from one load balancer vendor to another. Yowsers!

The part that keeps me fascinated is witnessing the awesomeness of continuous and unique collisions between theory and practice. Because we are responsible for "correct operation" of the whole architecture, traditional boundaries are removed in a fashion that allows us to freely explore the complete pathology of failures.

Pursuing a career in web operations places you in a position to be one of the most critical people in your organization's online pursuits. If you do it well, you stand to make the Web a better place for everyone.

## CHAPTER TWO

How Picnik Uses Cloud Computing: Lessons Learned

Justin Huff

PICNIK.COM IS THE LEADING IN-BROWSER PHOTO EDITOR. Each month, we're serving over 16 million people. Of course, it didn't start that way. When I started at Picnik in January 2007, my first task was to configure the five new servers that our COO had just purchased. Just three years later, those 5 machines have multiplied to 40, and we've added a very healthy dose of Amazon Web Services. Even better, until the end of 2009, the Picnik operations staff consisted of basically one person.

Our use of the cloud started with an instance on which to run QA tests back in May 2007. Our cloud usage changed very little until December of that year, when we started using Amazon's S3 storage offering to store files generated by our users. Several months later, we started using EC2 for some of our image processing.

It's safe to say that our use of the cloud has contributed significantly to our success. However, it wasn't without its hurdles. I'm going to cover the two main areas where Picnik uses the cloud, as well as the problems we've run into along the way.

Picnik runs a pretty typical LAMP (Linux, Apache, MySQL, Python) stack (see Figure 2-1). However, our servers don't do a lot when compared to many other sites. The vast majority of the Picnik experience is actually contained within an Adobe Flash application. This means the server side has to deal primarily with API calls from our client as well as file transfers without the need to keep any server-side session state.

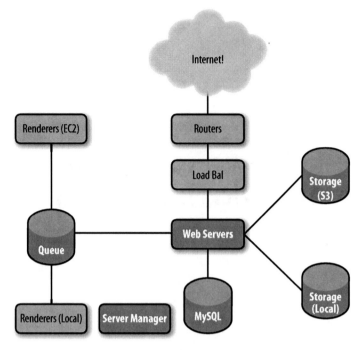

Figure 2-1. *Picnik's architecture*

Flash has traditionally had a number of security restrictions that limit its ability to access local files and talk to servers in different domains. To bypass these restrictions, certain save operations from Picnik are forced to go through our server in what we call a *render*. During a render, the server reconstructs the final image product and then either posts it to a remote service (such as Flickr or Facebook) or returns a URL to the client to initiate download to their computer.

Where the Cloud Fits (and Why!)

Storage

In the beginning, Picnik used an open source project, MogileFS, for file storage. Most of our servers had several spare drive bays, so we loaded them up with large SATA drives. Most of our backend services are CPU-bound, so they fit in nicely with I/O-bound storage. This strategy worked reasonably well until our need for storage outpaced our need for CPUs. Amazon's S3 service seemed like it'd be the easiest and cheapest way to expand our available storage.

We didn't actually do a lot of cost modeling prior to testing out S3. One reason was that there weren't too many cloud choices at that time. Another was that S3 was highly recommended by several well-respected engineers. Finally, we never expected to grow our usage as much as we did.

We already had a framework for abstracting different file storage systems because developer machines weren't using Mogile, so it was relatively easy to add support for S3. In fact, it took only about a day to implement S3 support. We tested for another day or two and then rolled it out with our normal weekly release. This ease of implementation was another critical factor in our choice of S3.

Initially, we planned to migrate only our oldest files to S3, which we started right away in December 2007. Because these files were infrequently accessed, we were less concerned with the potential for performance and availability problems. This scheme worked great and S3 seemed to perform well.

The only downside was that we weren't moving files off MogileFS fast enough to keep up with our increasing growth rate. In addition, MogileFS was also starting to show some performance problems. Our solution was to do what several other large sites on the Internet were doing: store files directly to S3. We started out by sending a small percentage of new files directly to S3 and gradually ramped up until the vast majority of new files were flowing to Amazon (see Figure 2-2). Again, things worked great, and we moved on to other problems and features.

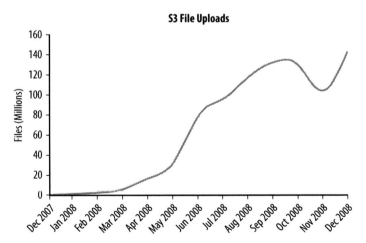

Figure 2-2. *Amazon S3 file uploads*

Although S3 has been fairly reliable, we have run into a few notable problems. The first problem we hit was *eventual consistency*. Basically, this means you can't guarantee that you can immediately read a file you just wrote. This problem was exacerbated when writing to the Seattle S3 cluster and then trying to read from EC2. We mitigated this by proxying all file access through our datacenter in Seattle. Unfortunately, this ended up costing a little more in bandwidth.

The second problem we ran into was Amazon returning HTTP 500 errors for requests. Our code had the ability to retry, which worked fine most of the time. Every week or two, we'd get a large burst of errors such that our retry logic was overwhelmed. These bursts would last for an hour or so. One day, I was looking at the keys that were getting errors and noticed that they all had the same prefix! As it turns out, S3 partitions data based on ranges of keys. This means maintenance (such as growing or shrinking a partition) can cause a drastic increase in the error rate for a particular range of keys. Amazon has to do this to keep S3 performing well. In our case, the error bursts were more of an annoyance because we also had MogileFS still available. If we failed to write to S3, we just wrote the file to Mogile instead. These events have become rarer now that our growth rate has stabilized, but Mogile is still there to handle them.

Many of the issues we ran into are actually inherent in building large-scale systems, so there is very little Amazon can do to hide them. It's easy to forget that this is actually a pretty huge distributed system with many users.

As our traffic grew, we became increasingly dependent on S3. During large parts of the day our Mogile install wouldn't have been able to handle the load if S3 were to go offline. Luckily, when S3 did have major problems it was not during our peak times, so Mogile was able to absorb the load. I should also mention that Mogile failed on us on at least two occasions. Both times, it was completely offline for several hours while I altered MySQL tables or debugged Mogile's Perl code. In those cases, S3 picked up 100% of our traffic, and our users never knew that anything happened.

One danger of "infinite" storage is that it becomes easy to waste it. In our case, I wasn't paying attention to the background job that deletes unused files. Because we end up deleting nearly 75% of the files we create, unused files can add up very quickly.

Even once we noticed the problem, we actually decided to more or less ignore it. All of us at Picnik had a lot on our plates, and it wasn't actually breaking anything. Besides, we had awesome new features or other scalability problems that needed our attention. What's interesting is that S3 gave us the choice of trying to hire and train more people or simply writing a check. All of that changed once we started approaching our credit card's monthly limit.

After months of tweaking, analyzing, and rewriting code, we finally came up with a scalable method of cleaning up our unused files. The first part of the work was to make sure our databases were actually purged of unused file records. Then the actual deletion amounted to a large merge-join between the file records in our databases and the list of keys in S3 (see Figure 2-3).

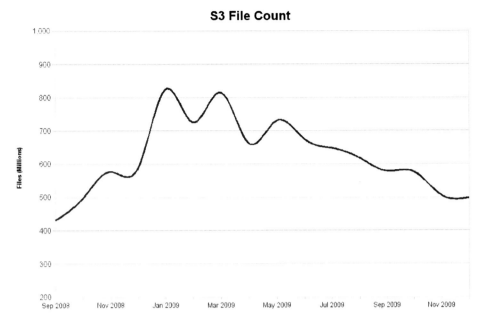

Figure 2-3. *Amazon S3 file count*

During the long process of implementing better cleanup systems we began to realize that S3 was actually very expensive for our workload. Our earlier analysis hadn't completely factored in the cost of PUT operations. In many S3 workloads, the storage cost dominates because the file is uploaded and then accessed occasionally over a long period of time. As mentioned earlier, our workload creates lots of files that are deleted in a few days. This means the cost of PUT operations starts to increase.

With this in mind, we worked hard at optimizing our MogileFS install for performance rather than bulk capacity and investigated high-performance NAS products. We ended up implementing a proof-of-concept Linux-based NFS system that is able to take over frontline storage. That means we'll need to store only the 25% of files that survive a week. These remaining files have a more S3-friendly access pattern.

Over the long term, it's not clear that S3 will still be a good fit. Although more traditional NAS hardware looks expensive, you can amortize the cost over a year or two if you're confident in that long-term storage need. On the other hand, many start-up CFOs (including ours) will tell you that it's worth paying a little more to maintain flexibility and degrees of freedom—which S3 offers. That flexibility matters more than whether those expenses are counted as operating expenses or capital expenses. As far as we were concerned, it was all an operating expense because it was directly tied to our traffic and feature offerings.

Hybrid Computing with EC2

One of Picnik's main server-side components is our render farm. When a user saves an image from Picnik, we often need to re-create the image on the server side. In those cases, the client sends the server a chunk of XML that describes their edits. The web server then packages up the XML with any required images and puts it into a queue of render jobs. A render server picks up the job, reconstructs the image, and returns the resultant image to the web server. Meanwhile, the client is blocked, waiting for a response from the web server. Most of the time, the client waits only a few seconds.

Although this is a typical architecture for scalable systems, we designed it with future use of the cloud in mind. In this case, the render servers don't require access to any internal services such as databases or storage servers. In short, they are ideal for running on EC2. In addition, we already had a homegrown configuration management and code deployment system called ServerManager.

Like S3, the actual implementation was quick and easy. Our internal render farm already consisted of VMs running on top of Xen, so all I had to do was make some slight modifications to our existing render VM image to fit into EC2's Xen stack and then package it up as an AMI. When the image starts, it contacts ServerManager to get a list of components it needs to install and run. One of those is our RenderServer code, which connects to the queue to pull work to do. The first thing I did was fire up a couple of instances to see how they performed—they did great!

The second phase was to implement the Holy Grail of cloud operations: auto-scaling. Our auto-scaling process is pretty easy, because everything runs through the queue. The goal of the auto-scaling code is to maintain an empty queue, because we have users waiting on the results of the render. Every minute, a thread in ServerManager wakes up and polls the queue stats (averaged over the last minute). It then calculates what needs to be done to maintain a target ratio of free workers to busy workers. Of course, there's some hysteresis to prevent unnecessary oscillation around the target ratio owing to small traffic and latency fluctuations. Sometimes it can take several minutes for an EC2 instance to start up, so the code also takes that into account. All this was tuned empirically over the course of a week or two. As far as control loops go, it's pretty darn simple. The final result looks something like the graphs in Figure 2-4.

Auto-scaling isn't always about typical capacity requirements. We've had cases where network latency to EC2 increased, or we released a code change that slowed down our rendering speed. In these cases, we auto-scaled "out of" the problem until we could rectify the underlying cause. In another case, we fixed a bug that was causing save failures for a small percentage of our users. The downside was that it increased our rendering load by 20%—right before Christmas. No problem! The spike in the graph in Figure 2-5 was caused by a performance problem in one of our NFS servers.

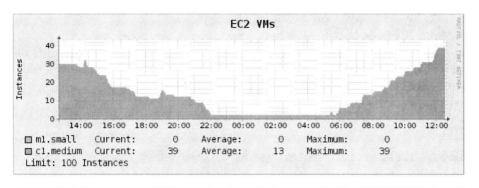

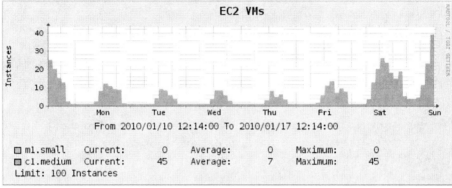

Figure 2-4. *Amazon EC2 instances, day view (top) and week view (bottom)*

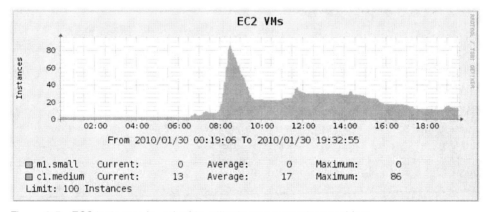

Figure 2-5. *EC2 instances launched to mitigate an on-premises problem*

This setup also works nicely for doing batch jobs. A while back we had to re-create a bunch of thumbnails for edit history. I wrote some code that submitted the jobs to the render queue and then updated the database record with the new thumbnail file. I didn't need to do anything special to allocate capacity or even run it at night when the load was lower. ServerManager just added instances to adjust to the new load.

From the financial side, our use of EC2 is clearer than our use of S3. We try to build out our internal rendering to meet our average capacity needs. At the same time, it's easy to convert CPUs doing rendering to CPUs doing web serving. This means the ability to use the cloud for render servers actually endows some dynamic characteristics on the web servers, which means it's easier for us to adjust to changing load patterns. It also allows us to more efficiently use our existing hardware by purchasing in convenient increments. For example, we can order a new cabinet in the datacenter and fill it with servers without worrying that we're wasting a large part of the cabinet's power allocation. The charts in Figure 2-6 illustrate the advantages of this "hybrid" model.

In general, the problems we've had with EC2 have all centered on connectivity. Although the Internet as a whole is very reliable, connectivity between any two points is less so. Normally, if there are problems between a network and your datacenter, only a small number of users are affected. However, if that network happens to be your cloud provider, all of your users are affected. These types of outages are probably the worst, because the problem is likely in an area that neither you nor your cloud provider pays money to.

When we've run into major issues (and it wasn't during a low-traffic period), our only option was to shed load. In the past, we had only one big knob to control how many users we allowed in. Now we can prioritize different classes of users (guest, free, partner, premium). Sadly, in most cases, you just have to wait out the outage. Either way, one of the first things we do is to update our Twitter feed, which is also displayed on our "It's raining on our Picnik" page. We don't generally blame anyone—the user just doesn't care.

We don't really monitor our EC2 instances in the same way we do our internal servers. Our Nagios install gets automatically updated with EC2 instances via ServerManager just like any other server. Nagios also monitors queue depth because it is an early indicator of many problems.

Cacti graphs the number of running instances (via the EC2 API) as well as cluster-level performance metrics. We don't bother adding individual instances into Cacti, because it doesn't really deal with clusters, let alone ones that dynamically change.

In fact, we don't really care about the performance of the individual instances. We already know they're a little slower than our local machines. This is OK because the auto-scaling system will still find an equilibrium given the set of resources it has available at a given point in time.

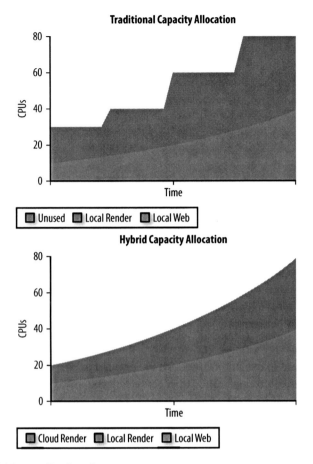

Figure 2-6. *Hybrid capacity allocation*

Because instances pull work from the queue, an EC2 instance that happens to be a little slower will simply do less work rather than falling over. This allows me to focus on higher-level metrics such as what percentage of the day we are using any EC2 instances. At the end of the day, traditional capacity planning focused on our web servers drives our hardware purchasing decisions. Render servers just get the benefit of any unused capacity.

Effective use of cloud computing resources requires a fairly "grown-up" attitude toward application architecture and configuration management/automation. The fact that we designed the render servers to be decoupled and that we already had a configuration management system in place made auto-scaling easy and very reliable.

Where the Cloud Doesn't Fit (for Picnik)

Picnik doesn't use EC2 for either our web servers or our MySQL database servers. Our web-serving layer is highly coupled to our databases, so it makes sense to keep the latency between them very low. That implies that they are either both in the cloud or both out of the cloud. Until very recently, disk I/O performance in EC2 was mediocre, so that necessitated keeping the DBs on real (and specialized) hardware. This might start to change with the introduction of Amazon's RDS, which is basically a nicely packaged version of MySQL on top of EC2.

Even though database performance might not be up to the task of a high-performance production server, I have toyed with the idea of using EC2 instances for DB slaves. These slaves would be primarily used for backups but could also be used for reports or batch jobs.

Another capability that was lacking from Amazon's cloud offering early on was load balancing. Although it is possible to have a decent amount of load balancing on an EC2 instance, you have to jump through a bunch of hoops to get any reasonable level of availability. Amazon eventually introduced a load balancer offering which eliminates many of those concerns.

The cloud landscape is changing very quickly. When we started working on Picnik, cloud offerings were sparse and untried, so we decided to run our own servers. If we were building Picnik in today's landscape, there's a reasonable chance we'd do things differently.

Conclusion

Although a lot of hype surrounds applications that are entirely cloud hosted, hybrid applications are probably the most interesting from an operations perspective. Hybrids allow you to use the cloud to get the most out of the hardware you purchase.

Hybrid applications also underscore the point that traditional operations best practices are exactly what are required for any cloud application to succeed. Configuration management and monitoring lay the foundation for effective auto-scaling.

With the cloud, it's less important to monitor each individual piece because there is very little consistency. What are important to monitor are high-level metrics such as how many files you're storing on S3 so that you can be aware of impending problems before they get out of hand.

Always try to use the best tool for the job, unless you have a really good reason not to. Like databases, some things just don't perform well in the cloud. By having a foot on both sides, you can more easily pick and choose from the options.

## CHAPTER THREE

Infrastructure and Application Metrics

John Allspaw, with Matt Massie

IN ANY SIZE WEB OPERATION, gathering metrics is about as important as plugging servers into a network. For infrastructures that are growing, it's even more important. Imagine designing a car without any of the dials or indicators in front of the driver. Now paint the windshield black. That's what it's like to run a web operation without metrics.

This chapter is about gathering metrics regarding your backing infrastructure, and the material presented here will overlap with other chapters in this book about user-facing metrics and monitoring. We're going to discuss not just the types of metrics you should gather and keep an eye on, but also what you can do with them to better enable you to react to various issues. We'll also go over what makes a great metrics collection system.

Gathering, storing, and displaying metrics for a growing web application is quite a feat, but there are a number of great tools that can do most (if not all) of the heavy lifting for you. The differences between the most popular ones are items for a blog post, not for this chapter. The important thing is that whatever tool you choose or build, it should be something you can depend on. You should be able to treat your metrics like a microphone—always on and always recording what is happening with your infrastructure.

One thing I want to note is that there should be a distinct difference in your mind between metrics collection and monitoring with the intention of alerting. Although some tools can do both, the concerns with each of them are quite different, and the scope of their operations is also quite different. Metrics collection in this context has nothing to do with what those metrics will be used for once they are gathered and stored. If you want to alert as a result of their values, feel free. Also feel free to correlate those metrics with other business-level metrics in a spreadsheet given to you by your friendly neighborhood Product Management person, "standard" benchmark data from your hardware vendor, or any other thing that you can think of. In the car analogy, your gas gauge usually has two different pieces: the actual gauge telling you how much gas you have and the red light next to the "empty" side of the gauge, alerting you when you're about to run out.

My point is that the automatic gathering, storage, and display of the metrics in your application and infrastructure should be considered different from (but related to) the alerting of staff members on anomalies and issues that are detected in that data, because that's only one of the use cases.

This chapter is meant to explore the reasoning behind collecting, storing, and displaying metrics about your infrastructure, and the approaches you might want to consider when doing so. We're going to discuss some real-world scenarios where having these metrics will enable you to better operate your web application.

Although this chapter is not meant to be specific to a particular tool, we will cover what makes a metrics collection system, and we will focus on an existing tool (Ganglia) to illustrate these points.

Time Resolution and Retention Concerns

One of the challenges with recording data on a timeline is to keep the size of the data manageable for the purposes that you're going to use it. Disk space is indeed cheaper these days than it used to be, and it's possible to keep many terabytes of metrics data without issue. However, making sure that data stays queryable and movable (if need be) throughout its growth is a sensible idea.

Some systems aim to keep high-resolution metrics in a relational database. This solves the issue of being able to query the data independently and also having the ability to manipulate the data with SQL, which is a relatively straightforward and comfortable thing to do for most engineers. And because collecting metrics almost never involves deleting data, you'll probably end up with a relatively nonfragmented database, which almost certainly helps with performance and in keeping the size efficient.

Personally, I haven't found too much to be lacking in what became a de facto standard storage system for keeping metrics: the Round Robin Database (RRD). The basic idea of the RRD is that the format will drop increasing levels of resolution on its data, on purpose, as time goes by, once it reaches a predescribed period (hour, day, week, month, year) of your choosing. It does this with the assumption that most metrics data is interesting only for recent time periods and has the benefit that the RRD's datafile won't grow past a certain point. This means you won't have to worry about disk space becoming an issue with your metrics.

Many systems have RRD resolution definitions that lean toward being conservative with disk space and start to drop the highest resolution after the first hour passes. Is this OK for your needs? It might or might not be, depending on what the metric is, how far back in the past you'll be using the data, and how important the individual metric is in the context of the whole application. I have seen organizations keep 10-second intervals for thousands of metrics for years, and I've seen other successful companies keep only 15-second intervals for only the last hour, one-minute intervals for the last day, and five-minute intervals for the last week. You'll obviously want to set your definitions to lean on the more granular side, because you can't go back in time to get more detail.

How long you retain that high-resolution data is also up for grabs. Personally, I never had a need to find out what the user CPU on server www125 was between 12:34:50 and 12:34:60 on February 10, 2005. But I've been very interested in the peak of all web servers for each week in 2005, so I've kept maximums and averages for longer than I've kept the raw data. Just like resolution, metrics retention can be adjusted to less granular levels later if you find it's a problem to manage.

When you're deciding how much resolution to keep for your metrics, try to think about how they'll likely be used. Will you be looking at them for insight into what is causing an outage or degradation? If so, you'll most likely want them to have fine resolution, less than a minute. Will you be using the data for capacity planning on a three-, six-, or nine-month timeline? If so, you'll want to make sure you can keep details about maximum and minimum values for that far back in history.

You'll also want your data to help you gain historical awareness of patterns. Metrics collection systems really shine when you can use them to answer questions such as these:

- What is the peak hour(s) of the day, day(s) of the week, or month(s) of the year for a particular resource?

- Is there any seasonality pattern to any metrics, such as summertime lows, holiday highs, peaks during school opening, and so forth?

- How do maximum (peak) values compare against minimum (valley) values?

- Do peak and valley relationships change as your users spread out more across the globe, covering more time zones?

Locality of Metrics Collection and Storage

If you're an organization that has more than one physical presence, or you use a cloud infrastructure whose physical location isn't quite known, you'll run into the issue of having multiple collection systems and the question of how to aggregate those metrics into a single place for easy comparison and cross-location correlation.

This is commonly found in websites that are being served from multiple datacenters. Let's say we have web servers and databases in two different datacenters, and we're geographically load-balancing the traffic across the two. I'll definitely want to know what the total traffic (say, Apache requests) is quickly and easily, without having to look at two graphs or values and adding them up. Our tool should be able to collect metrics locally in each datacenter, to keep the cost of gathering and transporting metrics low. At the same time, you'll also want to be able to aggregate data from multiple locations. Figure 3-1 shows an example of this.

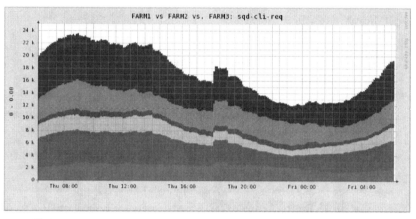

Figure 3-1. *Flickr photo-serving requests, gathered and aggregated from six datacenters*

Whatever metrics collection tool you use, being able to get metrics in and out easily should be considered mandatory.

Layers of Metrics

At Flickr, we have at least three different types of metrics collection:

- Application and business-level metrics stored in a database (MySQL) on a daily basis, gathered nightly (less than daily isn't needed for these purposes)

- Feature-specific, application-level metrics stored in a database (MySQL) in real time (as those events happen)

- Higher-resolution systems and service-level metrics stored in the RRD (with Ganglia) on a 15- or 60-second basis

High-Level Business or Feature-Specific Metrics

These metrics are usually for tracking website-specific events. In the case of Flickr, this means values for photos uploaded, user registrations, average photo size, total disk space consumption, Pro accounts sold, help cases logged and resolved, and so on. Because these are generally used for long-term trending for forecasting product or capacity planning needs, the daily resolution is fine. Adding higher resolution more than once per day wouldn't change any of the results and would only increase the amount of time it would take to run reports or make it a pain to move the data around. Gathering these metrics once a day can be as simple as a nightly cron job working on a replicated slave database kept solely for crunching these numbers.

Because we store these metrics in a database, being able to manipulate or correlate data across different metrics is pretty straightforward, because the date is held constant across metrics.

For example, it might not be a surprise that during the holiday season, the average size of photo uploads increases significantly compared to the rest of the year, because of the new digital cameras being given as gifts during that time. Because we have those values, we can lay out others on the same dates. Then, it's not difficult to see how average upload size can increase disk space consumption (because the original sizes are larger), which can increase Flickr Pro subscriptions (because the limits are extended, compared to free accounts).

When you have metrics that are this high level, you can't be surprised that product-oriented people in your organization are also extremely interested in this same data. Although you might need disk space consumption for capacity planning for your storage needs, they might look at the data with a different perspective. This usage data can help with the timing of feature launches, for example. Site usage can inform product road maps, product road maps can inform capacity planning, capacity planning informs budgeting and infrastructure expectations, and on and on. You'll be very glad you're storing these metrics in a simple and portable format, because the audience for them could be anyone in your organization.

One of the most useful things about application-specific metrics is having the ability to track user interactions. For example, on a social networking site, users can make "friends" with other users, upload a photo, or comment on another user's page. Recording these events when they happen means the time scale isn't on regular intervals. This is opposed to gathering CPU metrics, which is normally done on a regular interval—say, every 15 seconds. This is also different from the daily summing of events shown earlier. When correlating these nonperiodic events with periodic events, you'll want to make sure the time scale is held fixed.

An example of this type of nonregular event at Flickr was when we launched a feature that allowed you to import various email address books, correlate those names and emails with members on the site you might not already be contacts with, and allow you to batch-add them. If we did only daily roll-ups of how many contacts were being made, we certainly would have seen a jump with that one data point, but we wouldn't have seen what the jump looked like right after we launched, and how the jump sustained over hours after the launch and into the following week. The same applied to when we launched the tagging of people in photos. Knowing this information could help to guide us in how we release features in the future, so before we launched features, we would prepare the metrics collection (in these cases, a summary table in MySQL).

System- and Service-Level Metrics

This is the category of metrics that you will see graphed on the screens of ops engineers' laptops. These are the values gathered and displayed by tools such as Cacti, Ganglia, Hyperic HQ, Zenoss, Munin, and all of the others that you've undoubtedly seen throughout your career. The intervals for collecting these system resource metrics should absolutely have some high resolution for them to be valuable for characterizing capacity, troubleshooting issues in real time, and correlating load across different clusters of backend infrastructure segments.

Most tools capture all of the basics you're used to: CPU, network, disk (both space utilization and I/O utilization), memory, and so forth. These should be considered the foundation of insight into what is going on with your infrastructure. I'll argue that if *all* you know about your servers are these metrics, consider yourself blind. Knowing that over an hour's time you reached 12% system CPU usage doesn't tell you much about how your application is behaving—which is the whole point. The layers of application and service metrics will give needed context to what those resources are actually being used for, as shown in Table 3-1.

Table 3-1. *Layers of metrics*

	Example	**Example metrics**
Application layer	Web page or API call	Breakdown: type, latency, rate, etc.
Services layer	Services: Apache, MySQL, etc.	Apache: request rate, response time, busy workers, etc.
		MySQL: query type breakdown (select/insert/update/delete), query rates, busy/sleeping connections, etc.
Physical layer	CPU, memory, disk, network	CPU: user, system, % wait, etc.
		Memory: used, free, cached, etc.
		Disk: space utilization, I/O rates, % wait, etc.
		Network: packets/bytes in/out, etc.

Having these metrics recorded in close proximity to each other, if not in the same tool, yields great advantages. With them, you can answer questions such as these:

- How much CPU time (user and system) does the average web request use?

- What percentage of time is the slowest API call spending on a database query, versus pure time in the application?

- How much is the application relying on filesystem cache, as opposed to in-application buffers?

- Does the response time rise and fall with the request rate, indicating that they have a shared resource that they rely on?

- What percentage of the frontend requests is for web pages, for AJAX, for RSS feeds, or for API methods?

- What is your largest page response in terms of size?

- Does the size of the response change proportionately with the response time?

- What is your slowest database query, and how often is it called?

- What is your most popular database query, and how often is it called?

The answers to these questions will guide you as to which optimizations are worth making, which path to take when starting to troubleshoot an issue, and what resource usage should be deemed "normal" for your application so that you can set alerting thresholds on your monitoring appropriately.

Providing Context for Anomaly Detection and Alerts

The main reason you'll want to collect metrics in the first place is so that, as you would with your gas gauge, you have some idea of what the infrastructure is doing and where it's headed. One of the benefits of knowing where your resources are growing (or shrinking) is the ability to make forecasts. Using forecasting to predict your infrastructure's sizing needs is called *capacity planning*, and there are a couple of books written on the topic already, so we won't cover that here. Suffice it to say that medium- to long-term forecasting can be more art than science when it comes to predicting infrastructure usage. It can be difficult if not impossible to rely on metrics collection alone to provide confidence surrounding *organic* growth experienced by social web applications, and the *nonorganic* step-function growth that can happen surrounding feature releases that exponentially drive user engagement.

Metrics collection gets really interesting when you're looking for anomalies in your usage. When you get some warning or critical alerts on various pieces of your system, you should be able to find those values on a graph somewhere among all of the metrics you're gathering. Got an alert that says CPU usage on a web server is unacceptably high? Yep, it's right there on that graph. Hit the maximum number of connections on a database? Yep, it's right there on that graph. Anything that your monitoring system would alert you to, you should be gathering historical data for, so you can investigate the circumstances that caused that alert to occur.

The topic of automatic anomaly detection in time-series data is vast and interesting, and some of the greatest thinking related to web operations has arisen within the context of forecasting computer system usage. Some papers that come to mind are Jake Brutlag's "Aberrant Behavior Detection in Time Series for Network Service Monitoring," presented at the 2000 LISA Conference (*http://www.usenix.org/publications/library/proceedings/lisa2000/brutlag.html*), as well as Evan Miller's "Holt-Winters Forecasting Applied to Poisson Processes in Real-Time" (*http://www.evanmiller.org/poisson.pdf*).

When things go awry, metrics collection gives context to alerts. You want your alerts to be concise—tell you exactly what they detected, and when—whereas your metrics will tell you what happened leading up to each alert.

Your metrics collection tool is the eyes and ears of your infrastructure. It's the place you'll go to at the first sign of trouble, so you can look around and find any correlating events that can help you diagnose or resolve the issue. Having all events lie on the same timeline also means you can easily see what events happen in what order.

Log Lines Are Metrics, Too

As we're all aware, some of the best metrics and usage indicators can be found in the logs that applications write. At Flickr, we logged a number of different metrics that could be used to track events over time.

Apache 2.x has support for microsecond resolution for response time in its logs. MySQL can log queries that take over a certain threshold of time, and the Percona build of MySQL allows dynamic tuning of that threshold. Squid will give you the response time and the action of the request (cache MISS, HIT, etc.). Logs contain a treasure trove of information, and treating that information as though it was metrics data is a worthwhile thing to do. Figure 3-2 shows an example of this.

A coworker at Etsy, Mike Brittain, has some great examples of trending metrics found in error logs. When he worked at CafeMom.com, he collected and graphed the types of errors and their rate with Munin, another metrics collection tool (see Figure 3-3). More information and code for how Mike does this is available on his blog, at *http://www.mikebrittain.com/blog/2009/12/17/munin-plugins-code-deployment/*.

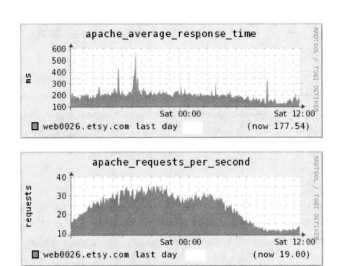

Figure 3-2. *Apache metrics taken from log lines*

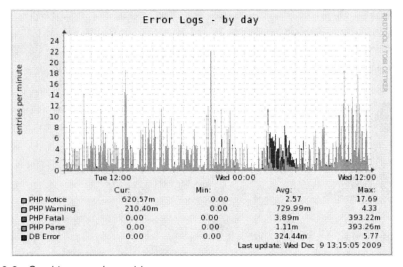

Figure 3-3. *Graphing error log entries*

Also, an excellent project dedicated to tracking various log formats in Ganglia is available at *http://bitbucket.org/maplebed/ganglia-logtailer/*.

Correlation with Change Management and Incident Timelines

Changing production systems brings risk. Keeping track of when the last change was made to your production environment is invaluable when tracking down a site degradation or outage, even just to eliminate (or include) the code push as a cause of the issue. At Flickr, we always found it helpful to have the timestamp of the last code deploy right in the header of our metrics pages (see Figure 3-4).

Figure 3-4. *Putting a timestamp of the last code deploy in the Ganglia header*

This meant we could quickly line up any issues that we saw on the graphs below the header with the last known code deploy.

In another example by Mike Brittain, he graphed the number of minutes since the last code push with Munin (see Figure 3-5). This makes lining up a code push to any resultant effects on the infrastructure easy once he can line up this graph against CPU, network, or any other metric he's gathering.

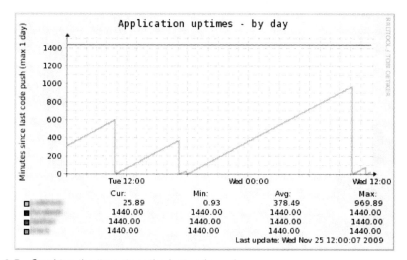

Figure 3-5. *Graphing the time since the last code push*

Making Metrics Available to Your Alerting Mechanisms

At the beginning of this chapter, I mentioned that monitoring systems built to alert on metrics can be and sometimes are different tools than the system collecting the metrics. Nagios is an example of a monitoring/alerting tool that is commonly found alongside metrics collection systems.

One of the advantages of having a metrics collection system focus entirely on gathering metrics is the ability to find integration points for alerting on the value metrics. At Flickr, Ganglia was our metrics collection system, and Nagios was our monitoring and alerting system. In some cases, we tied the two together to create more sophisticated alerting criteria. Giving Nagios awareness of metrics gathered by Ganglia allowed for a more advanced monitoring approach in which a fault could occur not with a single node reaching a critical threshold but with a multiple-value subthreshold *pattern*.

For example, let's say you have a cluster of web servers, and they are running Apache. And let's say they ask backend infrastructure such as databases running MySQL or Postgres for information used to build web pages. A common scenario that can come up is a database query taking longer than expected for whatever reason. The number of total active database connections increases, because they aren't closing as quickly. As a result, the number of busy Apache processes waiting on those connections is also increasing as they wait for their results. Both the web servers and the databases have maximum values for those processes held open, so there are warning and critical thresholds as a percentage of their maximums that you'd want to be aware of.

Do you alert on both values (busy Apache processes and open database connections), for every node in the web server and database cluster? What if only one database (or one database cluster) of many is seeing this issue, or one subset of web servers? At Flickr, pointing Nagios at various metrics being collected by Ganglia meant we could alert on a critical percentage of web servers reaching a critical value of busy Apache processes, but only if a critical percentage of database servers were reaching a critical value of open and busy connections.

Being able to handle these and more complex couplings of systems and metrics meant we could keep our alerting noise down, and page someone in the middle of the night only when a commonly known but complex scenario arose.

Another example is being able to alert on *acceleration* of values. Alerting systems have some notion of history but not in the same levels of detail that metrics collection systems have. For example, if your application includes the ability to upload photos or video, and you have a relatively well-known usage pattern for that activity (such as a daily peak and valley), you can alert on a high- or low-water mark for changes in that rate. You might expect a drop in uploaded photos, for example, when the U.S. East

Coast goes to bed for the night. The difference between peak of the day and valley of the day might be 40%. But do you expect a 40% drop over one hour? Not a drop to zero, but a sharp drop over a short period? This might be something worth alerting on.

This integration of monitoring systems and metrics collection is common, and a good number of open source projects and documentation are built just for this purpose:

- Integrating Nagios and Ganglia (*http://www.monitoringexchange.org/inventory/Check-Plugins/Software/Misc/check_ganglia*)

- Nagios and Cacti (*http://trac2.assembla.com/npc/*)

- Nagios and Munin (*http://munin-monitoring.org/wiki/HowToContactNagios*)

- GroundWork Open Source (integrates Nagios, Ganglia, and Cacti; *http://www.groundworkopensource.com/community/open-source/*)

Using Metrics to Guide Load-Feedback Mechanisms

Another advantage of collecting time-series metrics is being able to programmatically adapt your application to its own metrics. Safe and sophisticated feedback loops can be built, and there are a number of examples where this is useful.

In the world of cloud computing, where provisioning new instances requires only a simple API call to your provider, knowing when to turn up more instances or destroy existing ones can get tricky. If you're making those provision/destroy judgments based on resource usage being collected, it gets a lot easier. This is a common scenario in which to use metrics as a feedback mechanism.

I have an example of a large project at Flickr where this sort of feedback loop proved to be invaluable.

In 2007, Yahoo! decided it would shut down Yahoo!Photos. The plan was pretty simple: notifications to Yahoo!Photos users would go out that the service was going away, and they would have an option to take all of their photos along with metadata to another service, including non-Yahoo! services such as Shutterfly and Kodak Gallery. Flickr was one of the options given.

Coming up with the capacity estimates for this project was going to be a tough exercise. Although we had some metrics describing typical Yahoo!Photos users, in terms of frequency of upload, size of photos, and other factors, we really had no idea how many people would choose the Flickr option, and after they did, how their usage patterns would change. Because we're talking about a service that provided storage for over 10 years, it was going to be a huge amount of data, all consumed within a short period of time. Without saying how much exactly, I can tell you that in late

2009, Flickr consumed about 12 TB per day of storage. During this migration from Yahoo!Photos to Flickr for a short but sustained period of time in 2007, it was more than double that per day.

In preparation for the migration, we made our best guesses at the storage needs based on migration estimates and the existing volume and size of Yahoo!Photos data, allowing for a generous safety factor above that to make sure we wouldn't run out of storage before the migration was over. We had metrics for everything we could think of:

- Accounts migrated
- Photos migrated
- Photos processed
- Migration queue size
- Disk space consumption

We started the migration process for the users who elected to migrate to Flickr, and watched.

I'll skip to the good part: even with conservative guesses, we were *wrong*. Quite wrong. Even though we researched and were thorough in coming up with the capacity estimates for storage, the rate at which people wanted to migrate their photos to Flickr was much higher than we expected. If we migrated users' Yahoo!Photos data at the rate they were opting into the migration, we were going to run out of storage space with what we had deployed. We needed more storage, or uploads would stop on Flickr.

Thankfully, we realized this pretty quickly because our metrics collection was in place for tracking disk consumption, but we were going to be caught in the bounds of procurement timelines. The challenge was to buy, install, configure, and deploy more storage quickly so that we didn't run out of existing storage. The race to get more space deployed was up against the migration process.

To explain how we averted the crisis through metrics feedback, let me give you some background on how the migration process took place (as shown in Figure 3-6):

1. The Yahoo!Photos user is told that the service is going away, and the user is presented with a list of options. If she picks Flickr, her account goes into a queue for migration.

2. When her migration task comes up in the queue, her account is locked on Yahoo!Photos, preventing any changes from happening. An API-to-API communication between Yahoo!Photos and Flickr occurs, which gathers data about the photos needing to migrate.

3. Flickr consumes and processes the photos and metadata from the Yahoo!Photos account.

4. The Yahoo!Photos account is written to Flickr storage and databases.

After the migration was finished, the account was unlocked on the Flickr side and notifications went out to the user notifying her that she could now use her new Flickr account with freshly migrated photos. An individual account didn't take very long, but there were a lot of accounts. Basically, the process was a massive asynchronous version of creating a new Flickr account and batch-uploading the photos.

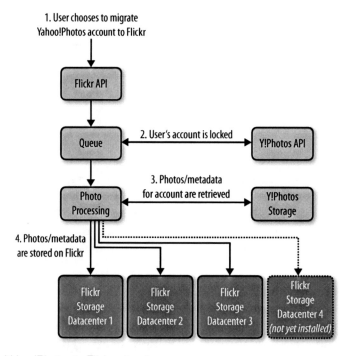

Figure 3-6. *Yahoo!Photos to Flickr migration process*

Because we knew how much storage we were consuming for the migrations and how much space we consumed for "organic" (nonmigration) growth, if we made some worst-case assumptions we could forecast how long we had until we ran out of space, in days. We gathered up another huge order of storage, one that was much more liberal with the numbers, and started the clock. We confirmed delivery and installation estimates so that we knew when the storage would show up at the datacenters and how long it would take before it was ready to take production writes.

Because we use Ganglia for our metrics collection, all it took was a three-line shell script to find the rate at which we were consuming storage, and expose that number to the API process that was working on the migrations. Because we stored photos in multiple datacenters around the United States, we made sure the API process could reach this value remotely, checking all of the datacenters that were taking migrated data. We modified the API process to look at that storage consumption rate. If the rate of consumption over the last hour was greater than that which would get us to the install date of new storage, the rate of migration on queued accounts would back off, and if it was below a certain rate, it would speed up. In the procedure I listed earlier, we inserted a step between steps 2 and 3 that would check the current consumption rate as people opted in to the migration (see Figure 3-7).

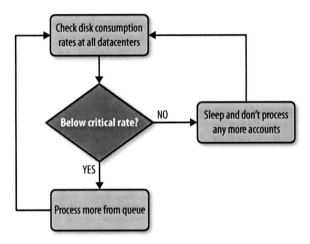

Figure 3-7. *Throttling the Yahoo!Photos migration by storage consumption feedback loops*

Because we were throttling the rate at which we migrated users who opted in to the migration queue, the accounts spent some time longer in the queue. Slowing down the process was the trade-off for actually being able to finish the process and not affect the current activity on Flickr.

In the end, the migration finished, and we never did run out of storage. In hindsight, our estimates were off, but not as off as we first thought; the initial spike in opted-in migrations brought enough concern to deploy more storage sooner, but it did taper off as time got close to the original storage limit.

The moral of this story is that we were able to leverage our metrics collection systems in multiple locations around the country to participate in a feedback loop that allowed for the safe migration of *petabytes* of photos from Yahoo!Photos to Flickr with minimal effect on the availability of either service.

A Metrics Collection System, Illustrated: Ganglia

As I've said, metrics collection systems should do the heavy lifting for you while you build and manage a growing infrastructure. I've given examples of how metrics collection can assist in the forecasting and troubleshooting of system and application anomalies, and it should be obvious that metrics collection should be considered mandatory, not optional. Without it, you're blind. With it, you're in control of your site's destiny.

As with all tools and their implementation, the devil is in the details. No matter if you're choosing an open source tool, using a commercial piece of metrics software, or writing a collection of scripts to gather application-specific metrics, they all have variations on the same ideas. How your tool collects, aggregates, stores, and serves your metrics will make a world of difference, and how you use (and rely on) it will largely depend on how easy those operations are.

To take a look at a real-world example, I asked Matt Massie to give his insight when he was designing and building a metrics collection system meant to scale with thousands of nodes across disparate physical locations. Ten years ago, Matt wrote the open source metrics collection tool called Ganglia, and although it was originally written with the High Performance Computing (HPC) industry in mind, it has become popular over the years with growing web infrastructures.

Because we've discussed the *what* and *why* of metrics collection, I think it's useful to hear Matt's thoughts on Ganglia as examples of what to consider when gathering metrics data and even creating your own collection utilities.

Background

Turn the dial back to January 1999.

America Online (AOL.com) was the most-visited website, and everyone was using dial-up modems to connect to the Internet. Mac OS 9 was the latest operating system from Apple, the Linux kernel was at version 2.2, and Windows users were all upgrading to Windows 98. Netscape Navigator was the most popular web browser.

At that time, I was working as a sys admin at the Washington University Medical Center in St. Louis and living in a small studio apartment. My apartment just happened to be across the street from where Pope John Paul II was going to be staying during his 31-hour whirlwind tour of St. Louis. For fun, I decided to set up a website to stream the visit live over the Internet. I called it the "popecam."

Keep in mind that this was 1999. Webcams were just starting to catch on, and I didn't have broadband to my apartment (almost no one did). I did, however, have access to the medical center network. I built the web server hardware using spare parts and ensured it had both an Ethernet and a modem card. I installed Solaris 7 (x86) on the box because it had the driver support I needed and a stable PPP server. I plugged the modem into my office phone jack and dialed into the server from my apartment.

Overall, the flow was (1) snap a picture with the webcam, (2) send the picture using FTP over the PPP link from my apartment to the web server at the medical center, and then (3) serve the image using an Apache web server over Ethernet to the world. I modified some C code written by Rob McCool that used multipart MIME encoding to "push" images to clients for video streaming. The system worked well, thanks to help from some friends (especially my buddy, Chuck) and was ready to go for the pope's visit.

Hours before a motorcade was scheduled to drive the pope through the city and deliver him to his temporary residence across the street, I opened my eighth floor window and began setting up the webcam tripod. I'll never forget the chill that went up my spine when I looked around and realized that snipers, on the rooftops across the street, were looking at me through their scopes and chatting into their radios. In retrospect, it was pretty dumb of me to think that setting up a tripod in my window wouldn't draw attention. I was so relieved when I was allowed to finish my setup and start the camera rolling (see Figure 3-8). Thousands of people tuned in to the popecam that day to watch the visit live, and my guestbook and inbox were flooded with thanks from people from all over the world.

Figure 3-8. *Image from the popecam taken January 26, 1999*

Before the pope's visit, I experimented a lot with camera position and sample rate. Even though I was able to send only one image every 15 seconds, I was still able to capture a picture of the pope as he sped down my street. I wanted a faster frame rate, but the PPP link was just too slow relative to the image size. I wanted my camera to have higher resolution and a wider field of view, but webcams at the time were not nearly as good as they are today. Even if I had a higher-resolution camera, I was still constrained by the PPP link.

You'll face similar questions when you're planning the metrics collection infrastructure for your web operations. How much bandwidth should be dedicated to passing metrics data? What is the best metrics resolution you can achieve for a given bandwidth budget? What metrics should be collected and how often? How should the data be visualized and shared with others?

Later that year, in the fall of 1999, I started work as a staff researcher in the Computer Science Department at the University of California, Berkeley, to help build software that made it practical to deploy, manage, and run clusters with thousands of nodes. Our team was also part of a government project that strived to advance science by creating a ubiquitous, continuous, and pervasive national computational infrastructure for universities and government research labs.

My focus was on designing and implementing the metrics collection infrastructure for this grid of large and distributed clusters. After a year of work and a number of false starts, I finally had a system working that I decided to name Ganglia. A ganglion is a cluster of interconnecting nerve cells typically found in the peripheral nervous system. The name was meant to imply that Ganglia was interconnected and didn't interfere with your central processing pipeline. I'll be the first to admit that the metaphor is tenuous and lost on most people.

Ganglia has been an open source project for 10 years now, and I've learned a lot from all the great people who've contributed to its success. As I share my experiences with Ganglia, I don't mean to imply that Ganglia is the only technology that addresses metrics collection, machine discovery, data aggregation, and visualization. Other tools, such as Cacti, Munin, and collectd, can be used to complement or replace Ganglia altogether for metrics collection.

This section also isn't meant be a Ganglia "How To," but more of a high-level conversation that I hope you'll find useful as you evaluate, install, or possibly build your own metrics collection software for your web operations.

A Quick Introduction to Ganglia

For people who aren't familiar with Ganglia, I'd like to take a moment to quickly outline the components and overall architecture. Table 3-2 provides details on each component in Ganglia.

Table 3-2. *Components of Ganglia*

Component	Purpose
Ganglia Monitoring Daemon (gmond)	Runs on every machine that you want to collect and announce metrics changes
Ganglia Meta Daemon (gmetad)	Collects state from pools of gmond resources, aggregates and saves them to time-series databases
Ganglia web frontend	Allows you to easily browse all the grids, clusters, and hosts in your metrics collection domain
Ganglia Metrics Tool (gmetric)	Used to publish custom metrics beyond the standard system metrics

The overall architecture of Ganglia looks like Figure 3-9.

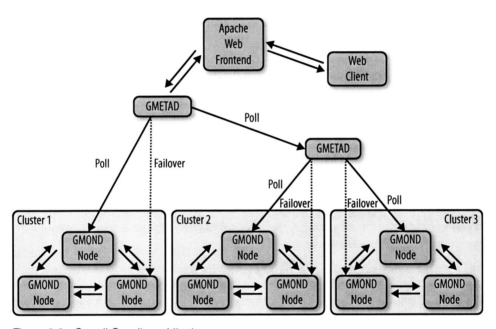

Figure 3-9. *Overall Ganglia architecture*

Each node in a cluster is part of a single local area communication channel. This channel is used to share information about changes in metrics state within the cluster. Gmetad is used to create a monitoring overlay that groups resources into a hierarchy.

Ganglia uses a number of techniques to keep metrics collection costs low in terms of both computational resources and management workload.

The need to keep collection and aggregation costs low

One of the requirements for a good metrics collection system is that it should use minimal resources. As we began to roll out Ganglia to more and more clusters at other universities, I remember worrying that Ganglia would rat itself out. The last thing I wanted to hear was: "Ganglia works well and I have great visibility into my computational resources now. However, looking at the Ganglia report, I see that Ganglia is the largest consumer of resources." Luckily, I heard that complaint only once, when I rolled out an embarrassing bug. (I'll provide more details on that later, when I talk about metrics time and value thresholds.)

Good metrics collection systems should keep management and configuration costs low. For example, adding new machines to a cluster shouldn't require any clicks in a GUI or pushing out a new configuration to every node in the cluster. Maintaining configuration on clusters with thousands of machines isn't easy, and a metrics collection system shouldn't add to that burden.

The need to automatically discover new nodes and metrics

Multicast is ideally suited for delivering messages to groups of machines. A multicast message will be delivered only to machines on a network that have explicitly subscribed to the same multicast channel. In contrast, a unicast message is delivered to a single destination machine, and a broadcast message is delivered to all machines on a network segment.

Multicast is used by systems such as Apple's Bonjour to allow users to, for example, automatically set up a network without any manual configuration, or find printers and file servers. Multicast is also widely used for commercial stock exchanges and multimedia content delivery networks.

The Internet Assigned Numbers Authority (IANA) reserves IPv4 addresses in the range 224.0.0.0 to 239.255.255.255 for multicast traffic. To make it easy for me to remember the Ganglia multicast channel in the beginning, I set the default channel to 239.2.11.71 because my birthday is 2/11/1971. Ten years later, that default address has stayed the same.

Multicast allows gmond to be started without a configuration file. By default, gmond will join the multicast channel 239.2.11.71 to send and receive metrics. In this default configuration, all gmonds on a network have information about the state of all machines on the same channel. This symmetrical listen-announce protocol allows each node in a cluster to automatically discover other nodes in a cluster as it saves their metrics values. This design also provides perfect failover because the state of the cluster is mirrored on each node.

Although this zero configuration approach is convenient, in practice it scales only to clusters with a few hundred or so nodes. For clusters with thousands of nodes, most people configure gmond for unicast messaging to a fixed set of machines. As a data point, a 90-node cluster sending metrics over multicast will consume, on average, about 27 Kb/s (55 packets/s).

The need to match network transport with your metrics collection task

The two most popular IP transports are Transmission Control Protocol (TCP) and User Datagram Protocol (UDP). Each protocol has different characteristics (see Table 3-3).

Table 3-3. *Comparison of UDP and TCP*

	UDP	TCP
Connection setup	Connectionless	Requires that a connection be built before data is sent
Data interface	Message based	Stream based
Overhead	Very little	More than UDP
Reliability	"Best effort" with no reliability guarantees	Reliable with all data being acknowledged
Transmission speed	Very high	Lower than UDP
Data size	Limited to a single MTU (about 1,472 bytes typically)	Unlimited
Multicast	Supported	Not supported

From this comparison, you can see that UDP is ideal for lightweight, local messages within a cluster, while TCP is better for sharing information between clusters distributed around the Internet.

I designed gmond and gmetad with the characteristics of UDP and TCP in mind. The comparison of gmond and gmetad in Table 3-4 highlights the unique design of each component.

Table 3-4. *Comparison of gmond and gmetad*

	Gmond	Gmetad
Transport	Lightweight UDP messages within clusters	Uses TCP exclusively to connect distributed clusters together
Message format	Compact binary format called External Data Representation (XDR)	Verbose human-readable Extensible Markup Language (XML)
Connection setup	Never connects to other processes	Pulls data from gmond and gmetad processes
Overhead	Keeps all state in-memory	Aggregates and stores all metrics to disk in time-series databases
Reliability	Failures require a reconstruction of the overall cluster state, which can take tens of minutes	Automatic failover to another gmetad or gmond to route around failures with all data stored to disk
Multicast	Used for discovery and zero configuration setup	Doesn't use multicast over the wide area network; hard to configure, and error prone

The need to implicitly prioritize cluster metrics

Gmond is targeted toward metrics collection for a large group of machines on the same local area network (LAN). As I've already mentioned, gmond sends messages using UDP, which is not reliable. To minimize the effect of lost messages and provide implicit prioritization, each metric that gmond monitors has unique settings for collection interval and time/value thresholds:

Collection interval

Defines the frequency with which gmond collects and processes a particular metric. It's possible for constant metrics such as the number of cores in a machine to be collected only once.

Value threshold

Defines the absolute value difference necessary between a collected value and the last reported value to cause the collected value to be sent. Only significant value changes solicit a message.

Time threshold

Maximum amount of time that can elapse before a metrics value is reported regardless of the value of the metric. This threshold is necessary to work around the fact that UDP is unreliable and to provide a way to calculate the age of a value. If one or more time thresholds have passed since we received an update, we know our current value for the metric is out of date.

At a high level, gmond follows these steps for each metric it monitors:

1. Collect the current value of the metric.

2. If the absolute difference between the current value and last reported value is greater than the specified value threshold, go to step 5.

3. If the current time is past our hard limit for sending the metric, go to step 5.

4. Go to step 7.

5. Send the value of the metric and save the value for later comparison (in step 2).

6. Use the time threshold to calculate the next hard limit for sending the metric by basically adding the time threshold to the current time.

7. Go to sleep for the collection interval.

8. Go to step 1.

This overall approach results in gmond sending messages only when a significant change in metrics has occurred. Also, randomness is added to the preceding calculations to reduce network contention. The last thing you want is thousands of machines collecting and sending metrics in unison.

Equally important to keeping metrics collection costs low is to keep them fixed. In the worst case, a message will be sent every collection interval for each metric collected, and in the best case, metrics will be sent only after the specific time threshold has passed. This range allows you to create a fixed budget for metrics collection unless, of course, there is a bug in your thresholds.

You should be very careful when you choose value thresholds for network metrics. When I first added network metrics collection to Ganglia, I accidentally set the default collection interval too short and the value threshold too small. I didn't notice this configuration error on my laptop, but it was painfully obvious when we began to roll out Ganglia to a number of large clusters. Every node began to send network metrics updates in response to other nodes sending network metrics, and Ganglia caused a number of very large network storms. Hopefully, you can spare yourself the embarrassment of this happening.

One feature that Ganglia doesn't have, but should, is metrics batching. If you're writing your own metrics collection system, make sure you support it. Batching metrics values together before sending them reduces the number of packets you send as well as the bandwidth you use. For example, every IPv4/UDP packet you send has a 14-byte Ethernet header, a 20-byte IP header, an 8-byte UDP header, and a 4-byte Ethernet trailer. Actually, these numbers ignore factors such as padding, VLANs, IP options, and IPv6 differences, but we'll use them for a back-of-napkin calculation.

Say you are sending metrics data that is 32 bytes in size. If you send ten updates without batching, it requires that ten 78-byte packets be sent, for a total of 780 bytes. With batching, you will send one packet that is 366 bytes in length, with 320 bytes for the metrics data. In this example, batching reduces the number of packets sent by 90% and cuts the bandwidth used by more than half. One downside of batching is that if a packet is lost, you lose multiple metrics updates instead of one.

The need to aggregate and organize metrics once they're collected

Before we continue, you should take a moment to look back at Figure 3-9, which shows the overall Ganglia architecture. Up to now, I've focused on the communication that occurs inside each cluster. Once you have metrics collection running on each of your clusters, you're going to want to aggregate, save, and view the data.

If a metric is valuable enough to collect on one machine, it's probably valuable enough to collect across all your machines. This is especially true for system metrics and less so for application metrics. For example, collecting MySQL metrics makes sense only on your database boxes, whereas you'll likely want to collect the one-minute load on all machines regardless of what applications are running on them.

The Ganglia Meta Daemon (gmetad) collects, aggregates, and saves metrics across a group of machines. This summarized data is passed to other upstream gmetads participating in the metrics collection hierarchy. This hierarchical delegation model allows you to create very large and useful decentralized metrics collection overlays. These overlays can span a single university campus or the globe.

For an extreme example, let's imagine we wanted every machine in the United States to be connected to a single large metrics collection overlay. We would have a single national gmetad that polled data from each of the 50 authoritative gmetads running in each state. Each state-level gmetad would collect metrics from each county-level gmetad. Each county-level gmetad would collect data from each city-level gmetad, and so on.

The root node in this case would not be overwhelmed by all the metrics data coming from every machine in the United States. It would only be reading summaries from each state and generating an overall summary for the United States. After all, it doesn't take a powerful computer to add 50 numbers together.

The Ganglia web frontend is typically installed on every machine running gmetad. The web frontend allows you to visualize the data that each gmetad has collected and navigate the overall metrics collection overlay using your web browser. For example, you could look at the gmetad for all of the United States to see the summary information for the United States and each state data source. You could then, for example, click a graph for Illinois and immediately be sent to the web frontend for Illinois for more details. In a sense, Ganglia allows you to zoom in and zoom out to get just the right picture of the data you are interested in. This tree of metrics values is the spatial component metrics collection, but there is also a time component.

Gmetad stores volatile metrics data to the RRDtool Round Robin Database (RRD). An RRD is designed to store and report the history of numeric data. A very useful characteristic of RRDs is that they do not grow in size over time. There are a fixed number of "buckets" for each internal archive in an RRD. As new data arrives, all the relevant archives are updated and older data is dropped. For a simplistic example, you could have 24 buckets for each hour of the day and 7 buckets for each day of the week. An RRD is ideal for finding trends in data over different periods of time. Mating this time-series data with the hierarchical delegation model explained earlier gives you a powerful tool for asking questions such as: "What is the trend in CPU utilization over the past year across the United States?"

As much as I wish it were so, Ganglia has never been deployed at quite this grand a scale. A more down-to-earth example would be something like the Grid3 group that used Ganglia to collect metrics from thousands of machines distributed across dozens of sites in the United States and South Korea for advanced physics research in 2003. The metrics data collected for Grid3 was plugged into other systems, such as Globus, which let people share computing resources for physics experiments.

Being able to aggregate data from pools of machines over different periods of time is also useful for capacity planning. Knowing that a single machine is at 80% CPU utilization is useful, but finding out that an entire cluster has been at 80% utilization over the past month is invaluable. Being able to see the "big picture" can help you plan hardware purchases, see bottlenecks in your processing pipeline, and gain insights into the dynamics of your web operations.

The need to provide convenient interfaces for creating new metrics and pulling out existing metrics for correlation against other data

I dealt with a number of security breaches in my early career as a system and network administrator. One of the larger attacks I helped investigate was a coordinated international attack on machines that were part of the Human Genome Project at a medical center. When I designed Ganglia, security was in the front of my mind. Because gmond runs on every machine you want to collect metrics from, a security vulnerability would cause quite a headache. It was important to me that people would trust Ganglia, because I hoped it would be running on a large number of machines.

In the past 10 years, there has been only one security vulnerability in gmond (fixed in version 2.5.5). A specially crafted message could cause gmond to segfault and crash. This denial-of-service vulnerability could not be triggered remotely, caused no privilege escalation, and did not allow arbitrary code execution.

When evaluating metrics collection systems (or building your own) you should think about how data flows into and out of the system. For gmond, you add/update metrics data by sending a UDP message, and you read metrics by connecting to a TCP port and parsing the XML output. When a client connects to the gmond TCP port (8649 by default), gmond will immediately dump the metrics data for all machines it is aware of and then close the connection. Clients are not allowed to query gmond for particular data. There is no RPC involved. There is also no way to explicitly request that data be deleted. Deletion is lazily handled using explicit data timeouts.

A Ganglia metrics update message contains the metrics value along with information about the update interval and amount of time to wait before deleting the metric. As long as a metric is regularly updated, it won't be deleted. When the first timeout is passed, Ganglia will report the data as being out of date. When the second timeout (for deletion) passes without an update, Ganglia will delete the metrics data completely and cease reporting the metric altogether.

Ganglia reports dozens of system metrics out of the box, including those for CPU, load, memory, disk, and network metrics information. To send your own metrics, there is also a command-line tool for generating and sending metrics updates, called gmetric. It's very easy to call gmetric from inside a bash script periodically called by cron. There is also a Google code project called embeddedgmetric that allows you to embed gmetric functionality inside your application. Both of these tools help make it easy to add any metrics you want to track to Ganglia. Be creative and add all the metrics you want. Let Ganglia worry about the details.

It's just as easy to pull data out of Ganglia. Just connect to TCP port 8649 on gmond, and it will dump all of the metrics it's aware of in XML. Even a simple command such as the following would work:

```
% telnet localhost 8649
```

Gmond will immediately close the connection once all the metrics data has been written. There is also a simple tool called gstat that presents a list of machines ordered by load. You can use gstat to create scripts for checking which machines are up or to see which machines are the least loaded and ready for more work. For scientific clusters running a Message Passing Interface (MPI) implementation, gstat can also be used to generate an MPI machine file with the least-loaded machines listed first.

Ganglia is designed to make it easy to collect metrics and observe trends in your data. Ganglia doesn't do alerting. However, it's pretty easy to pipe Ganglia data into other software such as Nagios to handle sending the alerts for you. There's also a simple Python script that generates an RSS feed of alerts for Ganglia data. Messages in this feed contain the URL to the particular portion of your metrics collection system that triggered the event.

There's even an OpenGL application that portrays each node in a cluster as a separate fish with characteristics that describe the state of the node. When a machine dies, the fish representing that machine flips on its side and floats to the top of the tank (*http:// sourceforge.net/projects/fish-monitoring/*); see Figure 3-10.

I could continue for pages listing all the cool tools that have been built to use the data that Ganglia exports. In the interest of space, I haven't even talked about the Ganglia Execution System (gexec), which uses Ganglia data to place work on the best possible machines in your infrastructure.

Figure 3-10. *Fish visual cluster monitoring*

Conclusion

Gathering, storing, and displaying metrics should be considered a mission-critical part of your infrastructure. Whether it's for troubleshooting on-the-fly, capacity forecasting, product launch planning, or application feedback mechanisms, you will be lost without the right metrics to give you a full view of what your infrastructure is doing. At Flickr and Etsy, we depend on these metrics on a daily basis to give context to our work.

All good metrics collection systems share the same traits:

- They can collect metrics while keeping collection and storage costs low.
- They can aggregate and organize metrics once they're collected.
- New devices can automatically be added to the system without disruption or overhead.
- New metrics can easily be added without disruption.

- Metrics can be pulled out as easily as they are put in, allowing for correlation with external sources of data.

- Metrics collection can be done on a global and physically separate scale while maintaining integration.

These traits allow for your metrics system to scale and provide the flexibility to measure and record all of the things you'll need to manage your site.

Matt Massie leaves you with this advice: think about security when you design how data flows through your system, and make it easy to export data to other applications. In the end, you want to create a system that people trust and can be creative with. Once you have your operations collecting metrics data, you may even find that tracking the data is actually fun and makes your life a little easier.

## CHAPTER FOUR

Continuous Deployment

Eric Ries

SOFTWARE SHOULD BE DESIGNED, WRITTEN, AND DEPLOYED IN SMALL BATCHES.
Doing so is good for developers, the product, and operations, too.

The batch size is the unit at which work products move between stages in a development process. For software, the easiest batch to see is code. Every time an engineer checks in code, he is batching up a certain amount of work. There are many techniques for controlling these batches, ranging from the tiny batches needed for continuous deployment to more traditional branch-based development, where all of the code from multiple developers working for weeks or months is batched up and integrated together.

It turns out that there are tremendous benefits from working with a batch size radically smaller than traditional practice suggests. In my experience, a few hours of coding is enough to produce a viable batch and is worth checking in *and deploying*. Similar results apply in product management, design, testing, and even operations. This is actually a hard case to make, because most of the benefits of small batches are counterintuitive.

Small Batches Mean Faster Feedback

The sooner you pass your work on to a later stage, the sooner you can find out how that next stage will receive it. If you're not used to working in this way, it may seem annoying to get interrupted so soon after you were "done" with something, instead of just working it all out by yourself. But these interruptions are actually much more efficient when you get them soon, because you're that much more likely to remember what you were working on. And as we'll see in a moment, you may also be busy building subsequent parts that depend on mistakes you made in earlier steps. The sooner you find out about these dependencies, the less time you'll waste having to unwind them.

Small Batches Mean Problems Are Instantly Localized

This is easiest to see in deployment. When something goes wrong with production software, it's almost always because of an unintended side effect of some piece of code. Think about the last time you were called upon to debug a problem like that. How much of the time you spent debugging was actually dedicated to fixing the problem, compared to the time it took to track down where the bug originated?

When bugs are found quickly, they can be fixed quickly. Take the example of Flickr, which practiced continuous deployment before being acquired by Yahoo!. As John Allspaw states:

> Amongst many Yahoo! properties, including the largest ones, which have quite dialed-in ops teams, Flickr's MTTD was insanely low because of this. Since only a handful of lines are changed when they are deployed, changes that do cause regressions or unexpected performance issues are quickly identified and fixed. And of course, the MTTR (Mean Time To Resolve) is much lower as well, because the number of changes needed to fix or roll back is not only finite, but also small.

Small Batches Reduce Risk

An example of this is integration risk, which we use continuous integration (*http://startuplessonslearned.com/2008/12/continuous-integration-step-by-step.html*) to mitigate. Integration problems happen when two people make incompatible changes to some part of the system. These come in all shapes and sizes. You can have code that depends on a certain configuration that's deployed on production. If that configuration changes before the code is deployed, the person who changes it won't know he's introduced a problem. That code is now a ticking time bomb, waiting to cause trouble when it's deployed.

When the explosion comes, it's usually operations that bears the brunt. After all, it would never have happened without that change in configuration (never mind that it also wouldn't have happened without that new code being written, either). New code is generally perceived as valuable forward progress. Configuration changes are a necessary overhead. Reducing the odds of them colliding makes everyone's life better. This is counterintuitive. It seems like having *more* releases will lead to increased odds of things going wrong. As we'll see, that's not actually correct. Slowing down the release process doesn't actually reduce the total number of changes—it just combines them into ever-larger batches.

Small Batches Reduce Overhead

In my experience, this is the most counterintuitive of its effects. Most organizations have their batch size tuned so as to reduce their overhead. For example, if QA takes a week to certify a release, it's likely that the company does releases no more than once every 30 or 60 days. Telling such a company that it should work in a two-week batch size sounds absurd—the company would spend 50% of its time waiting for QA to certify the release! But this argument is not quite right. This is something so surprising that I didn't really believe it the first few times I saw it in action. It turns out that organizations get better at the things they do very often. So, when we start checking in code more often, release more often, or conduct more frequent design reviews, we can actually do a lot to make those steps dramatically more efficient.

Of course, that doesn't necessarily mean we *will* make those steps more efficient. A common line of argument is: if we have the power to make a step more efficient, why don't we invest in that infrastructure first, and then reduce the batch size as we lower the overhead? This makes sense, and yet it rarely works. The bottlenecks that large batches cause are often hidden, and it takes work to make them evident, and even more work to invest in fixing them. When the existing system is working "good enough" these projects inevitably languish.

These changes pay increasing dividends, because each improvement now directly frees up somebody in QA or operations while also reducing the total time required for the certification step. Those freed-up resources might be able to spend some of that time helping the development team actually prevent bugs in the first place, or just take on some of their routine work. That frees up even more development resources, and so on. Pretty soon, the team can be developing and testing in a continuous feedback loop, addressing micro-bottlenecks the moment they appear. If you've never had the chance to work in an environment like this, I highly recommend you try it. I doubt you'll go back.

Let me show you what this looked like for the operations and engineering teams at IMVU (*http://www.imvu.com/*). We had made so many improvements to our tools and processes for deployment that it was pretty hard to take the site down. We had five strong levels of defense:

- Each engineer had his own sandbox that mimicked production as closely as possible (whenever it diverged, we'd inevitably find out in a "Five Whys" [*http://startuplessonslearned.com/2008/11/five-whys.html*] shortly thereafter).

- We had a comprehensive set of unit, acceptance, functional, and performance tests, and practiced test-driven development (TDD) across the whole team. Our engineers built a series of test tags, so you could quickly run a subset of tests in your sandbox that you thought were relevant to your current project or feature.

- One hundred percent of those tests ran, via a continuous integration cluster, after every check-in. When a test failed, it would prevent that revision from being deployed.

- When someone wanted to do a deployment, we had a completely automated system that we called the *cluster immune system*. This would deploy the change incrementally, one machine at a time. That process would continually monitor the health of those machines, as well as the cluster as a whole, to see if the change was causing problems. If it didn't like what was going on, it would reject the change, do a fast revert, and lock deployments until someone investigated what went wrong.

- We had a comprehensive set of Nagios alerts that would trigger a pager in operations if anything went wrong. Because Five Whys kept turning up a few key metrics that were hard to set static thresholds for, we even had a dynamic prediction algorithm that would make forecasts based on past data and fire alerts if the metric ever went out of its normal bounds.

So, if you had been able to sneak into the desks of any of our engineers, log in to their machines, and secretly check in an infinite loop on some highly trafficked page, here's what would have happened. Somewhere between 10 and 20 minutes later, they would have received an email with a message that read something like this:

Dear so-and-so,

Thank you so much for attempting to check in revision 1234. Unfortunately, that is a terrible idea, and your change has been reverted. We've also alerted the whole team to what's happened and look forward to you figuring out what went wrong.

Best of luck,

Your Software

(OK, that's not *exactly* what it said, but you get the idea.)

The goal of continuous deployment is to help development teams drive waste out of their process by simultaneously reducing the batch size (*http://startuplessonslearned .com/2009/02/work-in-small-batches.html*) and increasing the tempo of their work. This makes it possible for teams to get—and stay—in a condition of flow for sustained periods. This condition makes it much easier for teams to innovate, experiment, and achieve sustained productivity, and it nicely complements other continuous improvement systems, such as Five Whys, which we'll discuss later in this chapter.

The Quality Defenders' Lament

One large source of waste in development is *double-checking*. For example, imagine a team operating in a traditional waterfall development system, without continuous deployment, TDD, or continuous integration. When a developer wants to check in code, or an ops staff member thinks he's ready to push a release, this is a very scary moment. He has a choice: do it now, or double-check to make sure everything still works and looks good. Both options are attractive. If he proceeds now, he can claim the rewards of being done sooner. On the other hand, if he causes a problem, his previous speed will be counted against him. Why didn't he spend just another five minutes making sure he didn't cause that problem? In practice, how people respond to this dilemma is determined by their incentives, which are driven by the culture of their team. How severely is failure punished? Who will ultimately bear the cost of their mistakes? How important are schedules? Does the team value finishing early?

But the thing to notice in this situation is that there is really no right answer. People who agonize over the choice reap the worst of both worlds. As a result, people will tend toward two extremes: those who believe in getting things done as fast as possible, and those who believe that work should be carefully checked. Any intermediate position is untenable over the long term. When things go wrong any nuanced explanation of the trade-offs involved is going to sound unsatisfying. After all, you could have acted a little sooner or a little more carefully—if only you'd known what the problem was going to be in advance. Viewed through the lens of hindsight, most of those judgments look bad. On the other hand, an extreme position is much easier to defend. Both have built-in excuses: "Sure there were a few bugs, but I consistently overdeliver on an intense schedule, and it's well worth it," or "I know you wanted this done sooner, but you know I only ever deliver when it's absolutely ready and it's well worth it."

These two extreme positions lead to factional strife, which is extremely unpleasant. Managers start to make a note of who's part of which faction and then assign projects accordingly. Got a crazy last-minute feature? Get the Cowboys to take care of it—and then let the Quality Defenders clean it up in the next release. Both sides start to think of their point of view in moralistic terms: "Those guys don't see the economic value of fast action, they only care about their precious architecture diagrams," or "Those guys are sloppy and have no professional pride." Having been called upon to mediate these disagreements many times in my career, I can attest to just how wasteful they are.

However, they are completely logical outgrowths of a large-batch-size development process that forces developers to make trade-offs between time and quality, using the old "time-quality-money, pick two fallacy" (*http://startuplessonslearned.com/2008/10/engineering-managers-lament.html*). Because feedback is slow in coming, the damage caused by a mistake is felt long after the decisions that caused the mistake were made, making learning difficult. Because everyone gets ready to integrate with the release batch around the same time (there being no incentive to integrate early), conflicts are resolved under extreme time pressure. Features are chronically on the bubble, about to get deferred to the next release. But when they do get deferred, they tend to have their scope increased ("After all, we have a whole release cycle, and it's almost done…"), which leads to yet another time crunch, and so on. And of course, the code rarely performs in production the way it does in the testing or staging environment, which leads to a series of hotfixes immediately following each release. These come at the expense of the next release batch, meaning that each release cycle starts off behind.

You can't change the underlying incentives of this situation by getting better at any one activity. Better release planning, estimating, architecting, or integrating will only mitigate the symptoms. The only traditional technique for solving this problem is to add in massive queues in the forms of schedule padding, extra time for integration, code freezes, and the like. In fact, most organizations don't realize just how much of this padding is already going on in the estimates that individual contributors learn to generate. But padding doesn't help, because it serves to slow down the whole process. And as all development teams will tell you, time is always short. In fact, excess time pressure is exactly why they think they have these problems in the first place.

So, we need to find solutions that operate at the system level to break teams out of this pincer action. The Agile software movement has made numerous contributions: continuous integration, which helps accelerate feedback about defects; story cards and Kanban that reduce batch size; a daily stand-up that increases tempo. Continuous deployment is another such technique, one with a unique power to change development team dynamics for the better.

Why Does It Work?

First, continuous deployment separates two different definitions of the term *release*. One is used by engineers to refer to the process of getting code fully integrated into production. Another is used by marketing to refer to what customers see. In traditional batch-and-queue development, these two concepts are linked. All customers will see the new software as soon as it's deployed. This requires that all of the testing of the release happens before it is deployed to production, in special staging or testing environments. And this leaves the release vulnerable to unanticipated problems during this window of time: after the code is written but before it's running in production. On top of that overhead, by conflating the marketing release with the technical release, the amount of coordination overhead required to ship something is also dramatically increased.

Under continuous deployment, as soon as code is written it's on its way to production. That means we are often deploying just 1% of a feature—long before customers would want to see it. In fact, most of the work involved with a new feature is not the user-visible parts of the feature itself. Instead, it's the millions of tiny touch points that integrate the feature with all the other features that were built before. Think of the dozens of little API changes that are required when we want to pass new values through the system. These changes are generally supposed to be "side-effect free," meaning they don't affect the behavior of the system at the point of insertion—emphasis on *supposed*. In fact, many bugs are caused by unusual or unnoticed side effects of these deep changes. The same is true of small changes that only conflict with configuration parameters in the production environment. It's much better to get this feedback as soon as possible, which continuous deployment offers.

Continuous deployment also acts as a speed regulator. Every time the deployment process encounters a problem, a human being needs to get involved to diagnose it. During this time, it's intentionally impossible for anyone else to deploy. When teams are ready to deploy, but the process is locked, they become immediately available to help diagnose and fix the deployment problem (the alternative—that they continue to generate, but not deploy, new code—just serves to increase batch sizes to everyone's detriment). This speed regulation is a tricky adjustment for teams that are accustomed to measuring their progress via individual efficiency. In such a system, the primary goal of each engineer is to stay busy, using as close to 100% of his time for coding as possible. Unfortunately, this view ignores the team's overall throughput. Even if you don't adopt a radical definition of progress, such as the "validated learning about customers" definition (*http://startuplessonslearned.com/2009/04/validated-learning-about -customers.html*) that I advocate, it's still suboptimal to keep everyone busy. When you're in the midst of integration problems, any code that someone is writing is likely to have to be revised as a result of conflicts. The same is true with configuration mismatches or multiple teams stepping on one other's toes. In such circumstances, it's much better for overall productivity for people to stop coding and start talking. Once they figure out how to coordinate their actions so that the work they are doing doesn't have to be reworked, it's productive to start coding again.

Returning to our development team divided into Cowboy and Quality factions, let's take a look at how continuous deployment can change the calculus of their situation. For one, continuous deployment fosters learning and professional development—on both sides of the divide. Instead of having to argue with each other about the right way to code, each individual has an opportunity to learn directly from the production environment. This is the meaning of the axiom to "let your defects be your teacher."

If an engineer has a tendency to ship too soon, he will tend to find himself grappling with the cluster immune system (*http://startuplessonslearned.com/2008/09/just-in-time -scalability.html*), continuous integration server, and Five Whys master more often. These encounters, far from being the high-stakes arguments inherent in traditional teams, are actually low-risk, mostly private or small-group affairs. Because the feedback is rapid, Cowboys will start to learn what kinds of testing, preparation, and checking really do let them work faster. They'll be learning the key truth that there is such a thing as "too fast"—many quality problems actually slow you down.

Engineers who have a tendency to wait too long before shipping also have lessons to learn. For one, the larger the batch size of their work, the harder it will be to get it integrated. At IMVU, we would occasionally hire someone from a more traditional organization who had a hard time letting go of his "best practices" and habits. Sometimes he'd advocate for doing his work on a separate branch and integrating only at the end. Although I'd always do my best to convince such people otherwise, if they were insistent I would encourage them to give it a try. Inevitably, a week or two later I'd enjoy the spectacle of watching them engage in something I called "code bouncing." It's like throwing a rubber ball against a wall. In a code bounce, someone tries to check in a huge batch. First he has integration conflicts, which requires talking to various people on the team to know how to resolve them properly. Of course, while he is resolving the conflicts, new changes are being checked in. So, new conflicts appear. This cycle repeats for a while, until he either catches up to all the conflicts or just asks the rest of the team for a general check-in freeze. Then the fun part begins. Getting a large batch through the continuous integration server, incremental deploy system, and real-time monitoring system almost never works on the first try. Thus, the large batch gets reverted. While the problems are being fixed, more changes are being checked in. Unless we freeze the work of the whole team, this can go on for days. But if we do engage in a general check-in freeze, we're driving up the batch size of everyone else— which will lead to future episodes of code bouncing. In my experience, just one or two episodes is enough to cure anyone of his desire to work in large batches.

Because continuous deployment encourages learning, teams that practice it are able to get faster over time. That's because each individual's incentives are aligned with the goals of the whole team. Each person works to drive down waste in his own work, and this true efficiency gain more than offsets the incremental overhead of having to build and maintain the infrastructure required to do continuous deployment. In fact, if you practice Five Whys too, you can build this entire infrastructure in a completely incremental fashion. It's really a lot of fun.

Getting Started

Continuous deployment is controversial. When most people first hear about continuous deployment, they think I'm advocating low-quality code (*http://www .developsense.com/2009/03/50-deployments-day-and-perpetual-beta.html*) or an undisciplined Cowboy-coding development process (*http://lastinfirstout.blogspot.com/2009/03/ continuous-deployment-debate.html*). On the contrary, I believe that continuous deployment requires tremendous discipline and can greatly enhance software quality, by applying a rigorous set of standards to every change to prevent regressions, outages, or harm to key business metrics. Another common reaction I hear to continuous deployment is that it's too complicated, it's time-consuming, or it's hard to prioritize. It's this latter fear that I'd like to address head-on in this chapter. Although it is true that the full system we use to support deploying 50 times a day at IMVU is elaborate, it certainly didn't start that way. By making a few simple investments and process changes, any development team can be on their way to continuous deployment. It's the journey, not the destination, which counts. Here's the why and how, in five steps.

Step 1: Continuous Integration Server

This is the backbone of continuous deployment. We need a centralized place where all automated tests (unit tests, functional tests, integration tests, everything) can be run and monitored upon every commit. Many fine, free software tools are available to make this easy—I have had success with Buildbot (*http://buildbot.net*). Whatever tool you use, it's important that it can run all the tests your organization writes, in all languages and frameworks.

If you have only a few tests (or even none at all), don't despair. Simply set up the continuous integration server and agree to one simple rule: we'll add a new automated test every time we fix a bug. If you follow that rule, you'll start to immediately get testing where it's needed most: in the parts of your code that have the most bugs and therefore drive the most waste for your developers. Even better, these tests will start to pay immediate dividends by propping up that most-unstable code and freeing up a lot of time that used to be devoted to finding and fixing regressions (a.k.a. firefighting).

If you already have a lot of tests, make sure the continuous integration server spends only a small amount of time on a full run; 10 to 30 minutes at most. If that's not possible, simply partition the tests across multiple machines until you get the time down to something reasonable.

For more on the nuts and bolts of setting up continuous integration, see "Continuous integration step-by-step" (*http://startuplessonslearned.com/2008/12/continuous-integration -step-by-step.html*).

Step 2: Source Control Commit Check

The next piece of infrastructure we need is a source control server with a commit-check script. I've seen this implemented with CVS (*http://www.nongnu.org/cvs*), Subversion, or Perforce and have no reason to believe it isn't possible in any source control system. The most important thing is that you have the opportunity to run custom code at the moment a new commit is submitted but before the server accepts it. Your script should have the power to reject a change and report a message back to the person attempting to check in. This is a very handy place to enforce coding standards, especially those of the mechanical variety.

But its role in continuous deployment is much more important. This is the place you can control what I like to call "the production line," to borrow a metaphor from manufacturing. When something is going wrong with our systems at any place along the line, this script should halt new commits. So, if the continuous integration server runs a build and even one test breaks, the commit script should prohibit new code from being added to the repository. In subsequent steps, we'll add additional rules that also "stop the line," and therefore halt new commits.

This sets up the first important feedback loop that you need for continuous deployment. Our goal as a team is to work as fast as we can reliably produce high-quality code—and no faster. Going any "faster" is actually just creating delayed waste that will slow us down later. (This feedback loop is also discussed in detail at *http://startuplessonslearned.com/2008/12/continuous-integration-step-by-step.html*.)

Step 3: Simple Deployment Script

At IMVU, we built a serious deployment script that incrementally deploys software machine by machine and monitors the health of the cluster and the business along the way so that it can do a fast revert if something looks amiss. We call it a cluster immune system (*http://www.slideshare.net/olragon/just-in-time-scalability-agile-methods-to-support -massive-growth-presentation-presentation-925519*). But we didn't start out that way. In fact, attempting to build a complex deployment system like that from scratch is a bad idea.

Instead, start simple. It's not even important that you have an automated process, although as you practice you will get more automated over time. Rather, it's important that you do every deployment the same way and have a clear and published process for how to do it that you can evolve over time.

For most websites, I recommend starting with a simple script that just rsync's code to a version-specific directory on each target machine. If you are facile with Unix symlinks (*http://www.mikerubel.org/computers/rsync_snapshots/*), you can pretty easily set this up so that advancing to a new version (and hence, rolling back) is as easy as switching a single symlink on each server. But even if that's not appropriate for your setup, have a single script that does a deployment directly from source control.

When you want to push new code to production, require that everyone uses this one mechanism. Keep it manual, but simple, so that everyone knows how to use it. And most importantly, have it obey the same "production line" halting rules as the commit script. That is, make it impossible to do a deployment for a given revision if the continuous integration server hasn't yet run and had all tests pass for that revision.

Step 4: Real-Time Alerting

No matter how good your deployment process is bugs can still get through. The most annoying variety are bugs that don't manifest until hours or days after the code that caused them is deployed. To catch those nasty bugs, you need a monitoring platform that can let you know when things have gone awry, and get a human being involved in debugging them.

To start, I recommend a system such as the open source Nagios (*http://www.nagios .org/*). Out of the box, it can monitor basic system stats such as load average and disk utilization. For continuous deployment purposes, we want to be able to have it monitor business metrics such as simultaneous users or revenue per unit time. At the beginning, simply pick one or two of these metrics to use. Anything is fine to start, and it's important not to choose too many. The goal should be to wire the Nagios alerts up to a pager, cell phone, or high-priority email list that will wake someone up in the middle of the night if one of these metrics goes out of bounds. If the pager goes off too often, it won't get the attention it deserves, so start simple.

Follow this simple rule: every time the pager goes off, halt the production line (which will prevent check-ins and deployments). Fix the urgent problem, and don't resume the production line until you've had a chance to schedule a Five Whys meeting for root-cause analysis (RCA), which we'll discuss next.

Step 5: Root-Cause Analysis (Five Whys)

So far, we've talked about making modest investments in tools and infrastructure and adding a couple of simple rules to our development process. Most teams should be able to do everything we've talked about in a week or two, at the most, because most of the work involves installing and configuring off-the-shelf software.

Five Whys gets its name from the process of asking "why" recursively to uncover the true source of a given problem. The way Five Whys works to enable continuous deployment is when you add this rule: every time you do an RCA, make a proportional investment in prevention at each of the five levels you uncover. *Proportional* means the solution shouldn't be more expensive than the problem you're analyzing; a minor inconvenience for only a few customers should merit a much smaller investment than a multihour outage.

But no matter how small the problem is, always make some investments, and always make them at each level. Because our focus in this chapter is deployment, this means always asking the question, "Why was this problem not caught earlier in our deployment pipeline?" So, if a customer experienced a bug, why didn't Nagios alert us? Why didn't our deployment process catch it? Why didn't our continuous integration server catch it? For each question, make a small improvement.

Over months and years, these small improvements add up, much like compounding interest. But there is a reason this approach is superior to making a large upfront investment in a complex continuous deployment system modeled on IMVU's (or anyone else's). The payoff is that your system will be uniquely adapted to your particular system and circumstance. If most of your headaches come from performance problems in production, you'll naturally be forced to invest in prevention at the deployment/alerting stage. If your problems stem from badly factored code, which causes collateral damage for even small features or fixes, you'll naturally find yourself adding a lot of automated tests to your continuous integration server. Each problem drives investments in that category of solution. Thankfully, there's an 80/20 rule at work: 20% of your code and architecture probably drives 80% of your headaches. Investing in that 20% frees up incredible time and energy that can be invested in more productive things.

Following these five steps will not give you continuous deployment overnight. In its initial stages, most of your RCA will come back to the same problem: "We haven't invested in preventing that yet." But with patience and hard work, anyone can use these techniques to inexorably drive waste out of his development process.

Continuous Deployment Is for Mission-Critical Applications

Having evangelized the concept of continuous deployment for the past few years, I've come into contact with almost every conceivable question, objection, or concern that people have about it. The most common reaction I get is something like "That sounds great—for your business—but that could never work for my application." Or, phrased more hopefully, "I see how you can use continuous deployment to run an online consumer service, but how can it be used for B2B software?" Or variations thereof.

I understand why people would think that a consumer Internet service such as IMVU isn't really mission critical. I would posit that those same people have never been on the receiving end of a phone call from a 16-year-old girl complaining that your new release ruined her birthday party. That's where I learned a whole new appreciation for the idea that mission critical is in the eye of the beholder. But even so, there are key concerns that lead people to conclude that continuous deployment can't be used in mission-critical situations.

Implicit in these concerns are two beliefs:

- Mission-critical customers won't accept new releases on a continuous basis.

- Continuous deployment leads to lower-quality software than software built in large batches.

These beliefs are rooted in fears that make sense. But as is often the case, the right thing to do is to address the underlying cause of the fear (*http://www. startuplessonslearned.com/2009/05/fear-is-mind-killer.html*) instead of avoiding improving the process. Let's take each in turn.

Another Release? Do I Have To?

Most customers of most products hate new releases. That's a perfectly reasonable reaction, given that most releases of most products are bad news. It's likely that the new release will contain new bugs. Even worse, the sad state of product development generally means the new "features" are as likely to be ones that make the product worse, not better. So, asking customers if they'd like to receive new releases more often usually leads to a consistent answer: "No, thank you." On the other hand, you'll get a very different reaction if you say to customers, "The next time you report an urgent bug, would you prefer to have it fixed immediately or wait for a future arbitrary release milestone?"

Most enterprise customers of mission-critical software mitigate these problems by insisting on releases on a regular, slow schedule. This gives them plenty of time to do stress testing, training, and their own internal deployment. Smaller customers and regular consumers rely on their vendors to do this for them and are otherwise at their mercy. Switching these customers directly to continuous deployment sounds harder than it really is. That's because of the anatomy of a release. A typical "new feature" release is, in my experience, about 80% changes to underlying APIs or architecture. That is, the vast majority of the release is not actually visible to the end user. Most of these changes are supposed to be "side-effect free," although few traditional development teams actually achieve that level of quality. So, the first shift in mindset required for continuous deployment is this: if a change is supposedly "side-effect free," release it immediately. Don't wait to bundle it up with a bunch of other related changes. If you do that, it will be much harder to figure out which change caused the unexpected side effects.

The second shift in mindset required is to separate the concept of a marketing release from the concept of an engineering release. Just because a feature is built, tested, integrated, and deployed doesn't mean any customers should necessarily see it. When deploying end-user-visible changes, most continuous deployment teams keep them hidden behind "flags" that allow for a gradual rollout of the feature when it's ready. (See the Flickr blog post at *http://code.flickr.com/blog/2009/12/02/flipping-out/* for how that company does this.) This allows the concept of "ready" to be much more all-encompassing than the traditional "developers threw it over the wall to QA, and QA approved of it." You might have the interaction designer who designed it take a look to see if it really conforms to his design. You might have the marketing folks who are going to promote it double-check that it does what they expect. You can train your operations or customer service staff on how it works—all live in the production environment. Although this sounds similar to a staging server, it's actually much more powerful. Because the feature is live in the real production environment, all kinds of integration risks are mitigated. For example, many features have decent performance themselves but interact badly when sharing resources with other features. Those kinds of features can be immediately detected and reverted by continuous deployment. Most importantly, the feature will look, feel, and behave exactly like it does in production. Bugs that are found in production are real, not staging artifacts.

Plus, you want to get good at selectively hiding features from customers. That skill set is essential for gradual rollouts and, most importantly, A/B split-testing (*http://www.startuplessonslearned.com/2008/12/getting-started-with-split-testing.html*). In traditional large batch deployment systems, split-testing a new feature seems like considerably more work than just throwing it over the wall. Continuous deployment changes that calculus, making split-tests nearly free. As a result, the amount of validated learning (*http://www.startuplessonslearned.com/2009/04/validated-learning-about-customers.html*) a continuous deployment team achieves per unit time is much higher.

The QA Dilemma

A traditional QA process works through a checklist of key features, making sure each feature works as specified before allowing the release to go forward. This makes sense, especially given how many bugs in software involve "action at a distance" or unexpected side effects. Thus, even if a release is focused on changing Feature X, there's every reason to be concerned that it will accidentally break Feature Y. Over time, the overhead of this approach to QA becomes very expensive. As the product grows, the checklist has to grow proportionally. Thus, to get the same level of coverage for each release, the QA team has to grow (or, equivalently, the amount of time the product spends in QA has to grow). Unfortunately, it gets worse. In a successful start-up, the development team is also growing. That means more changes are being implemented per unit time as well, which means either the number of releases per unit time is growing or, more likely, the number of changes in each release is growing. So, for a growing team working on a growing product, the QA overhead is increasing polynomially, even if the team is expanding only linearly.

For organizations that have the highest quality standards, and the budget to do it, full coverage can work. In fact, that's what happens for organizations such as the U.S. Army, which has to do a massive amount of integration testing of products built by its vendors. Having those products fail in the field would be unacceptable. To achieve full coverage, the Army has a process for certifying these products. The whole process takes a massive amount of manpower and requires a cycle time that would be lethal for most start-ups (the major certifications take approximately two years). And even the Army recognizes that improving this cycle time would have major benefits.

Very few start-ups can afford this overhead, and so they simply accept a reduction in coverage instead. That solves the problem in the short term, but not in the long term—because the extra bugs that get through the QA process wind up slowing the team down over time, imposing extra "firefighting" overhead, too.

I want to directly challenge the belief that continuous deployment leads to lower-quality software. I just don't believe it. Continuous deployment offers significant advantages over large batch development systems. Some of these benefits are shared by Agile systems which have continuous integration but large batch releases, but others are unique to continuous deployment.

Faster (and better) feedback

Engineers working in a continuous deployment environment are much more likely to get *individually tailored* feedback about their work. When they introduce a bug, performance problem, or scalability bottleneck, they are likely to know about it immediately. They'll be much less likely to hide behind the work of others, as happens with large batch releases—when a release has a bug it tends to be attributed to the major contributor to that release, even if that association is untrue.

More automation

Continuous deployment requires living the mantra: "Have every problem only once." This requires a commitment to *realistic prevention* and learning from past mistakes. That necessarily means an awful lot of automation. That's good for QA and for engineers. QA's job gets a lot more interesting when we use machines for what machines are good for: routine repetitive detailed work, such as finding bug regressions.

Monitoring of real-world metrics

To make continuous deployment work, teams have to get good at automated monitoring and reacting to business and customer-centric metrics, not just technical metrics. That's a simple consequence of the automation principle I just mentioned. Huge classes of bugs "work as designed" but cause catastrophic changes in customer behavior. My favorite: changing the checkout button in an e-commerce flow to appear white on a white background. No automated test is going to catch that, but it still will drive revenue to zero. That class of bug will burn continuous deployment teams only once.

Better handling of intermittent bugs

Most QA teams are organized around finding reproduction paths for bugs that affect customers. This made sense in eras where successful products tended to be used by a small number of customers. These days, even niche products—or even big enterprise products—tend to have a lot of man-hours logged by end users. And that, in turn, means that rare bugs are actually quite exasperating. For example, consider a bug that happens only one time in a million uses. Traditional QA teams are never going to find a reproduction path for that bug. It will never show up in the lab. But for a product with millions of customers, it's happening (and it's being reported to customer service) multiple times a day! Continuous deployment teams are much better able to find and fix these bugs.

Smaller batches

Continuous deployment tends to drive the batch size of work down to an optimal level, whereas traditional deployment systems tend to drive it up. For more details on this phenomenon, see "Work in Small Batches" (*http://www.startuplessonslearned.com/2009/02/work-in-small-batches.html*) and the section on the "batch size death spiral" in "The Principles of Product Development Flow" (*http://www.startuplessonslearned.com/2009/07/principles-of-product-development-flow.html*).

Conclusion

I want to mention one last benefit of continuous deployment: morale. At a recent talk, an audience member asked me about the impact of continuous deployment on morale. This manager was worried that moving his engineers to a more rapid release cycle would stress them out, making them feel like they were always firefighting and releasing, and never had time for "real work." As luck would have it, one of IMVU's engineers happened to be in the audience at the time. He provided a better answer than I ever could. He explained that by reducing the overhead of doing a release, each engineer gets to work to his own release schedule. That means that as soon as an engineer is ready to deploy, he can. So, even if it's midnight, if your feature is ready to go, you can check in, deploy, and start talking to customers about it right away. No extra approvals, meetings, or coordination is required. Just you, your code, and your customers. It's pretty satisfying.

## CHAPTER FIVE

Infrastructure As Code

Adam Jacob

YOU'RE SITTING AT HOME, WATCHING A MOVIE AND EATING POPCORN, with your feet up and the family gathered around you. The phone rings—it's your on-call system administrator.

"The datacenter has been hit by a tornado—it ripped right through our cage. What do we do?"

Once you get over the obvious answer,* you start running down the list:

1. Pause the movie.

2. Sign up for an account with a cloud computing provider, to replace the raw computing, network, and storage resources you have lost.

3. Start uploading/downloading the off-site backups of your customer and application data to the new infrastructure.

4. Provision enough servers to bring the company back online, assigning an appropriate role to each new server resource ("web server," "database server," "monitoring server," etc.).

5. Change your DNS to point to your new infrastructure, with a "we got hit by a tornado" page.

6. Restore the customer and application data.

---

* Which, by the way, is *freak all the way out*.

7. Remove the "we got hit by a tornado" page.

8. Finish the movie.

One hour and forty-five minutes later, you've gone from business-ending natural disaster to finishing your family movie night. How did you do it? You built the original infrastructure as code: a series of interconnected services, relying on each other to bring each component of the system into the proper running state. All you had to do was apply that code to new resources and restore the application data, and you knew you would get the entire business back up and running from scratch.

This story illustrates the primary goal of treating your infrastructure as code:

> Enable the reconstruction of the business from nothing but a source code repository, an application data backup, and bare metal resources.

In a world of handcrafted infrastructure, where each component was lovingly built by a team of system administrators and software development engineers, the disaster scenario I just outlined would take weeks or months to recover from. Simply getting replacement hardware would take weeks—and once you had it delivered, the time it would take to hand-build it to run the application would take even longer (depending on the size of the infrastructure in the first place). Once all of that was done, you could start focusing on getting your application back up and running—but by that point, would anyone care anymore? You could achieve the goal manually, but if it takes too long, there might not be a business left to save.

In an ideal world, the single largest constraint on reconstituting the business should be the time it takes to restore the application data—it's the part that has real business value. You can speed up the process by which you acquire new raw resources, or the mechanism by which you configure those resources, but the application data restoration takes as long as it takes.

There are two steps to building your infrastructure as code:

1. Break the infrastructure down into reusable, network-accessible *services*.

2. *Integrate* those services together.

The recovery scenario I illustrated utilizes four different services:

1. A bootstrapping service, which provisions new bare metal resources

2. A configuration service, which configures each system and deploys the application itself

3. A backup service, which lets us retrieve our application data

4. A DNS service, which allows us to point Internet traffic at the new infrastructure

Each service operates independently of the others, but we integrate them together to rebuild the infrastructure. The bootstrapping service kicks off the configuration service, the backup service provides the application data to restore, and the DNS service makes the results publicly available.

Although this example focuses on rebuilding the business from scratch, these same principles apply to managing infrastructure on an ongoing basis. In fact, if you don't use these processes to manage your infrastructure, you're going to have trouble making sure you can rebuild it from scratch: reality will diverge from your carefully crafted bootstrapping code.

To understand how to build the entire infrastructure as code, you need to answer two questions:

1. What does a good infrastructure service look like?

2. How do we integrate those services together?

To learn what a good infrastructure service looks like, I'm going to enumerate 10 principles drawn from service-oriented architecture (SOA) and configuration management. Then I'll put it all together with an overview of how to approach the integration of those services.

Service-Oriented Architecture

The fundamental concept of an SOA is that each component of the system is broken up into network-accessible services, which are integrated to make a functioning application. You can think of it as taking a "primitive" approach to building an application. You break each part of the application down to its most primitive parts, and make each of those available over a network as a service, enabling you to create ever more flexible, powerful infrastructure with less overhead and time.

Through exposing each primitive component of the application as a service, application developers become free to compose new applications from the network prim-itives—resulting in easy reuse, clear encapsulation, and simpler troubleshooting. This approach powers some of the largest and most innovative sites on the Internet—it has become so fundamental to Internet architecture that it's considered a core competency of all Web 2.0 companies.*

Three lessons application developers have learned from service orientation apply directly to infrastructure as code:

* See *http://oreilly.com/pub/a/web2/archive/what-is-web-20.html*, "Services, not packaged software."

- It should be *modular*.

  "Do one thing, and do it well."

  In an SOA, each service is small—it does one thing, and allows other services to consume it. The complexity budget for any given service is tiny—the cost of integrating services is pushed up the stack to the application developer. By focusing each service in a narrow band, the services become easier to manage, develop, and test.

  The same is true when thinking about infrastructure services. By keeping the total space in which a given service operates small, you reduce its own complexity, and make it easier for others to reason about your behavior.

- It should be *cooperative*.

  "It takes a village."

  When you build primitive services exposed via network APIs, you encourage everyone to cooperate with you, rather than reimplement the same functionality. Each service must be designed to cooperate with others and have as few expectations as possible about the way in which it will be used.

  The cooperative nature of the service ensures that, as more people use it, the service itself becomes more useful. For infrastructure services, this nature is critical—as each piece of the infrastructure becomes integrated with the service, the ways in which they can cooperate with each other explode exponentially, in ways the original service authors could never have predicted.

- It should be *composable*.

  "It should be ready for anything."

  Once you have a bunch of nicely modularized services, you begin to compose them together into more complex applications. This is the moment where service orientation really begins to shine: as each primitive problem is solved, new applications can simply rely on it to provide the functionality required.

  Each component of the infrastructure gets a modular API, and you compose them together to automate the entire infrastructure.

For many of us, thinking about our infrastructure in service-oriented terms is easy. We're used to services such as DNS and LDAP inside our infrastructure. In an ideal world, each of these services would expose its configuration and functionality through easily accessible network APIs. In reality, many of them don't.* To automate all the parts of our infrastructure that don't provide configuration APIs, we need to talk about another discipline: configuration management.

Configuration Management

If you look for a definition of the term *configuration management*, you will be deluged with possible options. Every industry has its own meaning—for example, in the nuclear reactor industry configuration management is a vital component of ensuring that the systems managing the reactor are configured safely. The International Standards Organization has this definition:

> Configuration management is a management activity that applies technical and administrative direction over the life cycle of a product, its configuration items, and related product configuration information.–ISO 10007:2003, Quality management systems–Guidelines for configuration management

To me, configuration management means keeping track of all the stuff you have to do to take a system from "bare metal" to "doing its job." When a system administrator configures a system by hand and posts her notes on a wiki, she's practicing the most primitive form of configuration management. When a software developer writes a script to automate the deployment of her application, she's automating configuration management.

Configuration management is policy driven

Across every definition is a single commonality: configuration management is about *policy*. You look at a problem in your system, and you determine how the system should behave when it encounters that problem.

Each field has slightly different methods for implementing a policy, but you can boil it down to four steps, as listed here and shown in Figure 5-1:

1. Document what the problem is, and what the final result of any solution should be. (Setting the policy)

2. Write the code to do what you laid out in the policy. (Executing the policy)

3. Confirm that the final results are correct. (Auditing the policy)

4. Repeat the process so that you are certain you can reliably do it again someday. (Testing the policy)

---

* For example, Nagios (*http://www.nagios.org*) is a very common open source monitoring application that exposes very little of its functionality, and none of its configuration, through a network API.

Figure 5-1. *Configuration management policy*

A given implementation of the policy becomes a configuration management *process*. When you are determining whether a given configuration management process is successful, there is only one criterion: does the process correctly fulfill the policy, every time it is executed?

System automation is configuration management policy made into code

In 1995, I was partially responsible for a couple of BSDi boxes in the back of a dentist's office, rigged up to a bank of modems and calling itself an ISP. The biggest problems we faced were how many phone lines we could get delivered, and how quickly we could provision new customer accounts.

We had a configuration management policy around signing up new customers:

1. Get the customers' vital information.

2. Ensure that they can authenticate with the service when they dial in.

3. Provision an email account and website.

One of the first things we did was implement a manual configuration management process for that policy, which we cleverly called "The New Account Sign Up Process":

1. Get the customers' vital information via telephone.

2. Create an account for them on the server with the adduser command.

3. Create an entry for them in the database we used for customer tracking.

The process was taped to the top of the hutch on the cheap particleboard desk that all the customer support engineers shared. Customers would call in, we would walk through the process, and it seemed pretty simple to everyone involved.

But this was 1995, and the Internet was *hot*. Netscape had just gone IPO, Yahoo! was taking venture capital money, WebCrawler was the top search engine, and Amazon, eBay, and Hotmail were all founded. Only 9.6% of the population of the United States had Internet access at the beginning of 1995; by 1996, that number was 16.7%.*

That explosive growth meant our New Account Sign Up Process was having trouble keeping up with demand. It was taking long enough to sign people up that we were losing potential customers while they waited in line on hold. We were having quality control issues as well—we needed to input the users' vital information at least three times, and we were seeing pretty high error rates.

Our head system administrator at the time, whom I'll call Kevin, took it upon himself to improve the process. He took the outline taped on the hutch and wrote a Vim script that automated it. The new process looked like this:

1. Enter the customers' vital information into addcustomer.

All we had to do was run his addcustomer script, put in the vital information, confirm it with the customer, and *voilà*: customers fully provisioned.

Now, to me, this was the coolest thing ever. Kevin had turned our buggy, manual process into a simple, automated one. The owners of the ISP were ecstatic; the customer support engineers loved it. He was like a dorkier version of Batman. When the company was suffering, he could whip out a shell script and devise a way to save us all.

I learned a few important things from watching that experience:

- Having a process was good. It allowed us to cope with the influx of new customers, and provided Kevin the road map he needed to write any automation.

- Every manual step in the process was a potential source of misfortune—all it took was one mistake to throw the whole thing off.

- Being the guy who could write the script made you awesome.

Kevin took a configuration management policy and wrote code that cut out the manual steps of the current process, and the results streamlined it to the degree that the ISP could continue to grow at the pace the market demanded.

For problems such as these, the primary tools of the trade have long been scripting languages—starting with shell scripts, and moving toward languages such as Perl, Python, and Ruby. Essentially, this kind of automation almost always involves the use of a high-level programming language. This approach illustrates three more principles:

- It should be *flexible*.

* World Bank World Development Indicators, via Google; *http://bit.ly/4l69c6*.

"It should be capable of doing whatever is required."

No matter what your problem is, it's likely that you can solve it with a high-level programming language. Given even the most obscure and complex of policies, you can probably write a program to automate it—you are limited only by your knowledge and the facilities available in the language.

- It should be *extensible*.

"When something new is encountered, it's easy to extend."

When you encounter a problem the language has never seen before, such as a new protocol you need to speak, you can write a library to resolve it. This is a side effect of the language being general purpose—because it doesn't pretend to understand the sorts of problems it might be called upon to tackle, it behooves the designers of these languages to make them extensible enough that developers in the field can scratch their own itch.

- It should be *repeatable*.

"No matter how many times you do it, it works the same way."

When you write a piece of automation around a process, you cause that process to become repeatable. Given the same set of inputs, and the rest of the system functioning properly, you are going to get the exact same results. A side effect of being repeatable is being consistent—once you can rely on the results, you can also expect that the results will be correct.

Configuration management in system administration

System administrators have been concerned with configuration management from the inception of the job description. They're responsible for building, managing, and maintaining a group of computer systems. They're the people you call when your desktop isn't working, when the website is down, or when the printer is jammed.

The greatest skill that is common among all system administrators is the ability to *troubleshoot* a broken system. Even the most junior of system administrators has the ability to figure out why a file clerk's desktop can no longer print; the most senior of administrators has an almost supernatural ability to debug even highly complex systems from only the faintest of clues.

They develop this skill because they become intimately familiar with the way the system is supposed to behave and understand the typical process each component will go through to reach that behavior. In essence, they understand both the high-level policy of the system and the process required for each piece of the system to fulfill the policy.

System administrators like Kevin learned early that, to make their lives easier and their companies more successful, they needed to write automation. The instincts they honed while troubleshooting systems would often get distilled into scripts to help manage the systems. Doing this for common system administration tasks is no different from doing it for customer sign-up—except that we have an entire branch of tools made specifically to enable this kind of automation.

In 1993, Mark Burgess was a post-doctoral fellow at the University of Oslo, in charge of managing a group of Unix workstations. He was writing shell scripts as automation to keep the various systems configured properly but was frustrated by the minor discrepancies in how each Unix variant behaved—they made every script he wrote be covered in exceptions. In response, he wrote the first modern open source configuration management tool: Cfengine.

Mark brought a number of revolutionary ideas to automated configuration management, all of which are present in every modern configuration management tool created since then:*

- Declarative

  "It's about what you want, not how to do it."

  Rather than talk about *how* to do something, you should declare *what* you want done and let the tool determine how to do it on your behalf. For example, in Cfengine 2:

  ```
  packages: sudo
    action=installed
  ```

  would make sure that sudo is installed. This is opposed to the following, which focuses on how you install sudo:

  ```
  apt-get install sudo
  ```

  The declarative syntax has an additional side effect: for the things the tool knows how to manage, you can think about what you want the system to be like (the policy) and leave the process to the tool.

- Abstract

  "It takes care of the details for you."

  Under the hood, configuration management tools know how to map the description of the state you want a resource to be in to the mechanism the system has to fulfill it. They transform a package statement such as the one in the preceding bullet to the apt-get statement through auto-detecting the appropriate mechanism for your platform.

---

* There is a huge renaissance in configuration management tools: AutomateIT, Bcfg2, Chef (which I wrote), Cfengine, and Puppet are the most popular. Although they all differ (sometimes dramatically) from one another, they all embody the basic principles Mark Burgess pioneered.

- Idempotent

  "It takes action only if it needs to."

  Each resource is responsible for ensuring that it is in the proper state, and that means action is taken only if the resource *isn't* already properly configured. If the entire system is properly configured, no action will be taken.

- Convergent

  "It takes care of itself and relies on other services to do the same."

  Each resource is responsible for ensuring that it is in the proper state. With each resource acting as an autonomous actor, the system as a whole operates in a convergent manner; over time, each small act brings the system fully in line with the overall policy. In addition to the declarative syntax, the convergent nature of configuration management tools allows system administrators to focus on the policy, not the process.

System Integration

System integration is the moment when you bring everything together into a functional, fully automated system. As a discipline, it focuses on breadth—success hinges on understanding how each component of the system works and how they relate to each other.

In the beginning of this chapter, I enumerated the two steps you should follow to build your infrastructure as code, which happen to be the exact steps you use during the system integration phase of building your infrastructure as code. Because system integration is about bringing everything together, I'll use what we discussed earlier in this chapter to illuminate each step.

Step 1: Break the infrastructure down into reusable, network-accessible services

In our exploration of service-oriented architecture and configuration management, we identified 10 core principles of a good infrastructure service:

- It should be *modular*.
- It should be *cooperative*.
- It should be *composable*.
- It should be *flexible*.
- It should be *extensible*.
- It should be *repeatable*.
- It should be *declarative*.

- It should be *abstract*.

- It should be *idempotent*.

- It should be *convergent*.

To illustrate the process of evaluating a service according to those principles, we'll use two of the services identified earlier: the bootstrapping service and the configuration service.

The bootstrapping service. This service is responsible for delivering a working operating system, connected to a network, with a particular hardware profile. The policy at this layer is that, given a resource requirement, we can bring new resources online to fill the need with an API call.

Table 5-1 highlights the 10 core principles applied to the bootstrapping service as a design tool.

Table 5-1. *Bootstrapping service criteria*

Principle	Description
Modular	The bootstrapping process should only handle getting a resource network accessible.
Cooperative	The bootstrapping service should be capable of handing off work post-bootstrap to other services.
Composable	We need to be able to call in to the bootstrapping service from a variety of different services.
Flexible	An infrastructure with only one type of system to bootstrap is a rare bird. The service must be flexible enough to bootstrap many different kinds of physical systems (and operating systems).
Extensible	We need to be able to easily extend the bootstrapping service to bootstrap new kinds of resources.
Repeatable	It needs to produce the same system every time.
Declarative	We should describe the type of systems we need, rather than the details of how to install and build those systems.
Abstract	The underlying mechanism should be hidden. If we use PXE booting for bare metal systems or issuing commands to create virtual machines, our API interface should be the same.
Idempotent	Although the bootstrapping service itself does not need to be idempotent, the code that calls the bootstrapping service API does. If a server already exists to fulfill a need, we should not be bootstrapping any new systems to fill its role.
Convergent	It should focus on bringing each system up as quickly as possible, and allow them to bring themselves into alignment in future stages, without concern for the status of other systems in the bootstrapping process.

This service might be implemented via calls to a virtualization layer (such as Xen, KVM, or VMware), a cloud computing API (such as Amazon EC2, Rackspace, or Terremark), or raw PXE boot solutions.

Amazon EC2 is an example of a well-built bootstrapping service. Table 5-2 shows how it stacks up, using the criteria laid out in Table 5-1.

Table 5-2. *EC2 as a bootstrapping service*

Principle	Description
Modular	EC2 brings operating systems up on a network exclusively.
Cooperative	EC2 uses instance data to allow post-configuration of instances.
Composable	Many tools can make use of the EC2 API as a component.
Flexible	EC2 ships with a large number of flexible instance sizes and prebuilt operating system images.
Extensible	You can easily add your own operating system images to EC2.
Repeatable	Repeating the same API call yields similar results each time.
Declarative	You declare that you need a number of instances of a given type based on a particular machine image.
Abstract	Nothing about the EC2 API exposes the fact that it is using virtualization under the hood during instance creation.
Idempotent	Many tools built around EC2 allow for idempotent descriptions of system state, and Amazon's own CloudWatch service can provide similar functionality.
Convergent	When instances are launched in EC2, they are fully independent.

When you're evaluating your own options for a bootstrapping service, remember that the most important part is that you can make an API call to provision new systems. Although having all 10 attributes is great, if you can't call it as a service, you've failed before you have begun.

The configuration service. This service is responsible for taking a raw operating system all the way to running the applications necessary to fulfill its role in the infrastructure.

For example, let's assume we have just bootstrapped a new frontend application server running Ruby on Rails. Some of the tasks the configuration system will need to handle include the following:

- Installing packages, such as Ruby, Rails, and any needed libraries

- Creating users and groups

- Configuring system-level firewall rules

- Deploying the correct version of the application itself

Table 5-3 outlines the 10 core principles applied to the design of a configuration service.

Table 5-3. *Configuration service criteria*

Principle	Description
Modular	The configuration service should make the server capable of fulfilling its role in the infrastructure.
Cooperative	Many other services, such as the bootstrapping service or a monitoring service, need to cooperate with this service. It also will likely cooperate with many *other* services, such as services for source control, package distribution, and more.
Composable	It should make as few assumptions as possible about the way it will be called.
Flexible	The service must be flexible enough to fulfill a wide range of typical tasks out of the box.
Extensible	Because nobody can predict in advance the entire possible range of configurations that might appear in every infrastructure, the service must be easy to extend.
Repeatable	Given the same set of configuration inputs, the configuration service must produce the same results.
Declarative	The configuration service should have a declarative syntax, enabling you to think about configuration management policy, rather than execution.
Abstract	The service should provide abstractions both for how a policy is executed and for how individual servers are configured.
Idempotent	The job of the configuration service is ongoing, and it must be capable of doing only the work that is required to bring the system in line with policy.
Convergent	The configuration service should always be making progress toward bringing the system into a policy-compliant state.

Possible configuration services range from open source tools such as Chef, Cfengine, and Puppet to expensive commercial tools such as Tivoli, Opsware, and BladeLogic.

Let's examine Chef as an example of a well-built configuration service (see Table 5-4).

Table 5-4. *Chef as a configuration service*

Principle	Description
Modular	Chef can completely configure a system from scratch, including application deployment.
Cooperative	You can call out to other services from within Chef and easily retrieve data from Chef about the services that have been configured.
Composable	Chef can easily be integrated into preexisting systems and workflows through its REST API.
Flexible	Chef ships with the ability to configure a wide array of common-components.
Extensible	Chef extends Ruby, a third-generation programming language, making it easy to extend when you have a component it doesn't understand.
Repeatable	Given the same set of inputs, Chef will always behave the same way.
Declarative	The recipe (policy) language of Chef is declarative.
Abstract	Chef abstracts the implementation details of common resources.
Idempotent	All resources in Chef are idempotent.
Convergent	Each system managed by Chef is configured individually and will consistently make progress toward applying the policy defined in the recipes.

In a modern automated infrastructure, the configuration service takes a particularly central role. When you are designing your own systems, you want to focus on flexibility, extensibility, and cooperation above all. If the system is inflexible, it will likely fail to apply cleanly to your infrastructure. If it's difficult to extend, you won't be able to integrate it tightly with the rest of your infrastructure. If it can't cooperate with other services, you'll wind up duplicating a huge amount of data throughout your infrastructure.

Step 2: Integrate the services together

Now that you understand the shape of the bootstrapping and configuration services, we can look at how the two can be integrated together. Earlier we covered the four steps of policy-driven configuration management. This is the same pattern you'll follow during the integration phase. Here it is again, for reference:

1. Document what the problem is, and what the final result of any solution should be. (Setting the policy)

2. Write the code to do what you laid out in the policy. (Executing the policy)

3. Confirm that the final results are correct. (Auditing the policy)

4. Repeat the process so that you are certain you can reliably do it again someday. (Testing the policy)

The first step in the process is to make the goal of your policy clear:

> Provision a new server from bare metal to running application in less time than it takes to restore the application data.

Second, write the code (or take the steps) necessary to execute the policy:

1. Prepare the base operating system image for the bootstrapping service.

2. Write the configuration policy for each type of system in your infrastructure.

3. Configure the bootstrapping service to run the configuration service at launch and to accept data that tells the new system how it should be configured.

4. Write the code that launches the required new systems through the bootstrapping service in an idempotent way.

Now, confirm that when you run the code you've written, it works for you as designed.

Finally, get someone else to repeat the process you've created, ensuring that it can be done reliably without any knowledge that was missing from the policy.

Here you have created a policy for how systems are bootstrapped and configured—you know what the acceptance criteria are, can list the steps required to implement it, and can test that the policy works. Doing system integration this way is like building a layer cake: each layer builds on the deliciousness of the previous one to make the whole even more enticing.

Conclusion

Infrastructure as code is about enabling the reconstruction of the business from nothing but a source code repository, an application data backup, and bare metal resources. To get there, you follow a two-step process:

1. Break the infrastructure down into reusable, network-accessible services.

    Each service should have some combination of the 10 core principles of well-built infrastructure services:

    - It should be *modular*.

    - It should be *cooperative*.

- It should be *composable*.

- It should be *flexible*.

- It should be *extensible*.

- It should be *repeatable*.

- It should be *declarative*.

- It should be *abstract*.

- It should be *idempotent*.

- It should be *convergent*.

2. Integrate those services together.

   Build policies for how each service should function individually, and then start building policies about how they interact with each other to solve larger and larger chunks of your infrastructure. Follow the pattern of policy creation, execution, auditing, and testing set out in traditional configuration management:

   a. Document what the problem is, and what the final result of any solution should be. (Setting the policy)

   b. Write the code to do what you laid out in the policy. (Executing the policy)

   c. Confirm that the final results are correct. (Auditing the policy)

   d. Repeat the process so that you are certain you can reliably do it again some-day. (Testing the policy)

By following this process, you will create a powerful, flexible infrastructure that can be managed entirely as code.

## CHAPTER SIX

Monitoring

Patrick Debois

Story: "The Start of a Journey"

As a sys admin, I became fascinated by the powers of the Internet, and with it the power of the Web. Very soon, I started running my own website on one of the university computers. It was a platform for sharing links. I devoured every single computer book and magazine, went to all the user groups and conferences I could, and constantly surfed the Web for tips on how to structure my website. The site became popular, and some students started to rely on it for their daily work.

After running the site for some time, there was a major power outage on campus, and the web server didn't come back up. I got flooded with emails from students asking me to fix the problem. I quickly restarted the server and went back to tuning it and adding content. This was the first downtime the website experienced.

One morning, the website was down again and I found my mailbox full of emails. Dutifully, I restarted the server, but a few hours later the website was down again. I knew The Problem wasn't due to a power outage, as everything else was still online. And it wasn't due to the network, as my pings were showing no problems.

To automate the check to see if the website was down, I wrote a little script that did a simple HTTP request, and if the website didn't respond, it would send me an email. I was no longer relying on users to detect the problem. Most of the time I would be notified and was able to restart the website before any users complained.

After awhile I decided to execute the restart directly from the detection script. Although this wasn't solving the real problem, it required no more manual intervention from me, and now I could really concentrate on solving the issue. Finally, I found that there was a memory leak because of an old system library, which caused the process to increase its memory until it would become too big and core-dump.

The campus staff refused to update the library, as nobody else was experiencing similar problems. So, I decided to become proactive: again I wrote a little script that checked the memory size of the different processes, and if one of them was reaching an alarming state, I would send a clean kill to the process that was taking up too much memory. That way, I could keep the server up, and the users would not experience any downtime.

Finally, the staff updated the library. The server was running happily, and the website's popularity increased steadily. The fun continued until I checked the logfiles: the number of requests was decreasing at alarming rates. What was happening here?! My monitoring indicated that everything was running fine. Maybe I needed better content on the site....

I asked some key users, and the answer hit me in the face: "Your site is becoming unreliable. Sometimes it's so slow that it's unusable." My monitoring script had never complained because I didn't take response times into account. Again I extended my script to log response times, and after running it for some time I saw that response time was indeed increasing during the busiest hours of the days. So, instead of my usual morning checks, I logged on to the system during peak hours and saw that the load average on the box was almost 10! Everything kept on working, but response times were bad. I even noticed a kind of yo-yo effect happening: people would try to make a request to the home page when response times improved, and as a result, system load increased again.

I had assumed I had unlimited resources on the server, but in reality the web server was fighting to get the necessary memory. It started swapping, the CPU started to overload, and the timings were getting bad. After moving the website to a more powerful system, all was well again.

This story has the simplest technical setup you can think off: a single web server and nothing else. The first lesson to be learned is that there are always two views: the technician view and the end-user/business view. Monitoring isn't about setting up a system. It's there to support the business, to make sure they can do their work. That ability to work can be rephrased as keeping the website available.

Availability (A) can be expressed as:

$$A = \text{Uptime} / (\text{Uptime} + \text{Downtime})$$

The availability of a website is influenced by four major parameters as listed here and shown in Figure 6-1:

MTTD (Mean Time to Diagnose)
> The average time it takes to diagnose the problem

MTTR (Mean Time to Repair)
> The average time it takes to fix a problem

MTTF (Mean Time to Failure)
    The average time there is correct behavior

MTBF (Mean Time Between Failures)
    The average time between different failures of the service

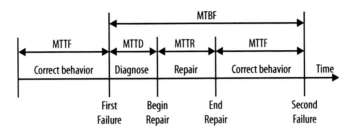

Figure 6-1. *Parameters influencing availability*

Therefore, *Availability* can be rewritten as:

    A = MTTF / MTBF = MTTF / (MTTF + MTTD + MTTR)

It is also typically expressed in terms of 9s, as outlined in Table 6-1.

Table 6-1. *Availability expressed in terms of 9s*

Availability	Downtime
90% (one 9)	36.5 days/year
99% (two 9s)	3.65 days/year
99.9% (three 9s)	8.76 hours/year
99.99% (four 9s)	52 minutes/year
99.999% (five 9s)	5 minutes/year
99.9999% (six 9s)	31 seconds/year!

I'm not saying that your business requires close to 90% or more availability. The availability your business requires is whatever the business expects. Users can be happy with downtime during weekends, or even during the day as long as that works for them. Your goal should be to increase availability by decreasing MTTD and MTTR and increasing MTTF. Each of these parameters can be broken into different parts that can be influenced by different measures taken.

Tables 6-2 through 6-4 give you an overview of how the parameters were influenced in the simple story.

Table 6-2. *Example influences of Mean Time to Diagnose*

MTTD parameter	Story example
The time it takes to detect the failure; also called *Mean Time to Detect*	Examples in the story are the script that checks HTTP availability, the performance monitoring, and the memory check. This is often where most effort is spent. Of course, detecting the problem is crucial, but it's only part of the complete Diagnose time. Because both Detect and Diagnose are abbreviated with MTTD, this often leads to confusion, but there clearly is a difference.
The time it takes to notify the correct people	The email the script sent is a clear example of a notification. It informed me that something was wrong.
The time it takes to respond; also called *Mean Time to Respond*	I didn't check my email all the time and it required me to go on campus, so even if it was detected and I was notified, it took me some time to respond. This time is often confused (sometimes even deliberately) with Mean Time to Repair, as both are abbreviated as MTTR. There is a world of difference between someone responding to you and someone fixing/repairing your problem.
The time it takes to understand what causes the problem	Luckily in the story, the restart was enough, and I could solve the problem without downtime. But if the library change had prohibited start-up, it's clear that the time it took me to find the cause of the problem added to the diagnose time.

Table 6-3. *Example influences of Mean Time to Repair*

MTTR parameter	Story example
The time to restart a service or to reset it back to a known state	A simple restart script instead of typing all the manual commands saved me time.
The time to fix the diagnosed problem	This time was reduced by executing the restart directly after the detection, because I assumed the problem was a known state.
The time spent to find the correct information	Getting the phone number of the correct university staff member, finding the correct command to type in, and even finding the correct password to log in to the server—all are examples of time spent finding information instead of solving the problem.

Both MTTD and MTTR are spent during downtime, so what can a monitoring system do to influence MTTF (Mean Time to Failure), even if all components are a given? The key here is to try to be proactive and improve things before they fail (see Table 6-4).

Table 6-4. *Example influences of Mean Time to Failure*

MTTF parameter	Story example
Detecting component fatigue	This includes proactive monitoring of the memory size and predicting failure.
Checking trends in capacity and usage	By checking the load average, bad response times could be predicted.
Design and component selection	This includes providing feedback on the availability versus the given design, and detecting weak spots for availability.
Monitoring service abuses	Conduct monitoring (i.e., network and application abuses) to predict failure.
Security checks	Proactively check the security state so that no vulnerabilities would be exploited (e.g., latest patch vulnerabilities, network ports open).

The second lesson of the story is that monitoring is a journey: it started with something simple and was improved along the way. I learned so much from this experience, but it took me several years to understand its full potential.

I hope I can speed up your learning by telling you three more stories about web operations, covering three steps to take while you are improving your skills. Let's start with the first step.

Step 1: Understand What You Are Monitoring

After graduating from university, I got a job managing websites at a government organization. We inherited a heterogeneous set of servers previously managed by different departments. Little documentation was available, and as we started exploring the environment, it almost felt like we were reverse-engineering. We made an inventory of all the servers we could find and started adding them to the monitoring: the first checks we added were those for availability using simple network pings as well as HTTP request checks and response times. To gather more information on what would cause problems we also added checks for memory, disk, and CPU usage in addition to checks for essential processes such as SSH, HTTPD, and NTPD. Looking at these results gave us a good overview of the situation we were facing.

Occasionally, we got emails from people stating that they couldn't access the website. When we'd check the website and the monitoring, we'd see that everything was working fine. We'd politely reply that as far as we could see, everything was working fine, and the problem was probably on their PC and they needed to reboot. In reality, we thought these cases were typical examples of PEBKAC (Problem Exists Between Keyboard and Chair).

Then one day my boss sent me an email saying that he too was experiencing problems accessing the website, and because he urgently needed some information, I had to come to his office ASAP. I opened his browser and typed in the URL. Nothing. I clicked the reload button. Nothing. I opened a command line and tried to resolve the server address and found the DNS server was not responding. Then I realized that because our monitoring script used an IP address to check the website, this was why it didn't detect the problem. I logged in to the DNS server for my boss's subnet and restarted it, and all was well again. To detect this kind of problem, we adapted the monitoring script and additionally started monitoring the DNS servers with an `nslookup` check to make sure we could detect that problem, too.

A few days later I met my boss at a meeting and asked him if everything was working OK. He replied, "Most of the time it's OK, but on the sites that require authentication I still have problems." My boss was one of the first people to access protected parts of the website. The management subsite required a login, with usernames and passwords stored in a database. As we had learned from the dependency of DNS, we had added the database server to the monitoring, too. We checked it by doing a simple SQL query. So, I opened the monitoring page and saw that the database service had been running green all the time. Hmm; I asked him to log on to the website, and *bang*, it failed. It turned out that although both the web server and the database server were working fine, the web server couldn't access the database server because of some firewall permission problem. Quietly I left the office: once again an end user had beaten our monitoring to detect that something was wrong. We enhanced our script that checked the website by making it perform an actual login.

I usually arrive early at work so that I can check everything before the majority of end users start their day. One morning I started receiving a lot of tickets to solve, complaining about the website being down. I checked the monitoring and couldn't find any problems: everything was green. Still, when I asked the users to try the web page, they couldn't reach it. I made them check the DNS, their gateway, and whatever else I could think of; no luck. I even rebooted the server, even though nothing was wrong.

After going back and forth through the configuration and the logfiles, I decided to call one of my colleagues from the networking group who was in the same building as the end users who were complaining. "Hey, can you try to check our website?" I asked. He answered, "No." I thought he was making fun of me and kindly repeated my question. "No," he answered again, and he continued: "There is a major power outage in the building and one of our core switches is down, so I can't help you with that."

I had just spent over an hour trying to figure out what was wrong. Nobody bothered to tell our group that there had been a power outage. If only I had known sooner. Later I learned that both the people responsible for the network and the people responsible for the housing had their own monitoring solution. The first step for us was to get access to their system so that we could verify the status if something failed. Then we continued to send each other alerts in case of a failure. Eventually, we integrated the different monitoring systems to have one overview.

Over time, the web servers evolved into a more homogeneous setup with the same parameters and configs. Some of these sites were running on underutilized hardware and others needed additional capacity. We decided to spread the websites over the different servers and load-balance across them. Besides performance and utilization, this also increased availability, because now the sites were running on multiple servers. So if one went down, the load balancer made sure users were redirected to a running web server. We did the same with the database servers by turning them into a high-availability cluster.

Our friends from the network department did the same: they added redundancy on their routers, switches, and firewalls. We were pretty sure we had eliminated a lot of the single points of failure in our architecture now. Managing our servers became much easier, because we could remove one of the web servers from the pool and do maintenance on it while everything kept running. We had made our monitoring site internally available to end users so that they could verify the state of the environment themselves. This helped them to understand if something was a site-wide problem or specific to their PC. After we introduced the redundancy levels, however, the end users got confused. They could not tell the difference between services per server and the global service provided through the load balancer. So, we introduced a service level in our monitoring display to make that difference clear to them. We did the same for other redundancy mechanisms for services such as DNS (NS records), Mail (MX records), and NTP clocks, and for disk redundancy such as RAID5 and mirrors.

The server team managed the load balancer because it was closer to the logic of the application, and more knowledge of HTTP was required to manage it correctly. When we wanted to make a change we would prepare the configuration on the passive load balancer and then switch from the active one to the passive one. We got so confident with this that we would do this kind of change during the day. But once in a while the failover would take more time than we expected, resulting in a failure of our checks. We could not understand it, as the load balancer was configured to take over imme-diately. We checked our historical logs to see if we could find indications of other problems. It turned out that in both cases when we experienced problems with the load balancer there had been problems with the firewall, routers, and switches. That explained it; nothing was wrong with our load balancer. That afternoon we got a phone call from the network department, asking us if we had changed anything on the load balancer. "Yes," we said. "We put on a new config, but the failover worked correctly; it's just too bad you guys had some problems with the routers, switches, and firewall." We continued the conversion, and it turned out that they had traced their problems to the failover of our load balancer: whenever it would fail over, their firewall would fail over because it would detect problems with the routing. It turned out that both failover mechanisms were tightly coupled together and would fail over together.

A lot of space in the preceding story was spent explaining the technical environment. The first step taken to resolve the issue was to identify the technical components that were used and how they depended on each other. A variety of dependencies were discovered along the way. Table 6-5 gives an overview of the dependencies typically encountered in web environments.

Table 6-5. *Example technical component dependencies*

Component	Example dependencies
Application	Application server, web server, email server, caching server, queuing servers
Mail server	Mail service processes, network, host, storage
DNS server	DNS service processes, network, host, storage
Application server	Application service processes, network, host, storage
Web server	Web server service processes, network, host, storage
Database	Database service processes, network, host, storage
Host	Device, OS device processes
Network	Device, network device processes
Storage	Device, disks, RAID controllers, interfaces
Generic device	Disk, memory, CPU, interfaces, housing
Housing	UPS, power, temperature

Often, dependencies are not under your control and instead are managed by different groups within your company. It will take extra effort to go beyond your own "silo" and get relevant information from other parts of your company. As you rely on them, it's crucial that you get a better understanding of "their" part. This will prevent you from spending useless time finding the cause of a problem or having blind spots on components your end users rely on for accessing your service. Table 6-6 outlines some typical examples of organizational boundaries.

Table 6-6. *Examples of different enterprise boundaries*

Enterprise group	Website dependencies
Desktop support	Can influence the browser, desktop settings, and antivirus/spyware software
Developers	Are often focused on changes in the application
Middleware group	Often runs databases, web servers, application servers, mail servers, caching servers, and queuing systems
Systems group	Provides the basic operating system, DNS, DHCP, virtualization, and cluster software
Network group	Is responsible for switches, routers, VPNs, Internet connections, proxy servers, and load balancers
Storage group	Manages SANs, NAS, volumes, and backup/restore
Datacenter group	Makes sure cabling, power, UPS, and cooling are working correctly
Security group	Is responsible for things such as firewall rules, security policies such as password policies, single sign-on, intrusion detection, and vulnerabilities

Such a division of responsibilities can significantly increase the time to repair in case the real cause of a problem is not immediately clear. A lot of negative energy is spent trying to prove a group's innocence, resulting in a longer time to resolve the problem. This extra time spent is called *Mean Time to Innocence*.* To reduce this ping-pong time, good cooperation and coordination is important. Clear procedures to escalate problems to different groups help to address this organizational issue. For a good understanding of a concern, people should at least have a minimal knowledge of each part they are supporting. Acquiring this knowledge only when problems occur is not a good base for good support. Continuous knowledge sharing helps to grow this overall responsibility. Larger organizations also have different levels of support: the first level has more generic knowledge that can solve the most common problems, and additional levels have increasing amounts of subject matter expert skill. This provides another way to escalate problems and avoids initial assignment to a specific group, but it can't avoid the problem when the problem area can't be clearly defined.

Organizational boundaries might stop at the firewall, but an Internet service has more dependencies than a service that is internally controlled. Good examples of external dependencies include ISPs, banners, RSS feeds, Internet mail/DNS servers, and ISP connections. The main difference between these internal and external dependencies is that for the external dependencies you don't have a view of how these services are provided. This must not stop you from monitoring these services, because they are still a dependency for the service you provide.

Now that we have detected all the dependencies between each component, the next thing to understand is what happens when each component fails. In a nonredundant system, you know that when one of the components fails, the complete service will fail. When the failure of one component has an impact on the service it is called a *Single Point of Failure.* This might result in complete downtime of the service, but it may also affect the quality of the service (i.e., performance degradation).

To avoid this, redundancy levels are typically added at various points in the architecture. These redundancy levels must be seen as safeguards in your environment and not as a way to compensate for problems at other levels. Usually, adding redundancy levels increases complexity, so don't fall for the overengineering trap. Table 6-7 outlines examples of redundancy mechanisms.

Table 6-7. *Examples of redundancy mechanisms*

Service/component	Redundancy mechanism examples
Application	Load balancers, state replication
Mail server	Multiple MX records for a domain
DNS server	Multiple NS records for a domain

* *http://beta.erinyes.org/2009/12/27/mean-time-to-innocence/*

Table 6-7. *Examples of redundancy mechanisms*

Service/component	Redundancy mechanism examples
Application server	Session replication, multi-instance installations
Web server	Web server service processes
Database	Cluster services, sharding
Host	Virtualization, clustering
Network	Multiple gateways, BGP, HSRP, VRRP, VRSP, multiple ISPs
Storage	RAID controllers, mirroring, multipathing
Generic device	Multiple network cards, CPUs, memory banks
Datacenter	BGP Anycast, GSLB

Dependencies can be classified as *serial, parallel, coupled,* or *chain* (*http://blog.lastinfirstout. net/2008/07/estimating-availability.html*). Figures 6-2, 6-3, and 6-4 show the differences among these three—in particular, the relationship between different components. The dotted path is the path of normal behavior, and the normal path is the failover path. In Figure 6-3, there is no alternative path if one of the components fails. In Figure 6-4, when one web server fails the second allows an automatic failover without any impact on other components. In the *coupled* dependency, when the firewall fails it causes the router, firewall, load balancer, and switch to fail over. (The *chain* dependency is an extreme example of a coupled dependency, where there is a complete switch from the left chain to the right chain, but it is not commonly used in web-related environments.)

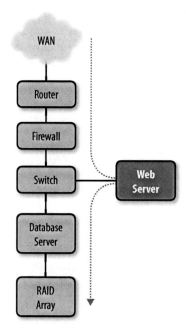

Figure 6-2. *Serial dependency*

In Figures 6-2, 6-3, and 6-4, we're assuming that the application is capable of handling the failover. Sadly, this is often not the case: an example of this is a connection pool that is not reinitialized when the database fails over. Furthermore, most applications need to store state somewhere, and often they store it on a local disk as well as in the database. This makes application redundancy difficult without code changes.

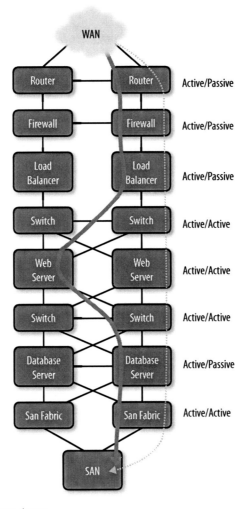

Figure 6-3. *Parallel dependency*

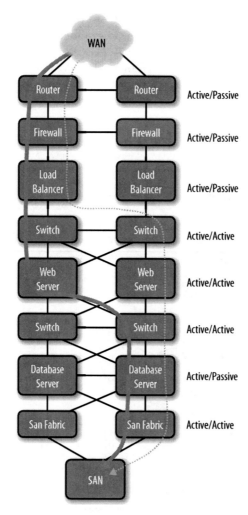

Figure 6-4. *Coupled dependency*

Also, don't forget to check your monitoring service's dependencies: when failures occur in a production environment you don't want your monitoring system to be affected. It is important that the moment you need your monitoring system the most, it is not failing because it had dependencies on production services. Here are some example dependencies:

- Using the production network to access your agents. Usually this is solved by using some sort of management network to connect to systems.

- Using the production DNS to look up hosts to connect to. Usually this is solved using a local hosts file on the monitoring machine, but be aware that this requires discipline for maintaining these across changes. Optimally, have a separate DNS infrastructure, replicated from the production environment.

- Using the production mail system to notify people. Instead, notify people in some other way, and cater it for alternative alerting in case mail fails or isn't available.

- Using the production Internet connections or proxies to connect into or out of the system.

- Using agents and information collectors. If this software malfunctions, your information might be inconsistent. You can usually solve this problem by performing the same checks by different agents in a rotation system.

- Using central storage to store the history. It should have its own redundant storage and backup system.

After identifying each component and understanding its dependencies, the next step is to work out how to check whether these services are available and whether the quality of the availability is appropriate. To do so, you should implement checks that focus on five levels: *availability* (Is it there?), *functionality* (Does it work?), *quality* (Does it work well enough?), *context* (Are all requirements fulfilled to keep it running?), and *credibility* (Would I trust it?).

The proof of the pudding is in the eating: nothing beats a functional check to see if the system is available. Sometimes these checks are not feasible because of restrictions such as the authentication mechanism. Quality metrics are usually good indicators of predicting failures at the functionality level, and focus on checking efficiency, throughput/performance, and workflow health. Most of the context checks tend to be proactive. Given the tight relationship between functionality and quality, these checks are often combined into one check: that is, performing the functionality and checking how long the transaction took. Checks can be either *in-flight* (while the end user is performing its functionality) or *simulated* (by playing a scenario a user might perform). Sometimes you may also want to perform a *negative* check—for instance, have you received no throughput in the past five minutes, or is the Telnet port disabled? Table 6-8 shows some examples of different types of checks.

Table 6-8. *Examples of different types of checks*

Types of checks	Examples
Availability	Can I access port 80? Is the HTTP process running? Are the disks mounted?
Functionality/ in-flight	An application is trying database requests; the OS is trying DNS lookups; the controller is trying disk writes; load balancers are trying to make requests from the web server.
Functionality/ simulated	Simulate making HTTP requests, making DNS requests, and sending mail.
Quality/utilization	By looking at the CPU and memory usage, we can see if the machine has enough processing capacity.
Quality/efficiency	Squid cache ratios.

Table 6-8. *Examples of different types of checks*

Types of checks	Examples
Quality/ throughput	Number of new subscribers, number of logins, number of incidents at the help desk, number of requests in/out, number of users in/out, number of database requests in/out, number of active connections over time, number of launched/terminated instances, mechanical turk money left (capacity).
Context	Configuration monitoring: checksum, packages; security monitoring: patches, ports, intrusion detection, virus scans; backup monitoring: provisioning checks, license checks, backups.
Credibility	Spam level of a mail domain, the SEO's reputation, SSL certificate verification, no explicit content.

The same check can often be executed from different points in the network: for example, a simple HTTP request can be performed from the Internet, just before the firewall, inside the firewall, before or after the load balancer, before or after the cache, from a different network zone, from another server on the same host, from the management network, or on the host web server. You don't have to perform it at each position, but you do need to understand what the check covers so that you don't leave any components unchecked.

Up until now, we have used a bottom-up approach to find all the servers and services required for our user's functionality: we started from the components and tried to map this into business services. Engineers often choose this approach because from their perspective, they don't have a full understanding of the business domain. This often results in a kind of reverse-engineering of the business services used by the systems they manage. Some monitoring tools provide you with features to discover these dependencies and rely on network discovery. This can help you to accomplish a portion of the work, but you will never fully discover the business level. The risk of going with the bottom-up approach is that it is easy to miss components to monitor or to misunderstand the importance of a component.

The business level is usually a high-level goal that a user needs to achieve. This is then broken into different transactions. For these different transactions the user uses the available services made possible by things running at the host level. Table 6-9 shows the different levels checks can be run against.

Table 6-9. *Different levels of checks*

Level	Examples		
Business	Management intranet site		Top-down
Transaction	Logging in, adding a document, sharing the link, logging out		
Service	Mail, DNS, web server, database, routing, firewall, LDAP		
Host	Servers, CPU, memory, switches	Bottom-up	

Given a dependency graph of a service you are checking, the closer to the business level you monitor, the more relevant the components you are checking. Therefore, functional checks performed on the higher business level are more complete checks. On the other hand, they don't provide you with insight into which component caused the failure or they will not detect failures in parallel or *coupled* dependencies. The best approach is to start the exercise from both perspectives and see if they map to both levels, resulting in a cross-check between the two approaches. That's why the user will always beat your technical checks; the user will be running the business and transactions all the time. If you have a lot of users, you can even use this to your advantage. Even with thorough testing, all combinations of input and output can't be tested. By closely monitoring usage statistics or the number of calls to the help desk, you can use these as indirect indicators that something is wrong, even if your (technical) monitoring doesn't show any problems.

Expanding your knowledge of all the relevant components both on the technical side and on the business side is the first step. Now that you understand this, the next step is to understand normal and abnormal behavior.

Step 2: Understand Normal Behavior

Over the years, I've done my share of election sites. It's one of those rare occasions that you can experience mass website usage in a very short period of time—a bit like the Slashdot effect but anticipated. After the government work, I got involved in building a portal website for a broadcaster that would launch by first covering the election and later turning into a major news site.

While we were setting up the new website we were also implementing a new monitoring solution for the web farm. It was the first time they set up a major Internet-facing website, and they demanded a much higher security standard because it was facing the Internet. None of the servers in the DMZ was allowed to connect back to the intranet. So, the agents running on that server to collect the metrics such as CPU, memory, and disk usage could not report back to a central monitoring console. To comply with this, we collected these metrics by logging in over SSH and running a few scripts. Additionally, SNMP agents couldn't send traps to the master, so we had to resort to polling the correct metrics.

A few weeks before the site went live we noticed that the load on all the machines was rising, even if no test users were connected. How could that happen? Well, the monitoring itself created the load: as everybody wanted to be 100% sure that everything was OK, check after check was added to the monitoring. And to be sure that we didn't miss any information, the polling frequency was made very short. As a result, the scripts running on the servers for monitoring were taking up a lot of memory and CPU usage. Also, as the number of machines and metrics increased, it took longer and longer to complete the entire monitoring check; and that resulted in overlapping cycles, again increasing the load on the machines because some checks were run in parallel on the same systems.

Careful analysis showed that a lot of the checks were checking the same thing: one script was reading the SNMP status of the interface and another was performing an actual ping to the interface. By looking at the different monitoring, we could reduce the number of checks. Also, we introduced different polling rates for different checks: we kept the HTTP request very frequent and reduced the CPU, memory, and disk check. We figured that the first check would indicate the problem as soon as possible, and the second check would only give us more information.

The work continued, and we asked some test users to try the site. One night, test users started to report that the system was down. A quick glance at the monitoring showed everything was green. I was still at work and wasn't experiencing any problems. I assumed the problem was a major outage on the ISP's side. To better detect such problems we placed several Internet probes outside our network to check the availability of the site through several of the major ISPs' networks.

Up until now, the websites had been fully supported during office hours and only at best effort after office hours. The new portal website was to be supported 24 hours a day, seven days a week. To hold a dry run with the support group, alert notification mechanisms were activated. After the first night, the guy on call came back and looked at us with an angry face: "Close to midnight I received the first alert and responded to it. And at 2:00 I got 25 alerts! They all seemed related to one problem, but I had to acknowledge the system 25 times! I fixed the problem and everything was green. And then at 4:00, the fun really began: the network ping was going up and down every minute. Finally, I shut off the alerting ... I'm never going to support your system like this, not in a million years, unless you make it saner."

We carefully analyzed the alerting and found three major issues. First, we should send out only one notification for a problem if the other alerts are a result of the first service failing. Second, during the night, backups were putting a high load on the production network, causing several pings to fail because of bad response times, resulting in up and down notifications. And third, if we want people to be on call, we need to keep the number of notifications low as much as possible. That meant no alerts of level information, or alerts from nonproduction environments in the evening.

We survived the night, and eventually the election site turned into a regular news portal. The peak load was gone, and the system continuously published new information. There was a steady increase in disk usage, and after a few months the system hit the threshold for disk space. This was absolutely normal, as things got published every day. To keep the disk volume under control we decided to activate an archival system that would migrate the old news to another system. So, once in a while the system would reach the threshold, and then after some time the archiving would kick in, releasing the disk space again.

The disk space kept on flirting with the threshold, and everybody grew used to it. We wouldn't even bother logging in to the system when we saw the warning, expecting it to turn green again. And then it happened: it turned red. We immediately logged in to the box and started a manual archival to free some space and restarted everything. The monitoring turned green again: mission accomplished. Five minutes later, we had a new warning, and one minute later it was red again. How could this have happened?! Postmortem analysis showed that a hacker was trying a kind of denial of service by doing a lot of requests. Although the site didn't have any difficulty coping with the load, the web server logged all the requests. And the logs were on the same volume as the data. If we had looked at the rate the disk was filling, we could have detected it. But the regular thresholds were just too slow in detecting the problem. Once again, monitoring was adapted, and we hoped for the best.

This story shows that even if you understand all your dependencies, it takes time to design a good monitoring solution.

One of the design decisions discussed in the story concerns how to collect the results of different checks. Various approaches exist, and your choice largely depends on who is responsible for triggering the check and collecting the results. A check can be performed by the monitoring system itself (*active* check) or it can be input from other tools (*passive* check).*

Passive checks are usually used when the monitoring does not have direct access to the component, or other tools have implemented the business logic to deal with the component, or the information is asynchronous (e.g., SNMP alerts). Also within a distributed collection of information, the central part acts as a passive check, getting information from other centralizing agents. Given the internal and external boundaries, collection of information from sources that fall under a different authority can be considered a passive check.

Active checks can be agent based or agentless. Agents are usually part of the monitoring software, but agents can also perform monitoring with standard interfaces such as SNMP, JMX, and WMI. Agents are sometimes built into products or require additional software to be run on the production systems, and they can constantly collect metrics. Agentless checks are polling based and usually don't go into depth but have the advantage of zero installation effort, because they use the remote login service already available as a service. This does introduce a dependency of the monitoring system on the remote login service, however, but often this is not an issue, as the remote login service is considered one of the highest priorities in monitoring to make fast problem resolution possible.

---

* http://nagios.sourceforge.net/docs/1_0/images/activepassive.png

All this information is collected and archived for future use, such as for trending information. To make this information useful good clock synchronization among all systems that are reporting is required. Use a reference clock and be aware of changes in summer and winter, or information from different time zones, before relating this information. The use of a 24-hour clock can help you avoid a.m./p.m. problems.

The more checks you introduce, the more resources might be taken away from your production systems: this can be bandwidth for transferring results, CPU power for calculating results, and so on. You need to find the right balance: monitoring too much is only a waste of resources and will decrease the overview; not monitoring enough will not alert you in time. Checks performed closer to the business level will have a better chance of detecting a real failure; checks performed at a lower level will give better insight into where things are happening. But these often come with a higher cost of using resources than just reading metrics.

Although most monitoring software comes with a variety of checks and metrics for your services and hosts, chances are you will end up writing some checks yourself. You can use your monitoring software's framework collection to report your information regarding the availability and quality of your checks. Good sources for information are usually exit codes of scripts and keywords in logfiles. The ease of use of the API and/or samples available on various websites will help you to write your own checks. Be sure to check how active your community is and how mature your monitoring solution's API is.

Monitoring is considered part of the operational environment and is usually managed by system or network administrators. It starts on a small system running in the background, and as the monitoring environment grows, more configuration and customization is performed. Although operational people are often the first to scrutinize new software to be deployed in production, their standards are often not applied to their own monitoring system. There is absolutely no reason for this: your monitoring is one of your most critical applications in operations, so treat it as one. Table 6-10 lists some common best practices in this regard.

Table 6-10. *Monitoring best practices*

Practice	Detail
Versioning	Version your checks and put them into a version-controlled repository.
Different environments	Use a different environment to develop or test new checks.
Testing	Treat your checks as normal code, and add tests to the code's functionality.
Usability	Create a good visual overview of all the components and their relationships. Indicating the failed monitoring checks and their relationship with the components helps an engineer to understand what might have caused a problem by simply looking at the dashboard.
Information architecture	Use different data representations, such as list views, map views, drill-down views, pie graphs, and trending information, and structure the data for easy navigation and to avoid information overload.

Table 6-10. *Monitoring best practices*

Practice	Detail
Code reuse	Don't rewrite your own business logic in checks when you can reuse the business logic from applications you are monitoring.
No hardcoding	Avoid hardcoded parameters in scripts. Use configuration files. This will also allow easier transfer between the different environments.
Deployment	Make it easy to deploy and distribute new checks.
Backup/ restore	Back up your monitoring data and understand how you need to restore it.
Monitoring	Monitor your own monitoring system. As the Romans once said: *"Quis custodiet ipsos custodes?"* (Who will guard the guards?)
Redundancy	Use high-availability functionality to do maintenance work on your monitoring.
Apply generic security principles	Don't use the same accounts for monitoring as for other functionalities. Run things with the least number of privileges needed. Don't store passwords in clear text. Limit access to the system. Don't use it as a playground for other tests. Protect your monitoring system with a firewall or proxy system to avoid access from compromised hosts.

Once all the information is collected and stored, the next thing to do is to analyze the results of the checks. A service or system can be available (Up) or unavailable (Down). Some monitoring systems also add a state when the system can't be reached (Unreachable) and when the system/service hasn't been checked (Pending).

As I explained, the availability of a system/service can have different qualities (e.g., performance timings, disk usage). These values are expressed in ranges. These ranges are then divided into subranges that express that the quality is optimal (OK), the quality has reached a level that requires preventive action (Warning), or the quality has reached a level that requires immediate attention (Critical). Thresholds are the values you define to specify when you transition from one state to another state.

Sometimes when building an environment for a new service, thresholds are difficult to define upfront: actual usage might surpass expectations or vice versa. Therefore, it makes sense to refine thresholds iteratively: define a set of thresholds based on a theoretical assumption, and then simulate the expected behavior in a test environment and make the translations to technical component usage. Because of the complexity of the usage and the systems we are building, it's hard to make exact models of the system, application, and user behavior. Therefore, we have to continuously inspect and adapt the thresholds. Trending really helps you define thresholds: most monitoring software will let you trend monitored values without alerting, and you can then enable alerting when you figure out the thresholds based on historical data shown in the trends.

Using thresholds for values will not tell you everything. Suppose a value has an upper and lower limit; you won't be alerted when the thresholds are not reached—for instance, in the case of a filesystem that has a warning level between 80% and 90% critical. The monitoring will not detect anything when the upper limit is not reached. Still, it's clear that something is bound to happen if the usage changes quickly. To detect such a change, the maximum *value change rate** over time can also be monitored. In Figure 6-3, you can see the expected volume growth is drawn with a line. Minimum and maximum levels would not have detected the sudden peak.

There are two additional states. When no current value is available, the value has a state of Unknown. And when the first check of this value is yet to be performed, the value has a state of Pending. While the system transitions between these different states, sometimes the value starts to oscillate among different ranges. If the speed of the transition is very high, the system is in a Flapping state. Monitoring systems can detect this by looking at the number of state changes over a period of time. If the state changes too frequently, the system can send only one notification with a state of Flapping.† Examples of this are thresholds for disk usage that vary between thresholds or unreliable links.

Depending on the business you are running, thresholds can have a strong relationship with time: this could be as easy as having different thresholds before or after office hours. More complex time relationships could be at the beginning or end of the month, or based on previous trending of usage patterns (baselines). It could also be a planned media campaign flirting with the limits of your capacity. This kind of benchmarking with previous usage is often used to detect indirect failures by a decrease in usage. It's important to understand that no past usage can predict the future: good examples of this are flash peaks caused by sudden community interest on social media sites, or a change in behavior owing to a big national sports event, or even religious events such as the start of Ramadan.

Now that we know there is a problem we can send out an alert. The simplest approach to alerting is to generate an alert for every component transitioning state. As described before, a lot of components work together to enable a business transaction, so one failure will likely fail other functionality we monitor. A good example of this is a network component: if a switch fails, possibly a lot of host services and business transactions can become unavailable. Still, we will monitor each component, so according to the simplistic approach, this will result in a lot of simultaneous alerts. Thanks to the work

* http://www.oreillynet.com/sysadmin/blog/2008/05/filesystem_monitoring_youre_do.html
†http://nagios.sourceforge.net/docs/2_0/flapping.html

we did in describing the dependencies, we can relate these alerts and group them together in one notification. The fact that we monitor each component separately will help us pinpoint the actual problem.

Managing alerts is not just about enabling alerts when states change: chances are that when you enable all alerts all the time, your engineers will not be able to sustain the support of the systems because of the large value of alerts, potentially resulting in *paging burnout*. It's clear that not having enough checks will result in a lot of time lost.

The same goes for having too many false alerts. This can be seen as having technical debt in your monitoring system. Another way to look at this problem is to ask yourself, does this alert require any immediate intervention? Alerts should be actionable. If an alert can be ignored or doesn't require human intervention, the alert is a waste of energy. Therefore, eliminating the noise is the real challenge. Too many alerts will also have the "boy who cried wolf" effect. Important alerts might be ignored because of alert overload. Within Six Sigma, there is a technique called failure mode and effects analysis* that can help you decide what is important to monitor: the basic idea is that you brainstorm the list of possible failures and then give each a score on detectability, frequency of occurrence, and severity. Then you multiply the scores and sort all the products to find the most important things to monitor.

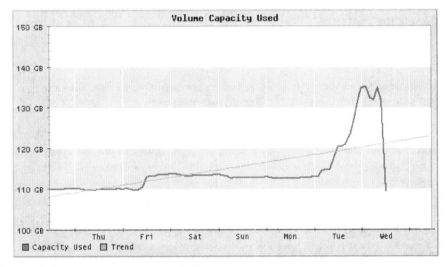

Figure 6-5. *Example value rate interpolation*

We've talked about redundancy mechanisms such as load balancing and clustering to improve the availability of a website. They can also serve to keep the alerting sustainable: with *N*+1 systems available and if *N* is large enough, we can put thresholds on

---

* http://en.wikipedia.org/wiki/Failure_mode_and_effects_analysis

the number of systems available in the cluster before we receive an alert—for example, send an alert only if 10% of the servers/capacity becomes unavailable. These thresholds are to be related to your capacity management expectations.

If possible, you should verify any failure checks before sending out an alert. You can do this by rerunning the same check before sending out the result, by cross-checking the results of the same check from different positions in your architecture, or by relating different checks together to verify if all checks fail. You need to be aware that conflicts can occur: one check might say green and the other red. Human verification is then required. Again, the goal is to have zero alerts, and if an occasional alert triggers human intervention, it had better be worth it. Some errors fail only some of the time; these are called *transient* errors. An example of this is a ping that occasionally drops a packet. These kinds of errors are usually handled by alerting only after *N* occurrences of the error.

What is normal system behavior needs to be related to normal business behavior. Similar to our component mapping exercise in step 1, this is one of the challenges. Limiting the alerts because you want to make the website sustainable is a good thing, but not if it doesn't align with the business requirements. The reverse is also true: sending out many alerts to make sure the website is up makes no sense if the business doesn't require it. It's part of the journey of monitoring to get this balance right. This brings us to the final step: "Be prepared and learn."

Step 3: Be Prepared and Learn

I remember the following very well: I was on call one night and sleeping. All of a sudden the phone rang. It wasn't my cell phone, it was my landline; nobody would call me at 4:00 in the morning, unless something bad happened. I raced down the stairs to take the call. I was greeted by my boss: "Why haven't you answered my calls? The site has been down for half an hour now, and you didn't respond to the alert. Can you please log in ASAP?" I muttered something like, "Yes boss, right away." I hadn't received any notification; had I slept through it? I went back upstairs to get my token and found that my cell phone battery had died during the night. So much for being alerted.... I logged in and tried the website. I was greeted by a beautiful stack trace indicating a problem with the application; it looked like gibberish to me. Nothing appeared to have changed since the previous day, so why did it fail? After looking around, I didn't find any problem with the disk space or memory, so I tried to restart the application server process. I still had the error. I knew it didn't have to do with the connection to the database, because monitoring showed that queries were still possible. I restarted the database anyway, but again, no luck. In the meantime, another half hour had passed, and I still had no solution. So, I decided to reboot all the machines. Everything came back online, but the error wouldn't go away.

I was puzzled, and I began to suspect a problem with the application. I didn't have a phone number for someone who could help me resolve the problem, so I called my boss, who told me he would try to get me the necessary contact information. In the meantime, as a last resort I decided to restore from backup. It took me 15 minutes to restore the latest backup. I compared the backup with the current configuration but couldn't find any difference between the two. At this point, it was 5:30 and still the site wasn't up. I began to feel desperate; the first end users would kick in at 6:00. Finally, my boss got me the developer's phone number. I explained the error to him, and he asked me to check the contents of a table in the database. The table was empty. "Is that normal?" I asked. "No," he responded. "We did experience it once during our tests, but we were never able to reproduce it." Because the application hadn't been updated for a week, I had no other solution but to restore the whole database again, as the data had been corrupted. With all the redundancy in place, we hadn't taken into consideration that it would take us three hours to restore the entire database.

The restore started, and there was nothing much I could do but wait. The end users started their day, and calls to the help desk were coming in at a high rate. I put up a web page stating that the website was down because of problems. Finally, luck returned to my side; the restore did the trick and the site was back up again.

The next day my boss had to report to management and explain the problem: "It was clearly an application fault that caused it," he said. "We need them to provide a better fix. Also, we need a contact list in case such a problem arises again." Another manager chimed in: "We need better communication to the end users and help desk." For two days, the topic remained hot and then slowly faded away. After two weeks, everybody was back to business as usual and the problem was considered only a temporary glitch—until one month later, when the inevitable happened again and the restore resulted in three hours of downtime....

At the start of this story, the problem with the website had already been detected. The next step was to notify the right person to handle the issue. A lot of different factors affect the selection of the correct person to be notified: this can be based on time (during or after office hours), which component has failed (network, server), the type of customer (premium, basic), the current active time zone, or a combination. Instead of assigning people directly to handle notifications, it makes sense to assign roles to notifications and people to roles. This allows for more flexible administration of notification rules. Each specific role can have its own email list for sending alerts. Again, sustainable assignment is crucial here: take into account holidays, family events, and birthdays to avoid alert aversion.

Usually one person is responsible for handling alert notifications. This person would acknowledge receipt of the notification in the monitoring system. If for some reason this person did not get the notification or was not able to acknowledge the notification, most notification systems allow you to resend a notification if it is not acknowledged within some defined period of time. This makes a *recording* of the event chain around an incident possible, allowing other people to keep track of what has happened. Popular notification mechanisms include email, IM (Yahoo!, Google Talk, and ICQ), SMS, and Twitter. Although some people consider such mechanisms to be reliable and fast enough for their usage, they don't provide guaranteed delivery. Therefore, most enterprises employ a texting or paging solution that guarantees timely delivery. Another thing to consider is whether the form of communication is in band or out of band: if you are using your production email servers, Internet connection, or telephone systems to send out notifications, be sure the notification can work independent of the production system.

This one person can easily become a single point of failure, so most enterprises have a primary and secondary on-call person, allowing for backup if required. Sometimes this is combined with informing the manager as well, allowing manual escalations. To ensure that no two persons start working on the same problem, acknowledgment is crucial. Some choose to have an acknowledgment silence the notifications and alarms, while others prefer to keep the notifications going until the problem is fixed, as a precaution. When the notification is silenced, after resolving the issues the alert and notification should be enabled again.

The responsibility of responding to notifications is usually rotated among people. Special attention should be paid when an alert happens during this rotation: a clear ceremony between both persons helps to transfer the knowledge of the work already performed on the case. Organizations often have a help desk and support organization with first- and second-line support using a ticketing system for issues. Linking the alerts to an incident allows people to follow up and enter details on the case they are working on.

During office hours, using a large display acting as an information radiator often complements this notification. Also, everyone involved can have a web page open to see the current state of the environment. This allows a kind of crowd monitoring, even when the primary person is not available/reachable for some reason.

While fixing the problem, consider the steps of *contain, eradicate*, and *recover*. These ideas are borrowed from security incident handling.* Containment helps in isolating the problem's cause: by removing a component or putting it offline, you can remove the cause and bring the system back online. If the system is not redundant, you can do this by shortcutting some functionality. After the containment, you can continue to eradicate the problem: fixing the config, restoring the backup, or doing whatever makes sense in your case.

Often, you will find yourself starting and stopping different components to reinitialize their state, hoping that will fix the problem. These steps should be automated as much as possible in start/stop scripts, or if they require human intervention they should be well documented. The location of logfiles, large files, necessary listeners, and so on should also be well documented. Make sure that before restarting the machine, you capture all the relevant information before it gets reset, too: determine the size of the process, make a heap dump, and collect the relevant metrics. This allows you to further investigate the problems even if restarts work fine.

* *http://www.cpni.gov.uk/Docs/FirstRespondersGuide.pdf*

If a restart doesn't work, you are often faced with the dilemma of finding the root cause or just reinstalling the whole box. Of course, it's difficult to predict which of these will be faster to accomplish. By automating the reinstallation as much as possible, you at least don't lose additional time. One person can't be a subject matter expert on everything: it makes sense to have a clearly defined escalation path to more specialist resources.

The last step is to recover the system by bringing the failed component online and operational again. In certain cases, the fix can be automated: if the system is in a known error state, a script could be executed to fix the problem automatically. Usually, this is a result of either a known problem or a problem that occurs frequently and whose fix has been well documented. It's clear that the human cost of being paged makes self-healing interesting. Still, this requires caution and a lot of careful checks to see if this is exactly the state that was expected.

With all systems in place, it's easy to overlook the time it takes to get physical replacements, possibly provided by third-party companies. Access to replacement material and tested backup and restore procedures is also crucial in terms of downsizing the recovery time. This is part of the preparation phase.

One major cause of failures that is often overlooked when fixing things is that before doing any investigation, one should check the list of changes made to the environment. Of course, this requires rigorous change management, registering all changes in one central place. Relating the changes to the different components helps in troubleshooting problems. Changes are not necessarily technical changes but can also relate to changes in business behavior (e.g., a new campaign started by the business). This, of course, relates to good capacity management.

Downtime itself is not necessarily caused by a malfunction; it can also be planned downtime for performing maintenance. This period is typically described as a maintenance window. In this case, the business has agreed to have some downtime. To avoid having unnecessary alerts, sometimes the monitoring system is silenced for that period. This can lead to missing other unrelated systems/services being down during the same period: therefore, only the related alerts should be disabled, not the complete environment notifications. After that, it is necessary for the monitoring system to be enabled again as soon as the service is considered stable; in too many cases, notification isn't reenabled until the next day.

Tracking and trending your critical alerts will help you make a case for improving your architecture or processes. Business owners are interested in new functionality, but when you relate business value lost because of problems, they will often approve further effort. But don't be upset if they don't go for the full 99.99% as well; if their business doesn't require it you have to accept that, too.

Conclusion

Monitoring isn't just about keeping the servers up and running. It's about keeping the business going. By understanding both the technical components and the business behavior, you stand a fair chance of reducing the time it takes to detect and repair problems. Accept that failure will happen, and be ready for it. In case the system does fail, be sure to radiate this information as feedback to everyone willing to listen, and improve things to avoid new failures. May the force of monitoring be with you.

## CHAPTER SEVEN

How Complex Systems Fail

John Allspaw and Richard Cook

WHEN I FIRST READ DR. RICHARD COOK'S ESSAY, "How Complex Systems Fail," I was convinced that he had written the piece specifically for the field of web operations. It is a concise and insightful article on the observations of failure and degradation that could have been inspired by years of experience running the distributed architectures for high-volume web companies. As I read through the observations in the essay, I kept remembering events in my own experience troubleshooting degradations and failures that happen when you operate a complex and fast-growing web application.

As it turns out, Dr. Cook is a physician, educator, and researcher at the University of Chicago. He really nailed this topic that spans across many different disciplines and fields. Whether it's structural engineering, space exploration, or patient safety in the medical field, complex systems all have commonalities when it comes to failure. Web operations is one such field.

How Complex Systems Fail

(Being a Short Treatise on the Nature of Failure; How Failure Is Evaluated; How Failure Is Attributed to Proximate Cause; and the Resulting New Understanding of Patient Safety)

By Richard I. Cook, MD, Cognitive Technologies Laboratory, University of Chicago

Complex systems are intrinsically hazardous systems

All of the interesting systems (e.g., transportation, healthcare, power generation) are inherently and unavoidably hazardous by their own nature. The frequency of hazard exposure can sometimes be changed, but the processes involved in the system are themselves intrinsically and irreducibly hazardous. It is the presence of these hazards that drives the creation of defenses against hazards that characterize these systems.

Complex systems are heavily and successfully defended against failure

The high consequences of failure lead, over time, to the construction of multiple layers of defense against failure. These defenses include obvious technical components (e.g., backup systems, "safety" features of equipment) and human components (e.g., training, knowledge), but also a variety of organizational, institutional, and regulatory defenses (e.g., policies and procedures, certification, work rules, team training). The effect of these measures is to provide a series of shields that normally divert operations away from accidents.

Catastrophe requires multiple failures—single-point failures are not enough

The array of defenses works. System operations are generally successful. Overt catastrophic failure occurs when small, apparently innocuous failures join to create opportunity for a systemic accident. Each of these small failures is necessary to cause catastrophe, but only the combination is sufficient to permit failure. Put another way, there are many more failure opportunities than overt system accidents. Most initial failure trajectories are blocked by designed system safety components. Trajectories that reach the operational level are mostly blocked, usually by practitioners.

Complex systems contain changing mixtures of failures latent within them

The complexity of these systems makes it impossible for them to run without multiple flaws being present. Because these are individually insufficient to cause failure they are regarded as minor factors during operations. Eradication of all latent failures is limited primarily by economic cost, but also because it is difficult before the fact to see how such failures might contribute to an accident. The failures change constantly because of changing technology, work organization, and efforts to eradicate failures.

Complex systems run in degraded mode

A corollary to the preceding point is that complex systems run as broken systems. The system continues to function because it contains so many redundancies and because people can make it function, despite the presence of many flaws. After-accident reviews nearly always note that the system has a history of prior "proto-accidents" that nearly generated catastrophe. Arguments that these degraded conditions should have been recognized before the overt accident are usually predicated on naïve notions of system performance. System operations are dynamic, with components (organizational, human, technical) failing and being replaced continuously.

Catastrophe is always just around the corner

Complex systems possess potential for catastrophic failure. Human practitioners are nearly always in close physical and temporal proximity to these potential failures—disaster can occur at any time and in nearly any place. The potential for catastrophic outcome is a hallmark of complex systems. It is impossible to eliminate the potential for such catastrophic failure; the potential for such failure is always present by the system's own nature.

Post-accident attribution to a "root cause" is fundamentally wrong

Because overt failure requires multiple faults, there is no isolated "cause" of an accident. There are multiple contributors to accidents. Each of these is necessarily insufficient in itself to create an accident. Only jointly are these causes sufficient to create an accident. Indeed, it is the linking of these causes together that creates the circumstances required for the accident. Thus, no isolation of the "root cause" of an accident is possible. The evaluations based on such reasoning as "root cause" do not reflect a technical understanding of the nature of failure, but rather the social, cultural need to blame specific, localized forces or events for outcomes.*

Hindsight biases post-accident assessments of human performance

Knowledge of the outcome makes it seem that events leading to the outcome should have appeared more salient to practitioners at the time than was actually the case. This means that *ex post facto* accident analysis of human performance is inaccurate. The outcome knowledge poisons the ability of after-accident observers to re-create the view of practitioners before the accident of those same factors. It seems that practi-

---

* Anthropological field research provides the clearest demonstration of the social construction of the notion of "cause" (cf. Goldman, L. [1993], *The Culture of Coincidence: Accident and Absolute Liability in Huli*, New York: Clarendon Press; and also Tasca, L. [1990], *The Social Construction of Human Error*, unpublished doctoral dissertation, Department of Sociology, State University of New York at Stonybrook).

tioners "should have known" that the factors would "inevitably" lead to an accident.* *Hindsight bias remains the primary obstacle to accident investigation, especially when expert human performance is involved.*

Human operators have dual roles: as producers and as defenders against failure

The system practitioners operate the system in order to produce its desired product and also work to forestall accidents. This dynamic quality of system operation, the balancing of demands for production against the possibility of incipient failure, is unavoidable. Outsiders rarely acknowledge the duality of this role. In non-accident-filled times, the production role is emphasized. After accidents, the defense against failure role is emphasized. At either time, the outsider's view misapprehends the operator's constant, simultaneous engagement with both roles.

All practitioner actions are gambles

After accidents, the overt failure often appears to have been inevitable and the practitioner's actions as blunders or deliberate willful disregard of certain impending failure. But all practitioner actions are actually gambles, that is, acts that take place in the face of uncertain outcomes. The degree of uncertainty may change from moment to moment. That practitioner actions are gambles appears clear after accidents; in general, analysis regards these gambles as poor ones. But the converse—that successful outcomes are also the result of gambles—is not widely appreciated.

Actions at the sharp end resolve all ambiguity

Organizations are ambiguous, often intentionally, about the relationship between production targets, efficient use of resources, economy and costs of operations, and acceptable risks of low- and high-consequence accidents. All ambiguity is resolved by actions of practitioners at the sharp end of the system. After an accident, practitioner actions may be regarded as "errors" or "violations," but these evaluations are heavily biased by hindsight and ignore the other driving forces, especially production pressure.

Human practitioners are the adaptable element of complex systems

Practitioners and first-line management actively adapt the system to maximize production and minimize accidents. These adaptations often occur on a moment-by-moment basis. Some of these adaptations include (1) restructuring the system in order to reduce exposure of vulnerable parts to failure; (2) concentrating critical resources in

---

* This is not a feature of medical judgments or technical ones, but rather of all human cognition about past events and their causes.

areas of expected high demand; (3) providing pathways for retreat or recovery from expected and unexpected faults; and (4) establishing means for early detection of changed system performance in order to allow graceful cutbacks in production or other means of increasing resiliency.

Human expertise in complex systems is constantly changing

Complex systems require substantial human expertise in their operation and management. This expertise changes in character as technology changes, but it also changes because of the need to replace experts who leave. In every case, training and refinement of skill and expertise is one part of the functions of the system itself. At any moment, therefore, a given complex system will contain practitioners and trainees with varying degrees of expertise. Critical issues related to expertise arise from (1) the need to use scarce expertise as a resource for the most difficult or demanding production needs and (2) the need to develop expertise for future use.

Change introduces new forms of failure

The low rate of overt accidents in reliable systems may encourage changes, especially the use of new technology, to decrease the number of low-consequence but high-frequency failures. These changes maybe actually create opportunities for new, low-frequency but high-consequence failures. When new technologies are used to eliminate well-understood system failures or to gain high-precision performance they often introduce new pathways to large-scale, catastrophic failures. Not uncommonly, these new, rare catastrophes have even greater impact than those eliminated by the new technology. These new forms of failure are difficult to see before the fact; attention is paid mostly to the putative beneficial characteristics of the changes. Because these new, high-consequence accidents occur at a low rate, multiple system changes may occur before an accident, making it hard to see the contribution of technology to the failure.

Views of "cause" limit the effectiveness of defenses against future events

Post-accident remedies for "human error" are usually predicated on obstructing activities that can "cause" accidents. These end-of-the-chain measures do little to reduce the likelihood of further accidents. In fact, that likelihood of an identical accident is already extraordinarily low because the pattern of latent failures changes constantly. Instead of increasing safety, post-accident remedies usually increase the coupling and complexity of the system. This increases the potential number of latent failures and also makes the detection and blocking of accident trajectories more difficult.

Safety is a characteristic of systems and not of their components

Safety is an emergent property of systems; it does not reside in a person, device, or department of an organization or system. Safety cannot be purchased or manufactured; it is not a feature that is separate from the other components of the system. This means that safety cannot be manipulated like a feedstock or raw material. The state of safety in any system is always dynamic; continuous systemic change ensures that hazard and its management are constantly changing.

People continuously create safety

Failure-free operations are the result of activities of people who work to keep the system within the boundaries of tolerable performance. These activities are, for the most part, part of normal operations and superficially straightforward. But because system operations are never trouble-free, human practitioner adaptations to changing conditions actually create safety from moment to moment. These adaptations often amount to just the selection of a well-rehearsed routine from a store of available responses; sometimes, however, the adaptations are novel combinations or *de novo* creations of new approaches.

Failure-free operations require experience with failure

Recognizing hazard and successfully manipulating system operations to remain inside the tolerable performance boundaries requires intimate contact with failure. More robust system performance is likely to arise in systems where operators can discern the "edge of the envelope." This is where system performance begins to deteriorate, becomes difficult to predict, or cannot be readily recovered. In intrinsically hazardous systems, operators are expected to encounter and appreciate hazards in ways that lead to overall performance that is desirable. Improved safety depends on providing operators with calibrated views of the hazards. It also depends on providing calibration about how their actions move system performance toward or away from the edge of the envelope.

As It Pertains Specifically to Web Operations

It will be difficult to tell that the system has failed

Overt failures such as server fires or a backhoe digging up the fiber optic cable are dramatic, easily detected, and—because they are well defended against—quite rare. Much more common are failures that degrade performance a little (or a lot) or cause portions of a system to stop working. Especially for distributed systems, central indicators may be nominal even though service is effectively down for some or even many users. For systems that involve server-side applications and lots of user input, failures may seem to be cases of "user error" and early reports of failure may be discounted because user-specific problems are so common.

It will be difficult to tell what has failed

Because complex systems involve tangled and shifting dependencies, the symptoms of failure are often nonspecific. This is a version of the notion of "action at a distance"; the consequences of failure are likely to be separated in time and space from the causes. When such a failure occurs, diagnosis may require very high levels of expertise to untangle the skein of components. This is problematic in the operational context because the people who are operating the system when it fails usually know little about the structure itself.

Meaningful response will be delayed

The combination of #1 and #2 will produce delays in responding to failures and these delays will be amplified by difficulties in communications related to diagnosis and repair.

Communications will be strained and tempers will flare

The people experiencing the failure (system users directly, system operators indirectly) will describe the problem in their own terms while the experts searching for the source of the problem employ an entirely different language. The result is that diagnosis typically involves repeated attempts to describe the problem and its context, often in a situation of escalating emotion. Especially for large systems, a deadly loss of information can occur as early reporters become frustrated with the process and leave. The problem reporters are often customers, and their dissatisfaction with the service that has failed for them is magnified by the inability of the problem handlers to do more than ask for more information. Nonoperational management will eventually hear about the operational problem and ask questions. Operations people will find themselves dealing with, on one side, the customer and point-of-contact representatives and on the other side nonoperational management, each demanding information and action. Pressure will escalate with time and some individuals will become angry.

Maintenance will be a major source of new failures

Hardware and software maintenance including routine maintenance and upgrades will cause many failures, directly or indirectly. "Simple" failures with catastrophic consequences induced by maintenance procedures are a recurring theme in IT. There are at least two reasons for this. First, because they fiddle with live systems, maintenance procedures themselves are inherently dangerous. Maintenance almost always involves some sort of suspension of operations with a subsequent restart, and starting complex systems is a recipe for the discovery of new dependencies. Second, although patches and upgrades may receive extensive testing before installation, it is virtually impossible to re-create the operating environment in enough detail for the testing to cover all the modes of failure available to the real, much more complex, system. Every maintenance activity is, ultimately, an experiment. Experienced owners of large, complex systems are reluctant to perform maintenance or upgrades, and this may lead to a kind of managerial paralysis: a working system, even one with known flaws, is a precious entity and so maintenance and, especially, upgrades are deliberately delayed because of fear of the failures that come from work on the system.

Recovery from backup is itself difficult and potentially dangerous

Although backing up, and its varieties (e.g., system checkpoints), is widely recognized as a good practice, actually using backups to recover from a complex system outage is relatively rare. The delays associated with #1–#4 above often contrive to make the most recent backup old enough that using it will lead to important data loss. Restoring from backup is a maintenance-like activity that is itself inherently hazardous, especially because it is an unfamiliar procedure, often one involving steps that the operators have never performed before. Not all managers recognize the complexity and uncertainty that accompanies a system restoration from backups. This can lead to pressure to use backups to restore system operations even before the cause of the outage has been determined.

Given all this, what should operations people do? Good system design is the best defense, of course, but operational people have to play the hand that the designers dealt them. There are a few things that can make operations easier.

Create test procedures that front-line people can use to verify system status

Make it easy for point-of-contact and operations personnel to test the system directly. For order entry systems that include credit card processing, for example, a useful test procedure might be a script that uses the system to create and place a real order, including credit card processing with a real credit card and email notification. Remote monitors of system performance may not show that the system is down. Fast, successful transaction processing, including all the ancillary processes, is good evidence that it is up. Conversely, slow processing or failure is strong evidence that something is wrong.

Manage operations on a daily basis

It's useful to practice communicating about system functional problems with the experts you will call on when an outage occurs. People—including experts—change jobs, go on vacation, call in sick, and go to lunch. Know who is available today and how to contact them. Formal printed lists or web-based call schedules are wonderful but not always current. An index card with the names, phone numbers, and email addresses of the people you might need to call if the system goes down fits in the pocket and can be handed to a deputy when you go to the dentist. Don't forget to include the name of the maintenance guy with the keys and the director of marketing who is always carping about how important uptime is. It's also quite interesting to call these people every once in a while as a test and as reinforcement regarding their potential roles. The reverse side of the index card is useful for writing down short notes about the time and nature of issues that arise during the day. If you save each day's card in a box you will soon have a nice operational log for the system. (Although there are many computer-based approaches to this sort of record, the manual method described is a good method for managing the difficult-to-categorize stuff of day-to-day operations that is hard to track with such apps.)

Control maintenance

Operational people don't usually perform software or hardware maintenance beyond routine backups, but they inherit all the problems that maintenance generates. Operations should control maintenance activities and regulate access to the running system. When maintenance is needed, access to the running system should be provided by operations and all maintenance activities should be examined by operations before access is granted. Systems people, especially programming types, are sometimes overconfident about the maintenance code and procedures they have generated. Maintenance activities need planning and careful observation from operations for two reasons. First, this sort of oversight makes explicit the changes and justification for them and generates records of the things that can be used when tracing back problems that appear in the system. Second, the first people to recognize that a new problem has appeared are the operations folks, and they benefit from knowing when and how the system has been altered. There is sometimes resistance from the software side to this kind of oversight, in part because of the belief that operations personnel will blame maintenance for any new problem that appears. This attitude can even lead to attempts to do maintenance "on the sly," that is, without letting the operations side know about it. There is sometimes a temptation to just "slip in this one little change" rather than go through a procedure that involves scheduling and notification and what some may consider bureaucratic process. Operations and not systems programming should control access to the system and oversee all the maintenance.

Assess performance at regular intervals

Operations can be hectic so that routine stuff gets put off indefinitely. Hints of future problems can often be found in current performance, and regular reviews of that performance is the best way to detect these warnings. Especially with distributed systems it can be hard to get a handle on performance, but this only means that it is even more important to look at it closely. A good deal of attention has been given to performance *measurement*—generally this means the automated tools that examine system logs and network hardware. But it is performance *assessment*—the examination and analysis of larger systems—that really matters. The performance measurement tools are only one source of information about system performance. The assessment is the detailed analysis of what these tools reveal in the context of operations. Such analysis is not done in a few minutes and often requires a good deal of data not gathered by the measurement tools, (e.g., transactions processed, the volume of transactions at different times of the day or week, relationships between measured values and recent maintenance).

Pay particular attention to things that might become bottlenecks under slightly different circumstances. Would a 10% increase in transaction rates lead to a full scratch volume? Is the pattern of user login durations suggestive of thoughtful users or poor system responsiveness? The goal of operations is to have every day be just another boring day. Achieving this boredom depends on foreseeing the future performance of the system and making adjustments accordingly.

Be a (unique) customer

The easiest way to determine that your system works is to use it as a customer would. If you can get information and perform transactions successfully it is likely that others can as well. You should be a regular user of the system and exercise its functions on a daily basis. Something taking too long? A page not displaying correctly? Some link is 404? It's far better for an operations person to identify these sorts of problems than to have a customer do it. Remember, not all browsers cooperate well with web-based services. Keep that old laptop and put Linux and a couple of different browsers on it for test purposes. Sure, your system works with the latest version of Explorer, but how about an older version of Opera? Stop thinking of Apple users as super-geeks and start thinking of them as customers—if it won't work with Safari, the people who use only that won't be using your site. Again, although others in your organization are supposed to take care of these issues, it is operations that will handle the calls from the field when they don't.

Further Reading

Cook, Richard I. (1999). "A Brief Look at the New Look in Error, Safety, and Failure of Complex Systems" (Chicago: CtL).

Cook, Richard I., and David D. Woods (1994). "Operating at the Sharp End: The Complexity of Human Error." In M. S. Bogner, ed., *Human Error in Medicine* (Hillsdale, NJ); pp. 255–310.

Cook, Richard I., David D. Woods, and Charlotte Miller (1998). "A Tale of Two Stories: Contrasting Views of Patient Safety" (Chicago: NPSF); available as a PDF file on the NPSF website at *http://www.npsf.org*.

Cook, Richard I., Marta Render, and David D. Woods (2000). "Gaps in the Continuity of Care and Progress on Patient Safety." *British Medical Journal* 320: pp. 791–794.

Woods, David D., and Richard I. Cook (1998). "Characteristics of Patient Safety: Five Principles that Underlie Productive Work" (Chicago: CtL).

Woods, David D., and Richard I. Cook (1999). "Perspectives on Human Error: Hindsight Biases and Local Rationality." In Durso, Nickerson, Dumais, et al., eds., *Handbook of Applied Cognition* (New York: Wiley); pp. 141–171.

Woods, David D., Leila J. Johannesen, Richard I. Cook, and Nadine B. Sarter (1994). *Behind Human Error: Cognition, Computers and Hindsight* (Wright Patterson AFB: CSERIAC).

## CHAPTER EIGHT

Community Management and Web Operations

Heather Champ and John Allspaw

RUNNING A LARGE AND POPULAR WEBSITE means you have a lot of people relying on your service to be fast and available, whenever they want it. If you're lucky, they'll form a community of people who will interact and relate to each other in all sorts of interesting and creative ways.

Web operations is usually thought of as a purely technical field, and for the most part, it is. But when your very technical service affects people's lives (for better or worse), operations and engineering have to take human elements into consideration, and that requires a good deal of collaboration and communication. Failure and the response to failure are common concerns in this field, and there's a uniquely human element to those topics that can make or break teams and products.

To highlight this topic, I interviewed Heather Champ, who for five years has guided Flickr's community through both clear and rough seas and has seen more than 40 million people join and use Flickr's service. I was lucky enough to stand beside her during that time, and thought she could give some insight into how community management and technical teams work together.

John: Heather, what do you do?

Heather: I am the director of community at Flickr. That's my "Big Kahuna" name. Essentially, I'm a community manager at Flickr. "Community manager" is a very nascent role within a web team. If you poll a room of community managers, you'll come away with a number of very different job descriptions.

At Flickr, community managers perform a variety of tasks. As editors and curators, we bubble up the interesting things that are going on within the "Flickrverse." Toward that end, we host global online events to engage our members. The most recent example of this is "Your Best Shot 2009" (*http://flickr.com/groups/yourbestshot2009/*), where we created a group and asked our members to share a single photo that was their "it" photo.

So, that's one aspect of our job: engaging with our members and bubbling up the good. Another is that we're a conduit between our communities and the team. For example, we represent the team within our Help Forum when we launch new features, to review and share the feedback and comments that will make Flickr "more better." So, I guess we're the grout between tiles or the glue between things. Or, you know, sort of the thing that's stuck between a rock and a hard place, I guess.

John and Heather: [laughter]

Heather: Ahem, anyway, a good community manager will know the pulse of what's going on, and as such, we support Flickr's Abuse & Advocacy team in resolving issues that arise when you have many passionate people from many backgrounds bumping up against one another on a daily basis.

John: What's an Abuse & Advocacy team?

Heather: In Flickr's case, it's a subset of the customer care team who monitors our high-priority "Report Abuse" queues. In addition to the tools that our members have on hand to delete comments or "block" other members, our Report Abuse queue enables our members to let us know when they stumble across content and/ or behavior that they feel may violate the Yahoo! Terms of Service or the Community Guidelines.

John: What's the relationship between community management and technical support?

Heather: In my mind, the Internet is a giant ball of chaos. While we can build sites to do certain things and perform certain functions, and a lot of time and preparation are spent in making sure there are backups of backups and that everything will fail elegantly, you just don't know. There are going to be times when things go wrong—someone trips and pulls the plug out of the wall. Or, other times a network will fail.

With a community site, it's important to be as transparent as possible with your members when things go wrong. More importantly, the people who are best suited to fix things (developers, engineers, and operations) shouldn't be taken away from that and tasked with communicating the state of the nation.

John: So, while it may be the operations or development team that's fixing things when there's an incident or an outage or a degradation, there's also a form of asynchronous communication to you and the community management team about what's going on—answers to questions like "how are things progressing as far as fixing the issue" and "what are the ETAs," that sort of thing.

And then you, as community management, turn around and communicate that to the wider audience of members.

Heather: It isn't only your external community that's going to want to know what's going on. Depending on the severity, it could be the internal VP of "Nanny Foony" or whatever.

A community manager can also channel updates to the customer care team, so they can respond to members as quickly as possible. This can greatly reduce the possibility of a mushrooming customer care queue. If the issue is such that the site is still somewhat or mostly operational, we open a topic within our Help Forum and direct members there from our blog, customer care email response, and even Twitter, for updates.

Really, a lot of it is just being *present*.

Also, if members are experiencing different things, you can communicate that back to the operations team, so they don't need to be fixing things and paying attention, like in a Help Forum, to what's going on.

All of this is a feedback loop of various aspects—internal and external communication. I think a lot of it is just really ensuring that the right people are doing what they should be doing.

John: It almost sounds like in addition to all of the systems that operations and development have in place to alert on things that could possibly go wrong (like Nagios, Ganglia, Cacti, etc.), community management should be used as a similar resource to inform where troubleshooting should go. Is that fair to say?

Heather: Yes, absolutely.

John: Can you talk specifically about Flickr, about when the shit does hit the fan? There is one of two ways it can go: either absolute chaos, running around with your head cut off; or a better way, the more ideal way, which is a deliberate and directed response. I'm thinking of a particular example. At some point in 2006, we lost a huge part of our photo storage due to a problem with some maintenance that was going on that was supposed to be transparent. A person working with the storage accidentally took about 20 terabytes of photos offline. At the time, we didn't have the redundancy in order to serve from a cold or replicated backup. In fact, the maintenance that was being done was in preparation for getting this replicated backup in place.

This was a catastrophic issue, because the vast majority of photos that were stored on the site were on these relatively few, but very large, storage devices. Can you talk about what happened then?

Heather: At that point in time, Flickr functioned a little bit differently in that whenever we launched a new feature or were making changes to the system, we would need to take the site down. Anyone who's been a member for a while will remember this as "Flickr is having a massage." Typically, when we need to bring a site down, or a site is going to be unavailable to people for a period of time, the ideal solution is to let people know ahead of time.

You came up to me and said, "So, Heather, we've got to take the site down." I'm like, "That's great, John. So, when do you want to do that? Let's start working on the message, and we'll make sure we get it up at least nine hours ahead of time." And you responded, "Well, we need to take it down immediately. In fact, we're taking it down right now."

It felt very frustrating, because we had to completely circumvent our process for letting people know what was going to happen. So, the site would just suddenly not be there. That can be difficult for some users, because if they were planning to do certain things at certain times, and the site's not available, we've thrown a monkey wrench in their day. This was right after Senator Ted Stevens had gotten up in front of the Senate and defined the Internet as being a "series of tubes." See Figure 8-1.

We decided at that point to do something a little different. We replaced the standard downtime message with the "Flickr dots" drawn as empty circles and information about our impromptu coloring contest, encouraging people to print out the "page" and do something with it. Once the site was back up, we encouraged our members to share what they'd done and add a specific tag. We then awarded a year of Flickr Pro to a "winner." In the end, we had close to 3,000 entries. My favorite one was a picture of a storm trooper holding the page, and the dots were two Death Stars (see Figure 8-2). Multiple people had cut out a circle and stuck their kitten's head through it. Children had colored them in; people had all sorts of pink and blue dots. In the end, we couldn't pick just one. I think we gave 14 prizes, and three months of Pro to everyone who entered.

When the universe hands you lemons, you make lemonade.

John: When there's a performance issue or degradation, or an outage, how does communication generally happen? I remember that if there was a problem, normally the operations person on call—in most of the scenarios—would be aware of it, or an operations person manning the member forums, if it was a subtler issue, would be aware of it.

Regardless, during the issue, there was always a constant stream of communication between you and me while it was being worked on, and while information was being gathered around it.

Heather: Right. If it happened during normal business hours, essentially we'd acknowledge the bug and then I'd wander over and be, like, "John, when you have a moment, let's sit down and talk." So, I'm not going to get up in your junk immediately.

If it was a weekend, I'd join the operations/engineering chat and make my presence known, and say, "Hey, when you guys are ready, we're going to acknowledge that there's an issue. Let me know if there are any updates, so we can do that."

John: In the case where there was an issue, if you were not 100% clear on what it was, you would communicate that there was an issue even if you didn't know exactly what was going on?

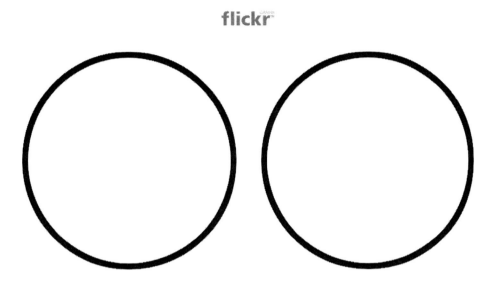

Figure 8-1. *Flickr's outage page , 2006: The Tubes Are Clogged*

Figure 8-2. *A Flickr member making the most of his time during an outage (photograph by Richard Clemens)*

Heather: Typically, I would just tell the community, "Hey, yes, there's an issue. The engineering team is looking into it. We'll get back to you." It's not the community manager's role—because typically we're not technical people—to define what is going on.

So, we acknowledge the problem so that people know that, yes, somebody is paying attention. And then it is our role—community management—to come to you—operations/engineering—and when it is appropriate, to know that you'll give us the lowdown on what we will share with the community in terms of what's gone wrong. I think it benefits everybody, internally and externally, to have that flow of communication, because if it's really big, it can start coming through PR, right? If the PR and marketing people get involved, everybody wants to know what's going on. It's really like air traffic control in terms of making sure the right people have the right amount of information.

But also, if you don't quickly acknowledge that there's an issue, things can blow out of proportion externally. The community really wants to have an idea, like, "Should I go have a cup of coffee, should I go take a walk, or should I come back tomorrow?"

If you are a part of a much larger corporation, depending on where you're situated in that company, a lot of people want to know what's going on. And if it starts coming through PR, you're going to get more and more pressure. So, really being ahead of that in terms of managing that flow of information is helpful for everybody. It just keeps people's blood pressure down.

If you've also established these channels, then if the VP of so-and-so calls you up and says, "Hey, John, what's going on?" it's not probably a really great time for you to get on the phone with your boss's boss's boss's boss and start talking about what's going on. You can tell them, "OK, here's the person you should talk to. Here's your incident manager."

Essentially, the community manager and engineering have an incident team going that's working on it, and they can manage that flow. So, you can have an update, like, "Here's the internal communication about what's going on and what we're doing to resolve it."

External communication usually is fairly close to internal communication. I don't think we've often had really different internal and external versions of what's going on. It's the Internet; everybody is doing the same kind of stuff. It's fairly obvious when pictures start disappearing; you know things are going wrong.

John: Would you say that it's advantageous to physically locate the community management and customer care teams in the same building, if not on the same floor, if not in the same office, as operations from a communications standpoint?

Heather: I would say it's very helpful, because you and I know one another really well. If something is really going wrong and you're going to bite my head off, and I've just come in at the wrong time, I know well enough that this is not the time. If those things are happening long distance with people who don't know one another, the community manager is just going to be making the situation harder.

John: How's community management involved with launching new features?

Heather: On launch day, the members of the team who will be shepherding the launch come together—for example, someone from the product team, engineers who've worked on the feature, the operations team, and community management; people who have a vested interest in a smooth launch. We'll sit together for a period up to and after the launch, ensuring that "everything is going according to plan."

As things are moved to the staging server for final testing, the community team will prepare the blog post, any new FAQs that will be published, and Help Forum topics for bugs and feedback.

That's just on launch day; a lot of prep work has gone into getting to that point. I think one of the most important things a team can do to prepare is work through and document what will happen if things go wrong—from the smallest thing to the worst thing you can think of, all itemized in a spreadsheet. The columns of the spreadsheet should identify things like what the community will experience and how the issue will be triaged: what the operations team will do, what the engineering team will do, what the community managers will communicate to the community, what the PR team will communicate to those who may contact them, and what will need to be communicated up the pipe. Not each type of issue will need all of those elements answered, but for a severe issue, it's incredibly handy to have this all sorted out beforehand, when calmer heads may not prevail during the issue.

If things go well, it will have been a colossal waste of time, but really, it's time well spent.

Otherwise, once a new feature launches, the team should be very present for the first 24 to 48 hours to make sure that what happens at launch is what's expected. I'm not talking about feedback on the feature, but ensuring that there aren't any unforeseen bugs, etc.

John: We haven't talked about the "go or no-go meeting."

Heather: So, those folks who are sitting around together on launch day will have met at some point previously for what we call the "go or no-go meeting." There's typically a hierarchy of who's got the final say, but everybody will have had an opportunity to give their feedback on whether or not that feature is ready to launch. This is the meeting where everyone steps up and signs off on moving toward an agreed-upon launch day. Typically, the operations team will have the final say, as launch has the biggest impact on that team. Essentially, at least at Flickr, the operations team always had the final say for the "go or no-go" before launch.

John: Yes, those meetings are really what gave everyone on the team confidence about the launch. If there was going to be a problem, it wasn't going to be for a lack of thinking hard on what the possible problems could be. Those meetings were actually pretty easy, because in most, if not all, cases, engineering and operations had been discussing things like worst-case scenarios and infrastructure needs throughout the development of the feature, not just on the day before launch. By the time this meeting happened, it didn't really come down to "go" or "no-go"; in most cases it was just really a decision of when to go.

Heather: Right. Yeah.

John: There was one particular launch that I remember, when operations (meaning, me) postponed a launch: Flickr Video.

Heather: Oh, yeah. We were supposed to go at 1:00 p.m., and I think we actually went at 6:30 p.m.

John: We wanted to make sure adequate switches and networking were put in place, when we realized a couple of places in the infrastructure weren't covered for the network jump we were expecting in a worst case. But the "press embargo" had come and passed, but we hadn't launched yet.

Heather: Yeah.

John: As nonideal as that was, was that OK?

Heather: It was OK.

John: What it came down to for me was the lesser of two evils. We could take the time to fix what was a potential networking bottleneck, and the press would publish stories about a feature that didn't exist yet. Or we could not fix what was a known potential network bottleneck, launch "on time" alongside the press releases, and risk the site coming down right after we launched the feature. Which is worse?

Heather: The site going down is worse. And while we were fixing the problem, the embargo ended.

TechCrunch posted "There's video on Flickr," but obviously there wasn't video on Flickr. So, we made up a finger puppet video that we posted. It said, "I hear there's video on Flickr," and we put it on Flickr Blog as a teaser, which said it was coming soon. I think the cat was out of the bag, so we played a little bit with that and sort of made the video of that. "So, I hear there's video on Flickr now, because I read about it on TechCrunch." The launch was pushed about five hours, and that was definitely tense, right?

John: Yeah, it was.

Heather: I saw a lot of people circling—that was a big launch for us. In the end it's a difficult call, but it has to be made. Because what you're looking for is the bigger picture: what will the impact be to the majority of people? You certainly don't want to launch something that's going to screw everything up. You have to stay the course and understand that people are making choices and decisions based on information, and that everybody appreciates and respects those choices.

That's part of it; that the stakeholder team understands that sometimes you're going to have to make difficult decisions. That might mean delaying a launch by some period of time. Or the word from various teams might be "no, this isn't ready and we're going to take another week"; not that that's ever happened with Flickr.

A lot of pressure can come into play, especially if you've got press embargoes lifting. That's going to make your PR people feel crappy, because they're certainly invested. These are their relationships with the press; they've stepped forward to work with these people; like, hey, this great thing is going to be happening. And when it doesn't happen, you've kind of left them a little bit high and dry.

Everybody has to understand what all of the stakes are. If you've done the "go or no-go" and you've done all your contingency planning, everybody should understand the choices that are being made, and why they're being made, and respect those and not try to arm-wrestle for different decisions.

John: At Flickr, what is the form of communication between community management and the rest of the internal groups? Is it mostly verbally in the office? Is it over IM? Or is it over the phone? Obviously, outside of office hours there's a lot over the phone.

Heather: All of the above. While it's easier when everyone's in the same room, there were Saturdays where everyone would dial in to the conference line and stay on the phone until the situation had been resolved.

When we're launching new features, I'll pick up my laptop and sit with the engineers and operations team, so I can keep my ear to the ground and also loop back to the team with the initial feedback coming from our members. For large, complicated launches, the various stakeholders in the launch will gather in our "war room" for the duration of the launch.

John: I think that getting together for launches is one of the most important things, culturally, at Flickr. When you're introducing change to the community, working together as a team raises confidence about any risks that come with that change.

I appreciate you taking the time to talk about this, Heather. I think it's extremely important for operations-minded folks to continually remind themselves that the technical work ultimately affects the people and the community their web application serves.

Heather: It was my pleasure.

## CHAPTER NINE

Dealing with Unexpected Traffic Spikes

Brian Moon

THE FOCUS OF DEALNEWS.COM, and its sister sites, is to find great deals on consumer products and let our visitors know where to find those deals. We handwrite every deal on the site, and many of our visitors visit the site multiple times per day. In addition, we have tens of thousands of people following RSS feeds and signed up for email alerts and newsletters, all so that they can get the best deals on the wide variety of products we cover. Because we are focused on consumer shopping, the holiday season from late November through the end of December is our busiest time of year.

How It All Started

In 2006, we hired a public relations firm to help us get the word out about the bargains people could find for their holiday gift buying. This had a noticeable impact on traffic the week of Thanksgiving (November 17–24): we hit all-time highs in every metric we tracked. We had added extra capacity in the summer, and everything went well. However, after sitting down and reviewing the statistics, we felt that our current infrastructure would not last another holiday season. Over the first few weeks of December, the web team talked about solutions. We had come up with a pretty solid plan to start implementing in preparation for the following year's big traffic rush. But that would be too late to handle traffic in the current holiday season.

Our content team had written a great article about when to buy HD TVs. The article proposed that the best time to buy would be after Christmas Day, not before. Unbeknownst to the web team, this article would be the one that the PR firm did the best job of promoting. They pointed it out to a blogger who wrote for the Tech blog at

Yahoo!, and he composed an entire article about the best time to buy an HD TV. On December 21 at 8:00 p.m. EST, that blog post was the featured article on the front page of Yahoo!. Now, we had been on the front pages of Digg and Slashdot at the same time already that season, and we handled that traffic with no problems. So, one would think that being directly linked on those sites would be similar to being linked on a page that is linked on the front page of Yahoo!. But I can assure you, Digg and Slashdot have nothing on Yahoo!.

Alarms Abound

I was just sitting down to eat dinner when my phone started to beep and vibrate. Nagios was reporting that our main database server was not responding. I simultaneously logged on to my laptop and dialed the phone to see if anyone else knew what was going on. At first, we were not sure what was happening. The database server was loaded with queries. But the queries were identical, and I recognized it: it was the query that was used to generate the cache for the front-page content. But why were so many running? We would soon hear about the Yahoo! blog post from our chief editor. It turned out that the PR firm had told us about the article, but as far as we knew it was going to be published after Christmas, not before. Figure 9-1 shows that at 8:00 p.m. EST, page views increased to a level that was abnormal for this time of day.

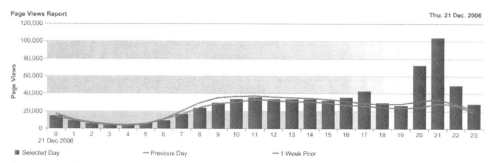

Figure 9-1. *Page views during Yahoo! front-page spike*

At that time, our infrastructure used a *reactive caching system*. This is a very traditional system and is usually the first example you'll find when learning about caching techniques for scaling websites. It works like this:

1. A request comes in for a page.

2. If the data needed is in the cache (a cache hit), the cache is used.

3. If the data is not found in the cache (a cache miss), code is run to generate the data needed.

4. The generated data is then placed into the cache for future requests.

That is a great starting point for caching. Unfortunately, it can lead to what is called a *cache stampede*. A cache stampede occurs when the code encounters a cache miss and a large number of requests are trying to access the same data at the same time. In our case, we were seeing thousands of requests per second for our front page. At the moment the cache for the front page expired, all of those requests ran the same query against our database server. The database server became overloaded and stopped answering new requests. And the requests it was trying to answer were being answered horribly slowly. This resulted in users either getting our maintenance page or simply watching the browser spin, waiting on an answer.

Putting Out the Fire

So, the cache stampede caused a rush on our database. Our first priority was to get the cache back in place. To do that, we had to start killing MySQL threads. A side effect of that, however, was that the requests waiting on the database server were now writing an empty cache entry to memcached. This made our front page blank. But, for the moment, that was fine. To get the cache filled again, we manually ran the function that created the cache for our front page. This refreshed the cache, and we had content again. Of course, we knew this was only a temporary solution—a five-minute solution, in fact. The cache would live for only five minutes before it expired.

Even with the cache in place, we started to see other problems. For one, the Apache servers had all reached their `MaxClients`. We had kept `MaxClients` set to a conservative number to avoid becoming CPU bound without knowing it. We had also never really been able to push these servers to their limits to know exactly what they could do. So, we increased `MaxClients` and restarted the servers.

Our success was short-lived, however: for each PHP request that came in and started an Apache client, a connection to our memcached pool was being created. This caused our memcached daemons to reach their connection limits quickly. So, we had to go through and update their configurations as well. We knew that memcached could handle lots of connections, so we proactively set its connection limits much higher than needed at the time in case we needed to make more adjustments to Apache.

At this point, we were doing OK. Requests were slow, but they were being answered. This gave us a moment to stop and talk about what we could do to return an expected level of service to our regular readers and also handle the flood of Yahoo! requests at the same time.

The first thing we did was to take a static snapshot of our front page. We placed this static file on just one web server, and then used our load balancers to direct any traffic that had "yahoo.com" in its HTTP referrer to the one server with the static page. This returned an acceptable level of service to our regular readers. However, it was less than optimal as Yahoo! visitors were getting an old version of our front page.

During the holiday season, we had already started on our new architecture. This is common for our team; we don't make changes to the live site during the busy season, which leaves time for us to start planning for the next year. In other words, we keep one eye on production and one eye on the next big thing. That year, the next big thing was our rearchitecture. The first piece of that architecture was a caching reverse proxy server. Squid was one caching reverse proxy server that was available at the time; however, Squid's main purpose is for use as a forward proxy, not a reverse proxy, and the documentation for using it as a reverse proxy was sparse at the time. The other feature missing in all the solutions we could find was the use of memcached to store the cache for the proxy server. Our front page changes every one to two minutes. Having a copy of our front page stored on each of our proxy servers was simply not acceptable for us. So, we wrote our own.

When writing the caching reverse proxy, we were open to whatever would be fastest. We tried Apache and lighttpd for the web serving, and wrote code in Perl, Python, and PHP for handling the proxy logic. After many, many tests, we found that the best solution was Apache with mod_php. We were a bit surprised; we did not expect this, despite the fact that we are predominantly a PHP shop. In the end, it was the PHP memcached extension that made the difference. PHP's memcached extension is written in C, whereas the memcached clients for Perl and Python are written in their native language. This means more overhead when compared to the PHP extension.

So, our idea was to stand up the caching proxy, with minimal testing at this point, to get us through the holiday weekend. It took a little while, but we got it up and running that same night. It performed very well.

Surviving the Weekend

We decided it was best to leave this in place through the Christmas weekend. Many people were on vacation, and we would not survive another hit like that without the caching proxy. It was a good thing we decided this, because on the 26th, the traffic came back from Yahoo!, this time even stronger (see Figure 9-2).

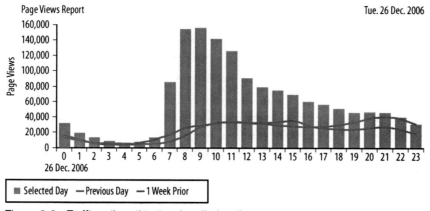

Figure 9-2. *Traffic spikes, this time handled well*

Not only did Yahoo! put the article back on its front page, but also our presence on Yahoo! made searches for the word *dealnews* break Yahoo!'s top 10 trending search terms. So, not only did we have traffic from the article, but also we now had traffic from people wondering what *dealnews* was and clicking on it from Yahoo!'s front page. All of this created a very long tail of traffic that day. Several members of the IT staff had taken that day as a vacation day, and although we knew about it, we did not have to do any work to keep the site up and running. I did not know about this spike until it had been happening for a couple of hours.

The only close call we had during this traffic rush concerned bandwidth. The connection we had from our datacenter was capable of bursting only up to 100 Mbit/s. During this event, we reached more than 80 Mbit/s. It was clear this was not going to be OK for another year.

Preparing for the Future

From the results of the second Yahoo! event, it was apparent that the caching proxy was a success. The next step would be to make our infrastructure stronger across the board. We now had nine months to prepare for the next holiday shopping season. We had already worked out an initial concept of our new architecture: it would be layered (the old way was very flat); requests would hit web servers, and they would use the cache or hit the single database server for data. The new system would be much more complex.

CDN to the Rescue

The solution to our bandwidth issues was to use a content delivery network or CDN. A CDN hosts files in multiple places on the Internet for quicker retrieval by client computers. The files are often loaded into a CDN's network on an on-demand basis. It works in some ways like a caching reverse proxy. For example, a request from a client comes in to the CDN for an image. If the object exists at the CDN, it is returned to the client. If not, the origin server (our servers) is asked for the data. The CDN then keeps a copy based on the caching headers our servers provide. The majority of the bandwidth being used during the Yahoo! events consisted of images, JavaScript, and CSS. These types of data are great for offloading to a CDN.

There are some negatives with a CDN. For instance, you lose a bit of control over your data. You can't simply change a file and upload it with the same name, as the CDN's servers have old copies and will not ask for a new copy of the object until it expires. Also, you have to change the way you think about your static content. CDNs don't work well with very short timeouts. Anything less than 30 minutes can lead to very erratic request patterns.

Proxy Servers

The proxy servers would be the front line of our system. Our goal was to serve as many requests from them as possible without having to use any other resources. These servers would do three jobs.

Their first and primary job was to serve cached requests directly from memcached. Memcached is a caching daemon that uses memory to store cache. It is designed to be a distributed system that lives on multiple host machines. One of the benefits is that the cache is shared. This means only one copy of an item is in the cache at a time. This was very desirable to us. The proxy servers would first check the memcached cluster for the given request URI. If it was found, the data would be returned immediately to the client, and the connection would be closed (this makes for incredibly fast requests). If the cache was empty, the proxy server would contact an application server. The data the application server returned would then be stored in memcached for later use. The application servers use standard HTTP headers to tell the proxy servers how to cache the content. Using standard HTTP headers means that even applications that we did not handwrite could be cached with little work.

The servers' second job was to serve what we came to call our *lightweight scripts*. These are scripts that require little to no overhead from our custom framework and are often logging, tracking, or redirection scripts that have fewer than 100 lines of PHP code and don't do any intensive database work or serve content. However, these scripts make up a large portion of our requests, so putting them outside our normal application framework forced us to ensure that they were lean and mean.

The last job these servers would perform would be to function as the origin servers for our CDN. If the CDN did not have a copy of an object, the servers would contact our proxy servers to get a copy. All of this data comprised static files on disk; we could have put it anywhere, but we decided we liked the idea of these servers being the first line of contact for all of our data.

Corralling the Stampede

The next step was to figure out how to avoid the cache stampede. There were two problems with how we accessed our data. The first problem was that the queries we were running were very complex. Our database is highly relational and normalized; we try to never duplicate data and always create good relationships between tables, resulting in a system that is very flexible and can gather data in any way we need. However, this is not good for performance.

The decision was made to denormalize (some prefer the word *optimize*) our data for use by our public facing application servers. In all, some 100+ tables were reduced to about 30 in this scheme. We did not lose our highly relational data. This would be a full duplicate of the relational data in a format that was easier to digest by our application servers. In cases where we had one-to-many relationships, we would gather the data from the many side of the relationship and shove the data into a TEXT field in a serialized format. This was one less join we had to use in our query. In cases where it made sense to keep some data in a relational format we would do so.

But simply having faster queries would not solve all of our data problems. The second problem was that we were relying on one database server (with a hot spare) for all of our data. The stampede therefore created a bottleneck of connections on the single server. To remedy this, we thought of a couple of possible solutions.

The first thing we tried was MySQL Cluster, which at the time was a new and promising MySQL solution that involved spreading data around to multiple servers along with multiple servers having the same data. MySQL Cluster is similar to RAID, but in a database and across multiple servers; everything is handled by the storage engine layer of MySQL, and therefore is transparent to the code that is making queries. In the end, we were too unfamiliar with the technology and did not feel we could get comfortable with it in the few months we had to prepare for the next year.

MySQL replication had been around for a long time. We had used it in the past with mixed success, but our problems with it were primarily on high-volume write tables that used the MyISAM storage engine. So, we decided to use all transactional InnoDB tables instead. We had hardly (if ever) seen a replication error on an InnoDB table, so we bought some servers and deployed them in a replication setup. The application servers now had four very fast MySQL servers to serve the data. We refer to this set of servers as our read-only database because the public facing application code would only ever read from it.

Streamlining the Codebase

We predominantly use PHP for our work; it is the language used in 99% of all of our web-based requests. PHP is, at its core, a templating language that is really good at getting data from a data source and then formatting that data for use by a client machine. Our codebase had drifted away from that core philosophy. However, it was doing a lot of data manipulation, a lot of business logic was happening during a user's request for a page on our site, and we were repeating data transformations on every request over and over.

Instead of doing this data transformation on every request, we thought, why not do it once? Now that we were keeping a second copy of the data in our read-only database, it was easy to tailor the data however we needed it. In addition to doing generic data manipulation, we could make changes to content for each publication on which the content appeared. Now there would be one copy in the read-only database for each publication on which a piece of content would appear. That copy of the content would be fully prepared for display on the publication, including URLs, images, and so on, all having the characteristics of the publication. This would make our codebase on the application servers much, much simpler. In essence, we wanted to be able to select all the rows from a single table based on a key with a small number of matching rows and display that data as it was coming in from the database. We nearly achieved just that. Some data manipulation still occurs, depending on which page on the site a piece of content appears, and we still do some changes on the fly to avoid having to recopy the entire database if factors change in how we display content, as a full recopy can take hours and is a drain on the systems.

Another way we changed our codebase was to control how developers accessed our data. In the past, we had adopted the policy of having data access be as direct as possible. We had tried using Object Relational Mapping (ORM) in the past and found it cumbersome and generally slow. However, the ad hoc queries spread throughout our code were causing more problems than they solved at that point. The solution was to create only a few ways to get to the data: limit sort options and limit filter options. If a new sort or filter was needed, the resultant queries would have to be tested and benchmarked, and the pages tested and benchmarked. And instead of working with objects as in ORM, we worked with set-based results. These are ready-to-use, simple arrays instead of complex objects with lots of overhead.

We had another tough decision to make. Do we add another layer of caching at the application server? It would essentially be the same old reactive cache that we had before. We didn't like this idea and really felt that a reactive cache was a bad solution as it leads to dependency that could fail us. You see, unlike on a social networking site, our traffic is concentrated: 40% of all requests are for our front page. If the reactive cache for this page fails, lots of requests will be extremely slow and this can cause problems. We decided that the read-only databases and code that queried them had to be ready to go without a cache at the application layer. We simply made that a requirement of our architecture and took the steps needed to meet that requirement.

How Do We Know It Works?

We did all this work over the course of several months. But how did we know we made any improvements? Although we ran simple benchmarks along the way to see how things were working, that is no substitute for a real test.

Luckily for us, our COO was previously with Keynote Systems. Keynote is a company that (among other things) can perform load tests on websites. In our opinion, the only way to make sure our production systems could handle the load was to test them, live, during the day when traffic was flowing. When I tell people this, they look shocked. But how would we know if it worked otherwise?

We scheduled a test. We notified our content team when the test was going to occur, and we provided test scenarios to Keynote that would accurately simulate the distribution of different types of requests. Keynote's systems could hit our website from several different datacenters with multiple clients per datacenter. The test scenario could also slowly ramp up the number of requests over time. This way, if things started to go bad, we could cancel the test with the push of a button.

The first test we ran did not tell us much. We had it configured to test the pages and all objects on them. The problem was that all it did was load-test our CDN provider. Because one page request to us would then generate 10–200 requests to our CDN, our servers never felt any load.

Next, we had the test ignore any objects that were on our CDN. This would focus the testing nodes on our servers and our servers only. We set the test to slowly ramp up to 600 concurrent connections over 30 minutes, which was the peak we saw during the Yahoo! event. The good and bad news was that nothing happened. The servers did not seem to even notice. Only the connections graph really moved in Cacti. So, we had to conduct another test.

This test ramped to 3,000 concurrent connections, and this time we saw something. Our application servers got a little busy—pretty busy, actually. From looking at our logs, we were able to determine that the problem concerned our proprietary ad server software. This was a bit of a surprise; this software had been our most solid for years. But we soon realized that our ad server software was now slower than the new systems we had put in place. After some investigation, we discovered some file I/O bottlenecks causing the poor performance. We moved those bottlenecks into memcached and tried our tests again.

This time, we decided that if all looked well at the midway point, we would turn off memcached to see how well the application servers and read-only database cluster could handle the load directly. The test completed without any cache. We stayed up the entire time. Load average, of course, jumped on the application and database servers, and response time doubled to about 1.2 seconds for the initial HTML to be returned. But all in all, it handled 3,000 concurrent connections with all requests coming from the database.

The Real Test

Of course, even this highly complex simulated test was not the real test. All of our previous tests were requesting pages from our servers from six datacenters. That is nothing like 50,000 unique clients out in the wild, all wanting your page at the same time. That test would come in November.

We all waited with anticipation for traffic to start ramping up. On the evening of Thanksgiving, the traffic started coming. It grew and grew and the servers never had issues. Our traffic that weekend reached peaks similar to those of the first Yahoo! event. And whereas before, the servers were overloaded and the site was not returning requests, this time, all was fine.

Compared to today's traffic, the Yahoo! event is an average day during our busiest time of year. I find myself almost wanting another big event like that to occur but bigger this time. I have still not seen the breaking point of this infrastructure. I know it has one, but we have never had the means to test it until it reached that point.

Lessons Learned

We learned a lot of lessons going through this experience. We have tried to apply these lessons to everything we have done since then.

The first lesson we learned is to always plan for five years away. Ask yourself: "Can my current solution make it five years from now?" Jared Spool, a user interface expert who talks about mapping your user's experience into the future, says that five years gets you beyond the current reality but does not get you into the realm of science fiction. That is to say, you can't know what technology will exist in five years that makes your decisions different. So, plan for five years, and tomorrow will probably take care of itself.

Another lesson we learned is to test the production systems. If we had not tested our production systems, we may not have found the old ad server code that was lagging behind. This could have caused problems during our next rush, whether it was expected or unexpected. It is a scary idea, but with proper planning, it can be done.

You may notice that in our solution we did not focus on just hardware, or just database schema, or just the software. We had to rethink the whole stack. I have heard some people say that a good system will never have to be refactored. I dispute that. I think you should strive to not refactor every three years, but when it is clear that your current solution is not going to work, you have to have the courage to rethink the whole solution. We rethought our code, our hardware, our network, and our database schemas. This created a much more scalable solution for the foreseeable future.

Improvements Since Then

We still have the same basic system in place today. However, we have made a few enhancements.

One of the key enhancements we made is that the population of the read-only database is now managed by an event-driven system which uses Gearman, a distributed job queue system, instead of on a schedule using scripts that were run via cron. This allows content to be pushed to the frontend as soon as it is ready. At first, we feared this would create an unpredictable load on our primary database. But it turned out that the opposite was true. The scheduled data migration was causing surges in database work. The server would be idle for minutes and then flooded with work to perform all at once. Likewise, the servers that moved the data would see similar peaks and valleys in their usage. If we experienced any unexpected event during these peaks, the database server would become unresponsive. Now the load is spread out based on the speed at which our content team creates new content.

Another enhancement we made is that now we operate two datacenters. The second datacenter has a full set of frontend proxy, application, and read-only database servers. In addition, the database is replicated over VPN from our primary datacenter. We use geo-IP-based DNS to send users to their closest datacenter. Plus, we have the ability to shift all requests to one datacenter after a short DNS timeout, allowing us to conduct major maintenance on a location and still serve content to our readers.

## CHAPTER TEN

Dev and Ops Collaboration and Cooperation

Paul Hammond

MOST ORGANIZATIONS SPLIT THEIR WEBSITE DEVELOPMENT AND SUPPORT into two separate teams. One team is responsible for creating new features and improving existing functionality. The other team is responsible for keeping the site up and running. These teams usually report to different managers and in some cases are in different business units or even different companies.

Splitting responsibilities in this way is common because superficially it makes a lot of sense. The two teams have different goals, and those goals require very different working styles. Software development is best done in long stretches of uninterrupted coding time in a quiet room. In contrast, an operations team needs to respond instantly when something breaks. It can be difficult to find people interested in working in both worlds, let alone people who are capable of doing both in the same day.

In this context, it's hard to argue against forming two distinct teams. Once that happens, the most obvious way to manage the relationship between these teams is through service-level agreements (SLAs) and a managed handoff of code. At regular intervals, the development team packages its work and hands it off to the operations team to deploy to production. This allows the developers to focus entirely on the most efficient way to add new features and allows operations to maintain control over the production environment. It allows management to clearly assign blame when things go wrong—if the site goes down, the ops team obviously dropped the ball; if the latest feature is late, the dev team has some explaining to do.

This setup is very common and is probably the worst possible way to ensure site stability or deliver new features.

In this scenario, developers have no incentive to make the site easier to support operationally. Code delivered by the development team is usually a black box; if anything unexpected happens the operations team has no way to fix the problem. Release documentation is patchy and is unlikely to include the scenario that caused a critical alert in the middle of the night. This structure also inhibits the development of new functionality. Building and deploying a new version of the site is time-consuming and expensive, and involves collaboration among many different teams. Deployments are risky for operations and the cause of many outages.

The traditional ops–developer divide also misses the point that both groups have a lot of useful information for each other. The performance bottleneck for most sites is in the application code: the development team is best placed to actually fix these issues, but the operations team has the metrics that are required to know what needs to be focused on. The development team has a much better idea about what might break, and how to fix it, but this is rarely documented.

Many successful Internet companies—including Amazon, Facebook, Google, and Flickr—are experimenting with alternative ways to organize these teams. A few companies have gone as far as removing the distinction between ops and development entirely; many more are finding the benefits of revisiting the relationship between ops and dev. This chapter explores some of these ideas, starting with deployment.

Deployment

In every team there is a point somewhere in the release process where a piece of code stops being owned by the developer(s) who wrote it, and starts being supported by a wider group of people. This handoff is the single most important interaction between your operational and development teams, but most groups pay no attention to it. Getting the handoff right can make a huge difference in how well different teams work together, but making changes to the process is hard as it requires cooperation and buy-in from everyone.

In many groups, code goes through multiple handoffs (code review, testing, QA, release management) before being put into production. As a codebase grows more complex and as the development team grows, deployment-related outages and integration bugs become more frequent until some kind of structure is put in place. As the process becomes more comprehensive, the amount of time it takes to prepare a release usually grows. Some teams experiment with weekly deploys, but they find that integration-related tasks can easily take two days or more. As a result, monthly release cycles are common; in the worst cases it can take over a year for code to be deployed to the site.

These infrequent releases make sense in the world of installed desktop software. Releasing too often causes real problems for your users. But if you're releasing a new version of your website only once a month, you're moving too slowly. The small start-ups nipping at your heels are releasing code multiple times every single day. They have much smaller codebases and less process, and the cost of a bad deploy is much lower for them. At the same time, huge companies such as Facebook and Amazon are also making production code changes multiple times a day and have built up the processes to ensure that they can do this without causing outages. Flickr deploys new code more than 10 times a day and has a great uptime record.

These companies have all found that frequent deploys are an essential part of making a service that people love.

Users are blown away when a bug they report is fixed in production 15 minutes after they report it. By responding in this way, you make it more likely that people will let you know about issues in the future, which makes your product better—especially if you can repeatedly iterate on the feedback rapidly. Being able to respond to critical data loss or security bugs in hours rather than weeks helps you keep your users' data safe.

But most importantly, frequent deploys aren't any riskier than weekly or monthly deploys. Many small changes, each independently tested and checked, are less likely to cause a significant outage than one big change.

The benefits of small changes are something we all understand instinctively: hanging a picture on a wall requires less preparation than renovating a kitchen. In the same way, correcting a single character typo in a configuration file or template is a lot less stress-ful than upgrading between major versions of your operating system (see Figures 10-1 and 10-2).

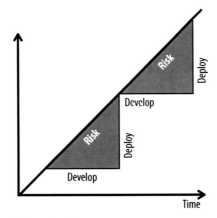

Figure 10-1. *Code change in large batches*

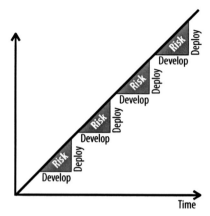

Figure 10-2. *Code change in small batches*

This is because the impact of a small change can be reviewed and tested ahead of time in isolation, and the impact of a mistake is easier to quantify and prepare for. It's significantly easier to spot a bug by reviewing a 10-line changeset than a 10,000-line one, and it's quicker to test just the functionality affected by a change than to retest the entire system. You can also ensure that every deploy changes only one area at a time, avoiding unexpected interactions between two components that both changed at once. Small deployments mean it's much easier to predict the impact of the change on your infrastructure before it happens, which in turn means preparing contingencies is much easier.

The real benefits of smaller changes become apparent once code is deployed. No QA or code review process is perfect, and sooner or later something unexpected will happen after a deployment. With a large deploy affecting multiple components, you may not even notice a problem—so many of your metrics will change at once that a significant improvement in one area may mask a serious degradation in service elsewhere. If you do notice something, it's impossible to know where to start looking for the root cause. At this point, a full rollback of all changes is usually the only option (unless your PR department has made sure that even that isn't a possibility). To reduce the impact of a bad deploy, one is usually run after hours, which means fewer people are around to help when things go wrong.

In contrast, if you've just deployed 30 lines of code, the bug is usually self-evident, especially if you can ask the engineer who made the changes earlier that day. If the bug isn't self-evident, its impact is usually minimized to one piece of functionality, and a rollback will be easier.

Frequent small changes work only if you follow these three rules:

- The build and deploy system has to be completely repeatable and automated.

- You have a close-to-perfect staging environment.

- Deployments have to be as fast as you can possibly make them, ideally less than five minutes.

Combined, these enable you to change one thing, run accurate regression tests, and roll out just that one thing without having to do lengthy QA cycles on the entire system. It means the developer who made the changes can track her changes as they're pushed out into production and quickly react to any problems that arise.

Most build and deployment systems are automated to some level, but few teams go as far as making it a "one-click" process. You need to know that if only one line changed in the source code, only one thing will change in your production environment. To do this you need to construct your build and deployment systems to be a single step, with no options and no chance of changes caused by differences in the environment in which it's run. Every additional step or option is a mistake waiting to happen; eventually someone will miss something and cause unexpected side effects when the code reaches production.

Flickr's main deployment system is web based and consists of two buttons: "stage" and "deploy." "Stage" checks out a fresh version of the code from source control, builds it, and pushes the resultant code to the staging server. "Deploy" pushes the code currently on staging into production and performs a number of post-deployment cleanup tasks.

Making the system web based means all builds are done on the same server with exactly the same environment. No errors are introduced by subtle differences in the configuration between different engineers' working environments—in particular, changes in library paths and versions of build tools can mean the same source code produces different results when compiled by different people. Being web based also provides a powerful incentive to avoid adding extra options because nobody wants to build a user interface for them.

Because the system is completely automated, we've found there's no benefit to having operations perform the code push. Developers who are allowed to push their own code take more responsibility for the changes they introduce; they're more likely to double-check a functional change before committing it, and they catch more bugs in prelaunch testing. It's more likely the original author of some code will be watching the state of the system as the deploy is happening, which means he's able to respond more quickly to bugs that show up postlaunch. By avoiding the need to schedule a deployment with another team, we avoid giving people an incentive to batch changes up into a larger push, which creates smaller, less risky changes.

Frequent deploys are hard to do properly. They work only if everyone involved takes the responsibility of a production code push seriously; people can do that only if they are given the tools they need to do their job. In most cases, automating the build and deployment process is a huge task, especially if it has been neglected.

Even if you don't go as far as letting everyone on the team deploy, you'll find that the benefits of an automated deployment infrastructure quickly pay off in less stressful code pushes.

Shared, Open Infrastructure

In most situations where operations and engineering have been split into different groups, you'll find that the support infrastructure has also been divided in two. Common examples include:

- Developers running their own dev servers and having no access at all to production hardware

- Engineering using a bug tracker and operations running a separate ticket tracker, with no links between the two

- Engineering and operations running independent metrics gathering and dashboards

- Engineering not being invited to the IRC channel used by ops

- Ops having no access or insight into the source code repository used by engineering

- Engineering having no access to the configuration management systems used by ops

In most cases, this happens for pragmatic reasons: members of one team try out a new system, find it makes their life easier, and never get around to telling the other groups about it. But sometimes the situation arises because one group doesn't trust the other group to not get in the way. Either way, it's a mistake. Having a shared infrastructure is one of the easiest ways to help your teams cooperate with each other. That doesn't mean all teams need to use the same tools all the time; you might find that engineering prefers IM-based chat while ops prefers to use IRC. It also doesn't mean you can't have different levels of access to tools where needed. But you should make sure everyone knows where the other team's tools are and that they have at least a read-only view of everything.

This approach is partially philosophical: it's important to understand that however you organize the teams, a large website is a complex, finely balanced, single system that you're all working on together. To do your job effectively you need insights into how other aspects of the system are functioning right now. To build trust you need to be transparent about what you're working on.

It's also a pragmatic approach: when debugging code or tracing a performance issue you sometimes need access to data in the other team's systems. If you don't know that data is there, you can waste weeks trying to collect it. If you don't have access, you can waste weeks trying to obtain it.

There are three small steps you can follow to improve this situation:

First, make a single web page somewhere that links to all your tools. Make it editable by anyone on the team. Encourage everyone to add new tools as they're developed or discovered. Whenever a team member asks where a particular tool is, tell her it's linked from the tools page. This means your team will find out about new tools and be able to find them again later.

Second, make sure your teams talk about the tools they use, especially when they use them to help solve an interesting problem. Flickr's engineering teams are always sending each other links to server metrics, code diffs, and our bug tracker as they collaborate on problems; over time this is an incredibly effective way to share knowledge about what tools are most useful for debugging a class of problem.

Finally, and perhaps most controversially, introduce a policy of giving everyone at least read-only access to all the systems you use. Remember, your ops team has root on every box in your datacenter; the ops team members should be trusted to look at your metrics and task tracker. Similarly, your development team is writing the code that runs your system; sometimes those team members need to inspect the state of a running system to isolate a bug that can't be reproduced on a development system. There's no risk in giving people read-only access to production systems unless you're handling personal user data or financial transactions, and even then there are ways to give limited access.

It's worth taking the time to periodically examine whether different teams are using overlapping systems and to see whether they should be merged. For example, Flickr's server configuration used to be stored in a Perforce repository, the application code in CVS. On a day-to-day basis, neither of the teams needed to interact with the other team's repository and very few people had ensured they had access. This became a problem only when someone needed access during an outage but didn't have the right permissions. These days, both teams store their work in a single SVN repository, which has made collaborating on common pieces of code much easier.

Once you start sharing systems, you'll probably find that there are ways you can join your systems. For example, Flickr's deployment system sends notifications to our IRC channel, and our installation of Ganglia tracks metrics fed from application code as well as system-level metrics. For example, Figure 10-3 depicts a Ganglia report from Flickr's background task processing cluster, showing the number of tasks in the job queue. This extra information is hugely helpful when managing an incident or planning for infrastructure growth, and it wouldn't be surfaced if our teams weren't cooperating on common infrastructure.

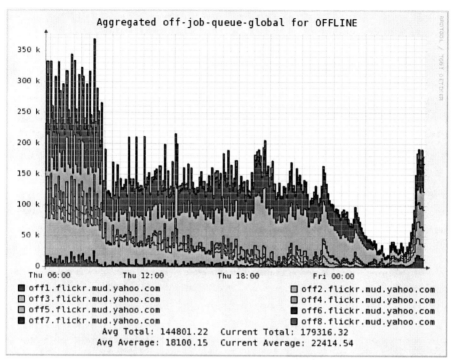

Figure 10-3. *Application-level metrics in system monitoring tools*

Opening up access as much as possible helps give all team members the information they need to do their job.

Trust

A common theme linking the areas of shared infrastructure and deployment processes is the idea of trust. You need to trust someone before giving that person access to the tools you rely on to do your job. If you're deploying multiple times a day, you need to trust that all the other team members have done their job—you don't have time to triple-check everything for everyone.

Trust is one of the most common areas of tension between development and operations. Most operations teams are slightly suspicious of their development teams, usually because they have been awakened by a pager too many times. Developers usually aren't any better, with deep misgivings about whether the operations team cares about the development team's deadlines. This mistrust between the teams is unhealthy and misplaced.

Trust is ultimately built on a sense of respect. If you respect someone's role, abilities, and judgment, it's easy to trust that this person will do the right thing. If you don't respect someone, every interaction with that person will be filled with second guesses, bad feelings, and frustration.

Most of the problems between operations and developers are caused by differences in opinion regarding the importance of the different roles of the two teams. We've already discussed why most companies have created two separate teams; an unfortunate side effect is that the stated goals of the teams are contradictory, especially when taken to extremes. For example, as an operations engineer, you're expected to minimize downtime and improve performance. One way to achieve this goal is to serve a completely static site with no JavaScript, CSS, or even images. If you insist on a simple architecture like this you'll easily hit your SLAs, but it's likely that your colleagues in development, design, product, marketing, and sales will miss theirs, and they'll be justifiably upset with you.

Members of the operations team have an unusual position of authority in most companies—they have root on their systems, and with it, absolute control over what gets installed. It's easy to abuse this power to achieve your aims at the expense of everyone else; this is a shortsighted move. Remember that despite the different goals, both teams are working to improve the business—and neither team can do it alone.

As an operations engineer, you should be able to trust that the development team isn't working against you. It's not. If development engineers care even slightly about the service they're working on, they won't want to deliberately make it less stable or slower (and if they don't care about the service, you're reading the wrong book). Of course, developers aren't perfect. It's likely they'll have different opinions on exactly where to draw the line when it comes to site stability and less experience with things going wrong. Most developers haven't developed a useful skepticism of shiny new things or a healthy paranoia about breaking things. Many operations teams respond to this by inserting themselves into the process as a gatekeeper of site stability. They argue that because the development team doesn't have a track record of getting things right, everything needs to be vetted before launch.

Doing this makes things worse, not better. It sends a clear message to the development team that you don't think they're responsible enough, which almost always leads to a self-fulfilling prophecy. It creates resentment and gives them no incentive to help you out. Developers will stop thinking things over too much before sending them to you because they know you'll be double-checking things before launch. But unlike a developer, an operations engineer isn't going to be able to read every line of code. He doesn't have quiet time to think through every eventuality, and he's not going to spot every problem. An extra layer of approval is supposed to increase the likelihood of catching bugs. In most cases, it has the opposite effect, as everyone assumes someone else is doing the hard work of actually checking things.

In any case, people will find a way around any approval process, intentionally or not. If it's too hard to do the right thing, people won't bother. At some point, someone on a deadline will decide to use her desktop machine to send the emails or run the cronjob on her account on a dev server. Suddenly you have an unmonitored, undocumented single point of failure, and nobody told you about it.

This leads to a negative feedback cycle. Ops says "no" because things break. Things break because nobody told ops about them. Nobody tells ops anything because ops always says "no" (see Figure 10-4).

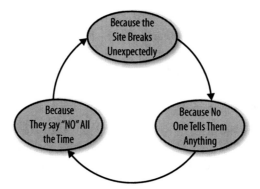

Figure 10-4. *The negative feedback cycle of saying "no"*

In contrast, many groups have found that sharing the responsibility for site stability and performance with the development team produces better results. If you trust the developers to write fast code that handles edge cases without taking down the servers, and if they know nobody will be double-checking their work, they'll respond by taking it seriously. They'll make mistakes, but no more than a typical operations engineer working in a new environment. They'll quickly learn when they need to seek a second opinion, and you'll have the time to concentrate on the interesting questions they raise because you're not doing checks on routine changes.

Of course, some large, complex projects will still need some level of review to ensure that there are no architectural problems. The earlier you can be involved, the better; it's easier to correct a mistake on a whiteboard than a mistake in written code. The only way operations will get invited to these meetings is if you're trusted to be constructive and not a roadblock. The easiest way to make that happen is to respect your colleagues enough to not second-guess them.

It'll take some time for a developer to adapt to the responsibility, especially on a large site, but our experience at Flickr is that it takes only a few weeks for a new developer to get used to being trusted and to start to take responsibility for his code. The benefits in productivity for both teams are well worth it.

On-Call Developers

One of the most common misconceptions about separating operations from development is that it requires members of the operations team to be the only ones who work on fixing production issues. This setup avoids the development interruptions that cause delays to new features but insulates developers from the realities of code running in a 24/7 production environment.

So far in this chapter we've discussed the need for operations to trust that developers have their best interests in mind, that developers should be allowed to deploy code without formal approval processes, and that developers should have access to production systems. This works only if developers take on responsibility for fixing problems with their code in production, which means they need to be on call.

At Flickr, the operations team operates a standard primary/backup pager rotation. In almost all cases, it's a known failure scenario and the on-call engineer can resolve the issue with a well-understood playbook. But every so often there's an issue the on-call engineer can't debug or fix by himself. In these cases, he'll call one of the developers for help.

This environment creates some useful social dynamics. As anyone who has carried a pager knows, avoiding being paged at 3:00 a.m. on a Sunday is a powerful incentive to keep things from breaking and to make sure ops has all the tools it needs to fix a problem without you. As an example, Flickr has a shared IRC channel; it's very common to see something such as the following from one of our developers:

```
[11:48:55] <myles> Sending 1% of video upload traffic to ATLAS. You can turn it off
by setting $cfg['video_upload_use_atlas'] = 0;
```

Over the years, the development team has learned that the easiest way to ensure that operations can fix as many problems as possible is to give them access to all of the development tools, and teach them how to use them. New functionality is usually built to be supported by others, with switches and documentation as needed. Two particularly interesting tools the development team has built to use during outages are live debugging and feature flags.

Live Debugging Tools

Most codebases are a black box to the operations team that supports them. They have no idea what the system is doing and no tools to inspect the state or trace the code. This leads to many operations teams resorting to tried-and-trusted low-level tools such as tcpdump, strace, and gdb when things go wrong. These produce large amounts of output and are difficult to parse, especially when under pressure to fix a live issue.

It's much easier to read:

```
[db] [shard1] SELECT * FROM Users WHERE id = 5806;
```

than pages of tcpdump data, especially when that data includes other requests that happened to be going to the same server at the same time. Binary wire formats and encrypted connections make examining low-level data dumps even harder.

At the same time, most developers sprinkle extra debugging code throughout their codebases to help them when they're building new systems. In most systems, these are stripped as part of the build process because they're considered unnecessary in a production environment. That's a mistake: the extra information a developer needs when building a system is generally the same information you need when debugging a live system.

Find a way to enable this debugging at runtime. At Flickr, any member of the technical team who is logged into his admin account can turn on extra debugging information by adding a parameter to the query string, or by setting a cookie. The idea behind the code is very simple:

```
if (is_admin()) {
  if ($_COOKIE['debugout'] || $_GET['debugout'] ){
    $GLOBALS['debugout'] = 1;
  }
}


function debug_out($message) {
  if ($GLOBALS['debugout']) {
    echo("<div class="debugout">");
    echo(HTMLSpecialChars($message));
    echo("</div>");
  }
}
```

Then, throughout our code, we include debug_out() statements. In most cases these calls are a null-op, but when needed they provide lots of useful extra information.

The most useful debugging data concerns what messages are sent between systems. You'll want to make sure you include the following:

Information about the request sent from the client
What is its IP, and what parameters were sent? This is incredibly useful to spot where an upstream system is sending the wrong data.

Information about how the request was routed internally
What class is responsible for running this request? Where is the code for that class?

Information about what requests are sent to backend systems
What SQL queries does the code run? What XML is being sent over the wire? What backend server is the application connecting to?

Information about data received from backend systems
What was the status code? What was the data?

Timing information
    How long did the request take to process? How much time was spent in parsing, waiting for backend systems, or generating a response?

Information about any errors or unexpected conditions
    What errors were seen? Were they handled by the code?

This might seem like a long list, but most codebases route all database queries or web service calls through a single code path. Adding some debugging information there should be enough to get you started.

The data exposed by this system might not give someone all the information needed to debug a problem, but it'll be a good start in almost all cases. This one piece of functionality probably contributes more than anything else to the sense of transparency between operations and engineering at Flickr, and all it takes is a slight change to the URL.

Feature Flags

As your site grows in scale and complexity the number of subsystems grows. It's likely you'll move toward an architecture where different pieces of functionality will be handled by different bits of infrastructure. Some of these clusters, particularly the database and web servers, are likely to be critical to your site. Other pieces of infrastructure will handle peripheral functionality. Eventually some of your infrastructure will fail in an unexpected way. When that happens, you'll want the ability to disable just the features that rely on it, and keep the rest of the site running. Feature flags make this possible.

Most applications have an internal configuration system, which is generally used to define things such as what database server the code should connect to. A great example of this is the WordPress *wp-config.php*. In Ruby on Rails applications the config is stored in the *RAILS_ROOT/config* folder; in a Django app it is stored in the settings file referenced by DJANGO_SETTINGS_MODULE. Flickr, like most PHP apps, has several includes that are referenced from all pages; the global config file is one of them.

If you have a config system such as this, extending it to add feature flags is easy. The most basic feature flag is a Boolean:

```
$cfg['enable_comments'] = true;
```

Once this is defined, you can liberally sprinkle conditionals based on this variable throughout your code:

```
if ($cfg['enable_comments']) {
    $comments = fetch_comments();
    // ...
}
```

The Flickr codebase exposes these config flags as a variable in Smarty, our chosen templating language, so that we can easily show the right thing to users:

```
{if $cfg.enable_comments}
 <form>
   <textarea name="comment"></textarea>
   <input type="submit" value="Post Comment">
 </form>
{else}
 <p>Oops! Commenting is temporarily disabled!</p>
{/if}
```

With this setup, recovering from the failure of a piece of infrastructure is, in most cases, a quick edit to a single file before pushing the update to all production hosts. This is easy to script, especially if you've already automated your deployment system.

As we develop new features, we consider how we'd handle partial failures, and include multiple feature flags for each piece of code. In particular, we have:

A single flag to disable each piece of noncore infrastructure
For example, Flickr has flags we can flip to disable all reads and writes to individual database clusters and flags to stop processing background tasks temporarily.

Flags for every external service you rely on
Flickr relies on many web services—both internal, such as Yahoo! Address Book and Delicious.com, and external, such as the Gmail address book, Snapfish, and Last.fm. In all cases, we can temporarily and gracefully disable the functionality that relies on these services in case they have an outage.

Flags to temporarily shed load if needed, a technique pioneered by news websites
They have learned to cope with the huge traffic spikes associated with a breaking story by serving a lite version of their site that requires fewer resources to serve. Many pages have computationally expensive elements that aren't absolutely critical; make sure these can be disabled if needed.

We also add new flags as new failure scenarios appear in production.

It's worth thinking very hard about what features are absolutely core to serving your site. You should be realistic about what features you can actually cope without. For example, it's possible for the Flickr operations team to disable photo uploads if needed—we don't need to stop people from viewing the billions of photos that are already uploaded just because our image processing servers are having problems.

You may want to consider introducing feature flags that selectively disable functionality for some users. If you have tiered account levels, or users with more aggressive SLAs than others, you may want to be able to disable functionality for some users to free up capacity for higher-value customers. This isn't appropriate for consumer-facing sites such as Flickr, but it may work in a business-facing context.

In systems that process incoming data, such as analytics products, it's worth ensuring that you can continue to collect data even if everything else is disabled. Your customers will feel much better about being told that they're not losing data, even if they can't see it right now.

Be careful not to take the idea of feature flags too far. There are many scenarios where you'd want to take the site down; it's not worth building contingency for these cases. Flickr has no feature flag to disable the serving of photos, nor do we have a feature flag to cope without our main database. We'd just take the site down.

You can also have too many feature flags. It is better to have one simple flag for a situation than dozens of similar flags that nobody in your on-call rotation understands.

It's worth involving everyone in the discussion around what feature flags to build. When you disable site functionality many of your users will contact you wanting more information; you need to understand the impact a degraded site will have on your customer care team. You should also make sure you're aware of the revenue impact of disabling each feature on the site and what SLAs you have with your partners. If possible, document these costs inline in your config file:

```
# if this is disabled for more than 10 minutes in any month
# we'll miss our SLA with ACME which will cost us $200k
$cfg['disable_awesome_integration'] = 0;
```

Intentionally degrading site functionality will be unpopular with many people, especially among your product and business teams. It's better to have the debate about the idea ahead of time while everyone is calm, and remind everyone that the alternative is to shut down the whole site. If that doesn't work, wait until the next site outage postmortem, and people will be more receptive to the idea.

Avoiding Blame

In a lot of teams nobody wants to be the sucker who broke everything. When something breaks, people point their finger at the person next to them:

> It can't be the transcoding system because that hasn't changed in the past three weeks. It must be a problem in our streaming servers.

> Well, ops did an upgrade on the OS on those boxes yesterday. I don't see why I should debug my code until they can prove it's not their problem.

> That OS has been in production in our Virginia datacenter for six months. The problem must be in the application configuration.

And so on (see Figure 10-5).

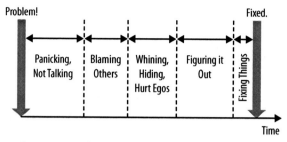

Figure 10-5. *An imperfect scenario for when things break*

Everyone has a plausible reason for passing the blame onto someone else, but nobody is stepping up and actually fixing things. Good teams know that until a fix has been pushed it doesn't matter who broke things, and every minute spent being defensive is another minute something is broken for users without a fix going out. They focus on trying every possibility until they've found what was broken.

It's really easy to prove your code or system has a bug. Proving that a simple system or piece of code is bug free is a known hard problem in computer science, even if you assume the expected behavior is clearly defined. It's impossible to prove any slightly complex system has no problems. In comparison, it's really easy to prove your code or system has a bug. When things are going wrong it's more productive to focus on trying to find causes than it is to try to find a way to push blame onto other people. Even if you don't find the problem you're looking for, you'll probably find things you can improve later (see Figure 10-6).

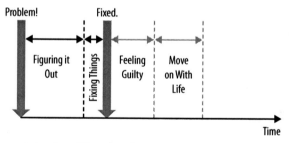

Figure 10-6. *Ideal scenario when things break*

This attitude is infectious. If someone is obviously working hard on trying to solve a problem, it's easier for others to join in and help out. Think about which of these is more motivating:

> The problem is not in the payment code, and I'm not even going to look at it until you check the transaction logs. I know the problem is in your system.

or:

> I'm stepping through the payment flow right now. I think the bug is there, but I've not found anything yet. Hey, could you check the transaction logs to see if you can see anything that might help me out?

Even if you're almost certain a bug wasn't caused by your system, rolling up your sleeves and trying to find a solution is usefully motivating.

Great teams have found that most production systems have enough redundancy and complexity that there is rarely a single root cause for a problem. Most problems are caused by two or more systems interacting in an unexpected way. Even in these situations people still resist patching the bug in their code for fear of being singled out for later blame—"The problem must have been in the login system if that's what we patched." In the scenarios where a fix could usually be applied in several places, it's best to very deliberately focus on the quick fix that is easiest to deploy, and worry about defining the right long-term changes once things have stabilized. This is possible only if each team member knows he won't create more problems for himself by being the person who fixed the problem.

One of the best ways to create a supportive blame-free environment during outages is to have inclusive, blame-free incident postmortem meetings. A discussion that tries to answer the question, "What did we do wrong?" will very quickly turn defensive. If instead you ask the question, "What could we do better next time?" it's much easier for the people involved to participate in suggesting improvements in themselves and others, without the appearance of blame. Jake Loomis covers the subject of postmortems in a lot more detail in Chapter 13.

Conclusion

This chapter covered many techniques and concepts that you can use to improve the development–operations relationship. The most useful and important is the understanding that site stability is everyone's responsibility and not just something that should be relegated to the operations team to handle on its own.

This is the case at Flickr. The team has many convictions about the best way to support and improve the product. The most deeply ingrained is that site uptime is more important than everything except the security and privacy of our members' data. This isn't true just within engineering—every team member, from design and product to ad sales and business development, is willing to drop what she's doing (even after hours) if there's something she can do to help keep the site up and running.

Thinking in this way removes the pressure to compromise on stability in the interests of some other goal. It leads to features that have been designed and built at every level to gracefully handle partial outages and provide switches and information that will be useful when things go wrong. It means that when things do break significantly, the response is coordinated and well thought through.

But if we move responsibility for site stability to someone else, where does that leave operations? Does this mean there's no role for the traditional operations team?

Even with the changes we've discussed, the members of the operations team remain the experts on site uptime. They're probably the first to be paged if something breaks, and they have the most experience anticipating and handling production problems. Sharing the responsibility among members of a larger group does not mean operations should lose their influence over how the site is run on a day-to-day basis; they are the ideal proponents for the ongoing emphasis on production stability.

That being said, having a common sense of ownership over the site does mean a reduced workload for the operations team. They'll spend less time advocating for preventive measures and less time fixing issues once they occur. This is a great thing—it means less downtime. It also frees up the operations team to work on the more important task of managing the long-term growth of the infrastructure that powers the site, which is far more useful than playing Whack-a-Mole with outages.

## CHAPTER ELEVEN

How Your Visitors Feel: User-Facing Metrics

Alistair Croll and Sean Power

IT OPERATORS ONCE CONCERNED THEMSELVES only with the health of their underlying infrastructure. The thinking went something like this: if the platforms on which the application was running were healthy, the user experience was good, too.

Today, we know this is not the case. A far larger percentage of the applications we build are web based and face a vast, unknown user base. End-user metrics are as critical to the success of a website as backend metrics. What's more, sudden problems with end-user metrics such as availability and page latency are often the first sign that something's wrong with the infrastructure.

Web operators need to know about four major categories of end-user measurements, as shown in Table 11-1.

Table 11-1. *The four kinds of end-user metrics*

Type of metric	What it's used for	Questions it answers	Who cares most about it
Web analytics	Tracks visitors as they use the site to see whether they did what you wanted them to	What percentage of visitors bought a product? Which segment of visitors is most likely to invite friends? Which content makes people stay longer?	Marketers and merchandisers, product managers
Web performance	Measures the health of the site from the outside perspective	How long does it take to deliver a page to a visitor? Where is the site slowest from? What percentage of the time is the site working properly?	IT operators and those responsible for service levels
Web Interaction Analytics (WIA)	Tracks how visitors interacted with the site	Where did visitors click? How many people scrolled to the bottom of the page? Did people see a button?	User interface designers, QA teams
Voice of the Customer (VOC)	Surveys visitors to measure satisfaction, capture demographic data, and ask for feedback and suggestions	How old are visitors? Which pages did people like the least? Why are people coming to the site?	Customer support, product managers

As a web operator, you'll care most about performance, because it's the thing over which you have the most control. Don't neglect the other metrics, however. Here's why:

- You'll be expected to help *install and maintain the tools* that collect these metrics. Many rely on JavaScript inserted into page templates, and this can slow down page load time or even break the site completely. As you release new versions of the site, you may have to coordinate upgrades with the owners of these other monitoring tools.

- To *understand the business impact of performance and availability*, you need to correlate site health with other metrics—particularly web analytics data. Otherwise, you won't know what downtime cost the business, or how much a speedup of the website improved revenues. We can't emphasize this enough: if you don't tie the fruits of your labor to a business metric, the suits won't care about all your hard work.

- Sometimes you'll *discover problems*—and possible solutions—through other metrics. We know of many operations teams that first learn of issues through customer feedback on the website.

Why Collect User-Facing Metrics?

IT has always collected some amount of data on the applications it's running, but until recently, this information stayed within the IT department. Syslog data, SNMP traps, and CPU history seldom made it out of the NOC.

MEASUREMENT

The Twitter Way

At Twitter, we collect and graph over 30,000 metrics that identify how effectively our systems are processing tweets in real time. Given the large amount of data that we collect hourly, standalone metrics from single servers do not generally give us actionable information. Grouping metrics together helps us to understand where the site is at any given time, and what impact deployments may have had on stability.

From individual metrics, we consolidate the data into a series of 10 important graphs. They include:

- Tweets per second
- Bandwidth
- Response time
- HTTP error rate
- Logged exception rate
- Process restart rate
- Queue sizes
- Server load average and number of processes
- Database load
- Memory

Any change in the graphs usually indicates that a recent deployment has impacted site performance. Therefore, the operations team constantly compares post-deployment site measurements against the previous state.

While the current state of the site is of the utmost importance to us, the deltas in our graphs tell the true story of where site performance is heading. Software deployments, restarts, and capacity limits affect these metrics; our goal is to permit change in a way that does not impact our top-line metrics and the outward-facing user experience.

Generally, I recommend that you collect data on your sites as soon as you can. In order of importance, you should collect errors per second (HTTP result codes that are not 200), average time to service a request, and the rate of exceptions on your application servers.

Already a wide range of tools are available to you to collect, process, and alert on this data. Open source tools such as Ganglia, Nagios, and RRDtool, combined with a few simple scripts, will give you new insights into your infrastructure.

—John Adams, Operations, Twitter

The rest of the business has also been collecting data—such as sales receipts, retail stores, employee productivity, inventory levels, call centers, and financial systems—and putting it into data warehouses so that the health of the business can be analyzed.

Web-based businesses have a unique opportunity to link IT data and business data. Never has there been a channel that's as easy to instrument and analyze as the Web, and today, the Web is the *default* channel for many industries. As a result, companies are trying to link business intelligence (BI) tools to IT operations data. In doing so, they can make smarter decisions and align business plans with capacity predictions.

Successful Start-ups Learn and Adapt

While big, established enterprises are trying to tie together BI and IT, however, it's start-ups that really live or die by the end-user metrics they collect. A start-up's one advantage is agility—its ability to react quickly. To do this, start-ups need to know what end users are experiencing.

For any website to succeed, it must learn from and adapt to its visitors. Websites are iterative: each release of an application should get the site closer to what its visitors want.* If you look at Internet giants such as Twitter, Facebook, and Flickr, you'll find that the business they're in today differs widely from what they set out to be.

That means collecting the four kinds of end-user measurement types we've seen; analyzing them properly; correlating them; and sharing them with the rest of the organization. As a web operator, you'll have a supporting role in analytics, VOC, and WIA; but you'll likely be in charge of measuring performance, latency, and uptime.

Performance Matters

We've known for three decades that responsive applications are better. Research by IBM in 1981 showed that as applications become more responsive, operators become more productive, and that this productivity increases exponentially as application response time dips below one second (see Figure 11-1).

---

* We can think of no better authorities than Eric Ries, Sean Ellis, Dave McClure, and Steve Blank on this subject.

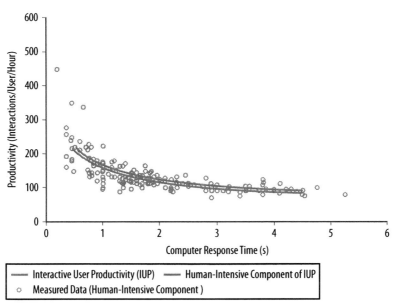

Figure 11-1. *User productivity as it correlates to computer response time*

One reason for this may be that humans become more engaged and involved in things when they're challenging, and this engagement makes them more productive. Mihaly Csikszentmihalyi wrote about this phenomenon in *Flow: The Psychology of Optimal Experience* (Harper & Row), where he describes the state of heightened awareness that athletes, artists, and others enter when their attention is captured.

To put attention into perspective, consider the following levels of responsiveness:

- If something responds within *10 milliseconds*, our brains think it's real. When we click on a button in a desktop operating system, the button changes color and shape to signal that it is now in a clicked state. Our brains believe that the button is real, in part because of this responsiveness. This is also why video gamers demand monitors with sub-10-millisecond refresh rates.

- If a conversation happens with *around 100 milliseconds* of delay, we're unaware of a delay. When international calls relied on satellites, there was an appreciable delay, leading to interruptions and uncertain, halting dialog.

- If an application responds *within a second*, we feel that we're interacting with it, and stay on task.

- If an application takes significantly *longer than a second* to respond, we become distracted.

* From Thadhani, A. J. (1981). *IBM Systems Journal* 20:4.

Despite this research, however, understanding what level of application responsiveness was "good enough" was largely anecdotal until recently. Analyst firms published studies on the "eight-second rule" of page load time, but there weren't any concrete studies showing how web performance correlated to business outcomes.

Recent Research Quantifies the Relationship

In recent years, proper research has replaced these anecdotal guidelines. Companies such as Google, Microsoft, Strangeloop, and Shopzilla have all shared research on the relationship between web performance and business key performance indicators (KPIs). All have concluded the same thing: faster web applications give a web business a significant advantage.

- Google's study* showed that adding delay *reduces the average number of searches* a visitor does each day even after the delay is removed. A similar study by Microsoft on its Bing search site revealed that slow pages affect other KPIs, *reducing the clicks, queries, and revenue per visitor.*

- Strangeloop's comparison of optimized and unoptimized visitors† provided further evidence of the role that end-user performance plays. The company used its web acceleration appliance to optimize half of the visitors' sessions on a site, and then compared the outcomes using web analytics. Unoptimized visitors *left sooner, returned less often, and were less likely to spend money*—and when they did spend money, they spent less of it.

- As part of a major overhaul,‡ Shopzilla redesigned its Shopzilla and BizRate properties, dramatically reducing web latency. The company found that important KPIs such as the *clicks-to-sessions ratio* (the percentage of people who clicked on a link and actually visited the site) increased after speeding it up. Its *search engine rankings* also improved. Although we'd long speculated that page speed influenced Google's page rank algorithm, this was only recently confirmed by the search giant.§

In other words, if your website is slow you'll get:

- Fewer search queries per user

- Less query refinement

- Less revenue per visitor

- Fewer clicks and lower satisfaction

- A longer time for visitors to click something

---

* *http://code.google.com/speed/files/delayexp.pdf*
† *http://www.watchingwebsites.com/archives/proof-that-speeding-up-websites-improves-online-business*
‡ *http://www.slideshare.net/timmorrow/shopzilla-performance-by-design-2433735*
§ *http://googlewebmastercentral.blogspot.com/2010/04/using-site-speed-in-web-search-ranking.html*

- Fewer searches per day

- Lower search engine rankings

What Makes a Site Slow?

At the simplest level, web applications are slow because of three things:

- The time the *server* takes to process the client's request

- The time the *network* takes to transmit the request and response

- The time the *client* takes to assemble and display the resultant content

It's more complicated than this, of course, for several reasons:

Service Discovery

At the start of any web visit, the client needs to find the server. This is generally done by a DNS lookup, although the client may have cached the server's IP address. Additional steps may be involved in finding the right server, including HTTP redirects that send a client elsewhere.

Every time the client needs to get content from a new server, it has to go through this service discovery process. As a result, a website with many components—a pattern which is increasingly common online—forces clients to resolve many sites and takes longer to load the page.

Modern web design relies heavily on third-party components for payment, embedded videos, links to social media feeds, monitoring, and so on. Each additional component is another point of failure for you to worry about and another source of delay for visitors, robbing you of the advantage of a fast site.

Sending the Request

Networks can be only as fast as the round-trip time between the client and the server. Part of this is just physics: it takes light 13 milliseconds to get from New York to Las Vegas, and your data won't get there any sooner than that.* The speed of the network between browser and content is the first factor in delay.

A web request can be simple: GET index.html. Often, however, a request is more complex, including cookies, URI parameters, and even POSTs to upload content. The larger the request, the longer the network will take to transmit it. If a page is secure, there's also a delay as the client and server negotiate encryption.

---

* We're hedging our bets, though (see *http://mblogs.discovermagazine.com/80beats/2008/08/13/entangled -particles-seem-to-communicate-instantly%E2%80%94and-befuddle-scientists/*).

Thinking About the Response

From the moment the request reaches the server, a new source of latency comes into play: host time. Whether retrieving a static object from memory or completing a complex request to backend third-party services, host latency affects performance. We're not going to dwell on backend delay, because it's covered elsewhere in this book; but host latency can be an important component of a bad user experience, and it's essential to track it from outside the website, as well as from the backend.

Remember that if your site relies on third-party components, you have to measure the host latency of those external sites as well, and you may have to craft service-level agreements (SLAs) with those providers to ensure that you can meet your own latency targets.

Delivering the Response

Once the response is ready, the server delivers the requested objects via HTTP. It's the delivery of these objects that accounts for most of the delay that visitors experience.

Although it might seem that bandwidth—the volume of data that can travel between the client and the server in a given period—dictates page latency, in fact the number of objects on a page, and where they come from, usually determines the time a page takes to load.

Web pages seldom consist of just a single object. For most pages, a container object (*page.html*) contains references to component objects (*image.gif, video.mov, audio.wav, movie.swf*) that must, in turn, be retrieved. Browsers have a limit to how many component objects can be retrieved at a time, so the time it takes to load a page is a combination of the number of objects, their size, the number that can be retrieved concurrently, and the available bandwidth.

To understand this, we usually express web page load time as cascade diagrams that show the container page and subsequent component pages (see Figure 11-2).

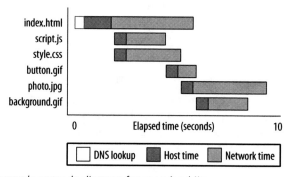

Figure 11-2. *An example cascade diagram for page load time*

At some point, the browser has enough information to start displaying the page, even though additional objects may still be retrieved.

Asynchronous Traffic and Refresh

Some applications include communication between client and server independent of a page. You see this when you drag a Google Map and the background tiles fill in independently; or when you type part of a search and the site suggests possible terms you may be looking for. These asynchronous communication patterns are increasingly common in Web 2.0–style sites.

Applications that include some kind of asynchronous update or refresh have a different set of latency metrics. We can't talk about "page load time," because a constant stream of updates are flowing to the browser. Instead, we measure metrics such as "messages per second" or "refresh time," the delay between when the user does something (types a character, drags a map) and when the content is refreshed (suggestions are updated, map is repainted).

Rendering Time

As clients become increasingly sophisticated, there's more for a browser to do. Rich Internet Applications (RIAs) built atop Flash, Flex, HTML5, Java, JavaScript, and Silverlight may have to launch; or media add-ons such as QuickTime and Windows Media Player may have to run. Even deciding how to lay out a complex page can take time. For sites that rely heavily on client-side rendering, it's essential to include this delay.

The good news is that when you're building a client for your site, you may be able to include code that measures latency and sends data back to you so that you know what your application is like for end users.

Measuring Delay

There are two basic ways to measure the delay we've looked at: synthetic monitoring (also known as active monitoring) and Real User Monitoring (RUM; sometimes called passive monitoring).

Synthetic Monitoring

Synthetic monitoring involves monitoring a site's performance through a series of regular, scripted tests of the website from multiple locations. It's analogous to internal monitoring via ping, TCP connections, or HTTP requests (see Figure 11-3).

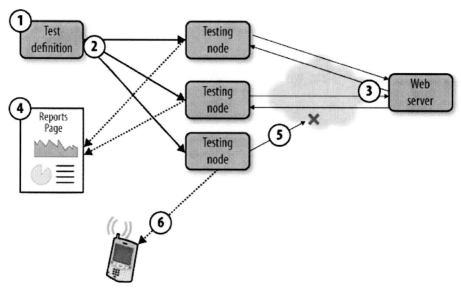

Figure 11-3. *The basic steps in a synthetic monitoring service*

Synthetic monitoring is great for checking whether something you know about is functioning properly. In other words, *synthetic monitoring shows you whether something is working*.

When to use synthetic monitoring

Synthetic monitoring and RUM are complementary technologies. Each plays a vital role in operating a web application at scale. But it's important to know when to use which tool.

Synthetic monitoring works well when you need to know about something *before* actual users encounter it. It's also good for creating baselines, because it can be performed at regular intervals regardless of visitor traffic. Use synthetic monitoring for:

- Monitoring key steps in your business transactions, such as the catalog page or comment process.

- Measuring the health of components that you don't control but that your business relies on. This could be a Facebook fan page, a payment service, or a form tool.

- Running the same test from different environments. Because the test is the same each time, comparing cities or carriers will tell you if you have a geographic region that's sluggish or an outage from a particular service provider.

Note that synthetic monitoring relies on the same principles as load testing, except that the goal isn't to break a site by overwhelming it with traffic, it's to estimate what the site's performance is like for real visitors at the time of the test.

Limitations of synthetic monitoring

Synthetic monitoring services are common and affordable. If your site isn't connected to the Internet, however, you'll likely have to deploy your own test server. There are a range of services from which to choose. When selecting a service, consider the following factors:

How easy is it to record and manage scripts?
> Your test scripts must stay in sync with your application, as each new release may break existing scripts and generate false alarms. You may need to devote considerable time to maintaining the testing systems for them to be useful.

What are the reports like?
> Higher-end services offer more advanced reports with granular details.

Is the alerting compatible with my backend monitoring tools?
> You'll want to send performance data from the outside world into the same management platform you're using to track backend health so that you can analyze it. Often, an external error will be the first sign that something's wrong.

Can I test all parts of my application?
> Modern sites include text messaging, email signup, Twitter activity, HTTP 5 WebSockets, server-sent events, embedded video, AJAX, and RIAs built in Flash, Flex, Java, and Silverlight. Be sure you know all of the components you need to monitor before you sign a contract.

Is the testing done by a script or a real browser?
> Some synthetic monitoring services emulate a browser, sending HTTP commands to your site and recording the results. Others, using an approach we call *browser puppetry*, actually take control of a real browser. The latter approach is costlier but tends to be less brittle as the site changes because the testing scripts are manipulating a browser's DOM rather than just sending text.

When an error occurs, what happens?
> Some services record the error in detail, capture the error message as it would be seen within a browser, and trigger additional tests such as traceroutes; others just forward an alert. More detail costs more money but makes it easier to fix problems.

Configuring synthetic monitoring

Setting up this kind of monitoring is relatively easy, particularly if you only want to measure the performance of a few key pages. Generally speaking, you just need to enter the URL to test, the testing interval, and any actions to take when an error occurs.

If you're doing more advanced monitoring, you may need to provide a "neutered" user account that can be tested without breaking things, as well as session parameters and other details the service will use to better simulate a real visit.

Remember, too, that synthetic tests consume server resources. We've seen sites where more than 50% of traffic came from synthetic monitoring scripts, and this was actually degrading the experience of real visitors (see Figure 11-4).

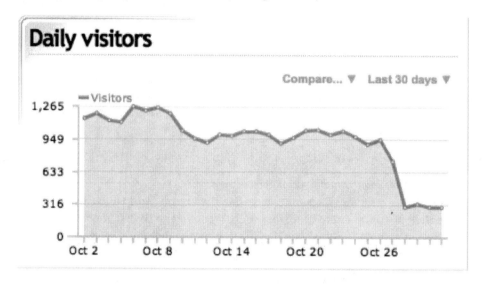

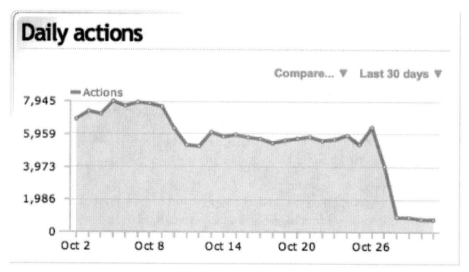

Figure 11-4. *Traffic patterns before and after filtering out a synthetic service*

Real User Monitoring

RUM does what the name implies: it watches actual visitors to a site, calculates the speed with which they receive pages, and then generates reports (see Figure 11-5).

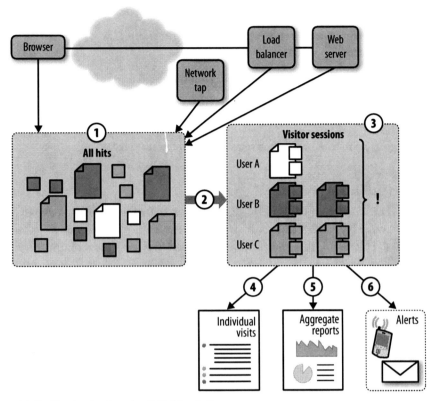

Figure 11-5. *The basic steps in all RUM solutions*

In this respect, *RUM shows you whether something is broken*, because you'll discover problems and slowdowns you weren't testing for and didn't know existed.

When to use RUM

RUM tools generate two kinds of reports, each of which helps you measure performance and diagnose problems:

Individual visitor reports

These are like having Firebug for every visitor to your site, letting you replay visits and review each page and object. You may also generate alerts based on an individual error (e.g., "If someone gets an HTTP 500 error, send me an email.").

Aggregate reports

These show what happened across all visitors—which pages are slowest, which objects have the most errors, and so on. You may generate alerts based on aggregate data over time (e.g., "If average page latency exceeds five seconds in a five-minute period, send an SNMP trap.").

Common use cases for RUM include:

- Reviewing problem sessions to diagnose a technical issue with the site

- Generating service-level reports for actual visitors to the site, particularly if you're running a Software-as-a-Service (SaaS) offering

- Identifying parts of the site that may need more regular monitoring

- Measuring the health of parts of the site you can't measure synthetically, such as checkout pages

- Alerting as soon as a problem is seen, rather than at intervals

Limitations of RUM

Although synthetic tools are all fairly similar, there's a big distinction between client-side and server-side RUM tools. The former rely on AJAX scripts or embedded agent code to collect information from end users as they visit the site; the latter use server logs, load balancers, or network taps to collect visitor information from the datacenter.

Client-side RUM sees the user's experience within the browser, so it can measure delays such as client-side rendering. Unfortunately, because client-side RUM is loaded only when your web page is successfully loaded and executed on the browser, it can't detect errors that prevent it from loading and won't work with some clients. What's more, because it's running within the browser sandbox, it can't see lower-layer data such as packet loss. It also can't calculate host latency for the first page on your site that the user visits.

Server-side RUM has the opposite problems. Because it's independent of a browser, it can see everything—even failed TCP connection attempts—with great detail. But it can't peer within the browser to see what's going on. Perhaps most significantly, because it requires access to the network and logging, and in some cases physical networks, you may not be able to deploy it in some hosted or cloud-based environments. Many commercial RUM solutions combine both client-side and server-side collection approaches to overcome this.

Configuring RUM

RUM tools are configured in two basic steps. First, you train the tool to understand the traffic patterns of your site; then you tell it what's important to watch.

By definition, a RUM tool will capture all traffic going to and from your server. Training the tool is necessary because every site is different. It involves the following steps:

1. Filter out unwanted traffic.

   You may not want to include certain kinds of web traffic in your measurement. Bots, other monitoring tools, web service calls, and traffic from within the firewall can all skew your understanding of the end-user experience.

2. Tell the system how to track individual users.

   Every website uses something to identify a unique visitor, whether that's a session cookie, a URL parameter, or even an IP address. In some RUM approaches—particularly those that use client-side scripts—this isn't necessary, because an instance of the script runs in each visitor's browser.

3. Tell the system how to assemble pages.

   It can be tricky to know when one page ends and another begins. Some pages may have asynchronous communication after the page has loaded (e.g., Google Suggest sends suggestions based on what a user has typed into a search box). The RUM tool needs to know what constitutes the start and end of a page, which is essential for measuring timing and calculating page counts properly.

4. Identify errors.

   Although every website has fundamental error types (e.g., HTTP 500) there may be custom messages that constitute an error (such as an apology page) but that look like a normal page.

Once the tool knows how to understand a visit and measure latency, you need to tell it what to watch. Most RUM tools start with a set of defaults: pages, users, cities, and servers are all good ways in which to segment the data, and they'll show you which of these are slowest or have the most errors.

Because of the vast amount of information a RUM tool is handling, however, it will often provide only high-level data on the site unless you specifically tell it to drill down—for example, to a part of the site that was just launched or a particularly high-value customer. In general, each segment you identify will then be used for reporting and can generate alerts or email notifications.

Building an SLA

One of the main reasons for web operators to collect end-user data is to build an SLA. Even if you don't have a formal SLA with clients, you should have internal targets for uptime and page latency, because site speed has a direct impact on business experience.

User-facing SLAs have several components (see Table 11-2). You need to be specific about these so that there's no doubt whether an SLA was violated when someone claims that a problem occurred.

Table 11-2. *The elements of a user-facing SLA*

SLA component	What it means	How it's expressed	Example
Task being measured	The thing being tested—the business process or function itself	This is usually expressed as a name or description of the test; avoid using just the URL or page name as it makes the test harder to read.	"Updating a contact record"
Metric being calculated	The element of latency that's being computed. If you can't control it, it shouldn't be in your SLA.	This is a measurement that is specific and can be reproduced across systems. You should know, for example, that "page load time" means "from the first DNS lookup to the browser's onLoad event."	"Host latency"
Calculation	The math used to generate the number	Unfortunately, this is usually an average. Don't do this. Averages suck. Insist on a percentile (or at the very least a trimmed mean), and a single bad measurement won't ruin an otherwise good month.	"95th per-centile"
Valid times	The times and days when the metric is valid. If you don't include this, you won't have room for maintenance. Some business processes matter at only certain times.	This is expressed as hours, days, and time zones.	"8:00 a.m. to 9:00 p.m., PST, Monday to Friday"
Test conditions (or filters)	The circumstances of the test or the visits included in the report: • For synthetic monitoring, this may be an agreed-upon external service provider. • For RUM, it may be all visits from a particular client, location, IP range, or some other segment.	This is expressed as operating systems, network locations, browsers, user accounts, source IP ranges, and so on.	"Domestic United States on a PC running IE7"
Time span	The time over which the calculation is performed	This is expressed as a time range, often a day, week, or month.	"In a 30-day period"

Apdex

One method of communicating service levels is the Application Performance Index or Apdex.* It's a measurement of how often the application's performance and availability are acceptable that's easy to calculate and can be used for comparison purposes.

Here's how you calculate an Apdex score:

1. Start with your performance target ("the login page should load in two seconds").

2. For each loaded page or transaction, decide whether it was delivered promptly. Apdex has three ratings for performance: if the page loaded within its performance target, the visitor was *satisfied*; if it loaded in less than four times the target, the visitor was *tolerating*; and if it loaded in more than four times the performance target or failed to load entirely, the visitor was *frustrated*.

3. Using this data, you then calculate the score as shown in Figure 11-6.

4. The result is a score from 0 to 1, where 1 means every transaction happened within the performance target and 0 means all requests resulted in a frustrated user.

$$Score = \left\{ \frac{(Satisfied) + (Tolerating/2)}{All} \right\}$$

Figure 11-6. *Calculating an Apdex score*

The strongest argument for Apdex is math: it's easy to roll up Apdex scores across sites, pages, or time periods just by totaling the satisfied, tolerating, and frustrated users.[†] It works even if different parts of your site have different performance targets. And it works whether you have only a few measurements—a test every five minutes, for example—or many thousands of measurements every second.

Visitor Outcomes: Analytics

So far, we've looked at the metrics you need to collect for web performance. These metrics don't mean much, however, unless you tie them to business outcomes. For successful web operators, monitoring is all about *knowing the impact*. And when it comes to web businesses, the place where those impacts are measured is within the practice of web analytics, which is where we'll spend the rest of this chapter.

How Marketing Defines Success

One of the best descriptions of marketing, by Sergio Zyman, formerly the CMO of Coca-Cola, is that it's about "selling more things to more people more often for more

---

* *http://www.apdex.org*
† When considering SLA reporting, remember that most executives won't understand anything more complex than a golf score.

money, more efficiently." Not every website is focused on e-commerce, though, so it's perhaps more accurate to define online marketing success as "getting people to do the things you want them to efficiently."

Of course, what you want visitors to do depends on the business you're in.

The Four Kinds of Sites

There are four fundamental web business models. Your site might fall into more than one of these—indeed, most sites do—but these four archetypes underlie every web property. Before you can decide what metrics marketing needs to analyze, you have to know what kind of site you're running.

Transactional sites

> Involve the completion of some kind of transaction, often a purchase. They define success by revenues from sales that happen on their site.

Collaborative sites

> Involve the creation of content. When valuable new content is added to the site, it benefits. On the other hand, spammers and trolls reduce the site's value.

SaaS sites

> Offer functional applications on a subscription or per-use basis. They thrive when their users are productive, renewing or upgrading their subscriptions and telling others.

Media sites

> Make money through advertising. They want to show content to visitors, along with marketing messages from sponsors or affiliate networks. They make money when they have many visitors (for sponsored or pay-per-view ads) or when visitors click ads (in a pay-per-click model).

Many popular web properties have more than one of these models. Google's Gmail is a SaaS site—offering a service whose goal is to make users productive—and a media site, featuring embedded ads. Amazon.com includes transactional aspects (the purchase of books) alongside collaboration (customer ratings and reviews).

Web analytics is about tracking the things that drive success for each type of site and identifying what makes those things increase—whether that's a particular advertising campaign, an improvement in performance, a mention on a social network, a particular pricing model, or even some compelling content or improved page design.

A (Very) Basic Model of Analytics

Here's a simple way to think about analytics, through a single visit:

A *visitor* arrives at your website, possibly after following a link that *referred* her. She *lands* on a web page and either *bounces* (leaves immediately) or requests additional pages.

In time, the visitor may complete an action that's good for your business, *converting* her from a mere buyer into something more: a customer, user, member, or contributor, depending on the kind of site you're running. On the other hand, she may *abandon* that action and ultimately exit the website.

The visitor has many external attributes—such as the browser she's using, or where she's surfing from—that let you group her into *segments*. She may also see different *offers* or products internal to the site during her visit as the basis for further segmentation.

The goal of analytics, then, is to maximize conversions by *optimizing* your website, often by *experimenting* with the website and analyzing the results of those experiments on various internal and external segments.

With the widespread availability of free analytics tools such as Google Analytics, most people know something about their site. But for most sites—even surprisingly big ones—analytics amounts to little more than a popularity contest, showing how many visitors stopped by. When you're serious about analytics, two things change. First, you care about outcomes—how many of those visits end in success—which means mapping visitors to the fundamental goals of your business. And second, you start to wonder how to improve things by looking at trends, or correlations within specific visitor segments.

Even if you're not in marketing, you should know some of the fundamental KPIs that marketers care about, because things you do on the operational side can affect them (and you'll be blamed when they go pear-shaped). Figure 11-7 shows some of these KPIs.

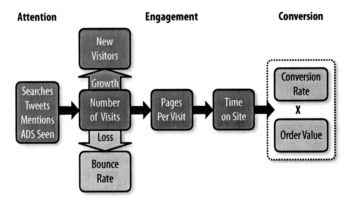

Figure 11-7. *A simple analytics model*

A given number of people visit the site. Some of them are new (which grows your audience); some are returning (which shows loyalty); and some "bounce" immediately (which may indicate that they didn't find what they wanted). Hopefully, visitors stick around for several pages and a decent amount of time, culminating in some kind of business outcome you want (such as a purchase). This is usually expressed in the form of a funnel, indicating abandonment (not buying) and conversion (buying).

There are plenty of good books on analytics, so we're not going to go into more detail here. But we will tackle one aspect of analytics: tying it to site health. Although this might seem like an obvious idea that will help prove the value of good monitoring, robust infrastructure, and lean site design, it's surprisingly hard to do.

Correlating Performance and Analytics by Time

The easy way to link site health and business outcomes is to put them on a graph together, an example of which is shown in Figure 11-8. If you see a sudden increase in site delay and a sudden drop in conversion rates, it's worth looking into. Over a long enough period of time you may even be able to calculate the correlation.

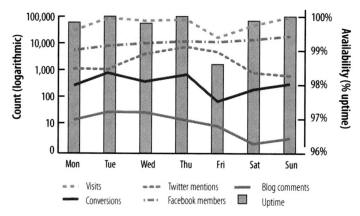

Figure 11-8. *Consolidating data manually by displaying multiple data sources in a spreadsheet using time as a common key*

There are several problems with this approach, however:

It relies on averages

> Without associating a single visitor to a single outcome, it's hard to get a precise correlation.

It's not well controlled

> You can't easily eliminate other factors with this method. Consider, for example, a successful web marketing campaign that drives up traffic—slowing down the site—and improves conversion rates at the same time. You might conclude that there was an inverse correlation between performance and conversion, when in fact the campaign would have been even more successful with the proper infrastructure.

Often, the performance measurements aren't coming from the users who are on the site

> If you have a synthetic test result showing that your site is slow from California, but nobody from California is on the site right now, any latency measurements aren't relevant to conversion rates.

For many companies, however, this is the best correlation they can get, because they rely exclusively on synthetic monitoring and don't have individual visitor performance data.

Correlating Performance and Analytics by Visits

The second way to correlate performance and business outcomes is to actually record the performance of each visitor's session. This means using a RUM tool and then getting latency measurements into the analytics package somehow. You can do this with JavaScript on the client that marks a visit as "fast" or "slow," for example; this is essentially what the research from Google, Microsoft, Strangeloop, and Shopzilla did. Or you can export logs from server-side RUM and combine them with web analytics logs separately, using cookies or usernames to associate sessions (see Figure 11-9). This is a lot of work, and likely involves a significant investment in data warehousing technology today, but vendors are quickly consolidating their solutions.

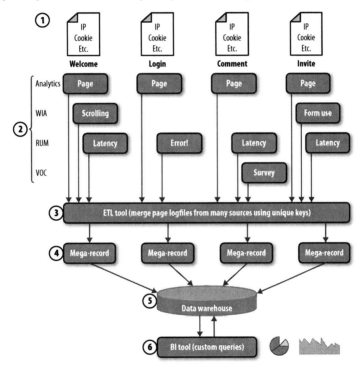

Figure 11-9. *Pulling together disparate data according to common unique keys*

One reason this is hard to do well is that RUM and analytics tools store data differently. Aggregate RUM data (segmented by city, by carrier, or by URL) is hard to match with aggregate analytics data (which is organized in terms of funnels and visitor sessions). The best way to combine the two without building a central repository is to mark visits according to a set of performance levels (such as the Apdex model of satisfied, tolerating, and frustrated performance) and segment goal funnels along these dimensions—in effect, creating a new analytics segment devoted to performance.

Other Metrics Marketing Cares About

We've concentrated on performance and analytics, because it's your job to manage the former and you know if you're succeeding by tracking the latter. But there are two other aspects of end-user monitoring we should touch on briefly, because on a modern website, everything's related.

Web Interaction Analytics

While analytics looks at a user's entire visit across many pages, Web Interaction Analytics (WIA) focuses on the usability and interaction within an individual page. This kind of data can help you pinpoint web ops problems, even though it's mainly used by application designers.

You may find that reported bugs aren't really bugs—users may be misunderstanding the user interface, clicking on buttons that aren't actually buttons, or not scrolling far enough to see controls. More advanced WIA tools capture mouse movements and keystrokes, and may help you to troubleshoot tricky application problems because they overlap with RUM tools somewhat.

Voice of the Customer

Voice of the Customer (VOC) tools ask visitors what's on their mind. They solicit feedback from people who visit the site, either by asking them to participate in a survey or by offering them a feedback button on pages.

VOC surveys are usually conducted to find out demographic and psychographic information about the site's audience. Here, too, there's useful data for the web operator. A few questions about operating systems and network speeds will show you what kinds of client environment you need to test for.

On the other hand, VOC feedback buttons are a "pressure valve" for frustrated visitors. These buttons let visitors express themselves when they see something they love—or hate. Sometimes this information includes a rating of the page they're on, which can suggest new pages to monitor. At the very least, your QA department should be entering visitor complaints gleaned from VOC feedback into the QA system.

How User Experience Affects Web Ops

With the newfound focus on end-user experience, your role as a web operator is changing. There's much more interest in what's happening online and every aspect of a website is tied back to the business outcomes tracked by analytics.

Many More Stakeholders

Lots more people want access to the data. Remember that they're not necessarily technical, and they're almost certainly not interested in backend monitoring data. Here are some tips for reporting end-user experience to the rest of the organization:

Train your stakeholders early

> From the outset, make an end-user experience report part of weekly meetings. If you need data from other groups to create correlated reports, set that expectation with them and demand it. The organization should start to expect your information regularly.

Don't keep changing things

> If you want to add a chart or table, put it into the report on a trial basis, in a separate section. See if it works, or if it confuses people, before you incorporate it into the overall report.

If performance is core, make it visible

> Invest in some TV screens and display things prominently. Make sure the company understands that the underlying web operations drive the business. When everyone else knows data is available, they'll come to you with questions and ideas, and you'll work better together.

Take baby steps

> Start with simple reports (such as uptime) and easy-to-understand figures (such as percentages or scores). Although percentiles and histograms are great, they're often hard to understand. If you have to explain a chart or teach someone statistics, your reports are too complicated: think golf scores, not stats classes.

Relate it to the business

> Every business metric can be tied to either revenue or cost. Make everything relevant. If you're reporting on trouble tickets, tie it to traffic on the Feedback page and the cost of providing service. If you're looking at survey responses, know how the mail server handled the initial mailing and the conversion and bounce rates. If you're seeing a spike in performance, find out what marketing did last week and whether the increased traffic from the campaign offset the drop in conversion rates from a slower page load.

Associate it to changes

> Rather than just showing a number, provide a trailing history and a percentage increase or decrease.

Monitoring As Part of the Life Cycle, Not Just QA

Sites change a lot. As Agile and Lean product development catches on, monitoring needs to keep up. The synthetic monitoring scripts and RUM configurations on which you rely need to do so, too.

This means your change control systems must include any monitoring you're doing—including web analytics instrumentation, WIA, VOC scripts, and any performance metrics. With each release cycle, find out:

- Have we added any new functionality that has to be monitored?

- Have we done anything to the site that will change how end-user measurement happens?

- Can we now decommission any existing monitoring?

- Have changes to the site affected any thresholds (such as "acceptable performance") that will now need adjusting?

- Are we supporting any new browsers, regions, subscribers, or carriers that need to be added to the synthetic tests we run?

- Are there any new error messages or diagnostic information we should be extracting from the site's responses with our RUM tools?

The Future of Web Monitoring

End-user experience monitoring is a thriving and rapidly changing field. It's the most analyzable, quantifiable part of a business, and new technologies emerge weekly. Here are some things to consider.

Moving from Parts to Users

The stack on which the modern Web runs can be deep and hard to troubleshoot. It's not uncommon to see a web application based on virtual machines in many locations, load balanced locally and globally, and running layers upon layers of abstraction. Consider a cloud, with a VM, running Java, with a Rails implementation atop that, serving HTML and CSS. Instrumenting the stack is tough, and setting meaningful thresholds is almost impossible.

As a reaction to this complexity, many web operators start with end-user experience rather than platform health. This "top-down" approach relies on external monitoring to trap errors, extract diagnostic information, and help you pinpoint the problem from the errors themselves. You can even build a "click here to send this error to us" apology page that sends a message to your team, including suitably obfuscated diagnostic data such as which server created the page and which datacenter it came from.

Service-Centric Architectures

With RIAs built atop Flash, Silverlight, Java, and AJAX, more and more of the communication between the client and the server occurs through web services. The IT industry is gradually shifting toward the service-oriented architecture (SOA) model, in part because it allows operators to separate the service they offer from the underlying infrastructure and in part because it encourages portability. Gone are the days of a few, large servers. They've been replaced by farms of commodity hardware using shared-nothing data architectures.*

This means you'll be responsible for sites that depend on myriad third-party services. What looks like server latency to your visitors is in fact backend delay from service providers on whom you rely. This means you've got to go monitor stuff you don't run—and even though you have no control over it, it can still break you.

Clouds and Monitoring

Cloud computing—elastic, on-demand computing resources that are paid for in a utility model—is reducing the barriers to entry for many start-ups, because no upfront investment is needed. It's also letting big enterprises experiment more, and making big-computing applications such as genomics, Monte Carlo simulations, and data mining accessible to anyone.

Despite all the fanfare, however, clouds are still young. And this means cloud computing has a "roof rack" problem. When you buy a car, it's clear which components are included (speedometers) and which are purchased after-market (roof racks). The cloud computing industry hasn't yet settled on these distinctions. As a result, some monitoring tools that were once sold by third-party vendors are now included in cloud offerings.

To further complicate matters, Platform-as-a-Service clouds (such as Google's App Engine) include measurement tools to show users what their bills will be like, while Infrastructure-as-a-Service clouds (such as Amazon Web Services) leave much of the work of instrumentation up to users.

APIs and RSS Feeds

Increasingly, site operators syndicate their content to end users and developers. We're in the middle of a shift from creating applications our users visit to publishing services atop which they can build. As a result, we'll need to monitor traffic across APIs and traditional mechanisms such as RSS and Atom feeds.

* *http://en.wikipedia.org/wiki/Shared_nothing_architecture*

Delivering an API to others

If you provide an API or RSS feed that is consumed by your users, you'll need to monitor it and guarantee its performance. The more real-time the information you provide, the more vocal those who consume it will become when it gets slow or goes away. As a result, you may need to set appropriate SLAs and provide timely information when downtime occurs. Note that downtime can also affect how much traffic others think you have: services such as Compete.com, Quantcast.com, and ComScore will under-report the usage patterns of your website when they can't read your APIs and feeds.

As a service provider, you'll want to work with your marketing department to help them understand basic API usage patterns. Together, you'll want to explore things such as:

- How long it takes until a user interfaces with your API
- Whether the user's behavior changes as a result of this
- Whether the user spends more time or less time with your application or website
- Whether this brings the user further along in your goal funnel
- How you can continue to track the user now that he is accessing a feed or an API rather than pages instrumented with JavaScript

Consuming an API from someone else

If you consume an API or RSS feed from a service provider, you'll need to measure it to identify problems. Every feed on which you rely is as essential as the servers you run. When those feeds break, do you handle the outage gracefully? How much extra delay does the external data introduce? You'll need to depend on your service provider for accurate information, and you may need to monitor the provider's services independently (e.g., using a synthetic testing service) to ensure that you can accurately pinpoint who is at fault when something goes wrong.

Most synthetic monitoring tools can monitor APIs and RSS feeds, though you'll pay more for those that measure external systems such as email and Short Message Service (SMS). Because simple testing won't be sensitive to data inconsistencies that often plague high-volume API systems, you may need to build your own in-house monitoring system or rely on a third-party API proxy service that can do it for you.

Rich Internet Applications

The growth of RIAs and dedicated mobile applications is changing the ways in which we monitor end users. Consider, for example, that web traffic to Twitter.com comprises only 20% of its total traffic.* The rest of that traffic comes from clients such as

---

* According to *http://twitstat.com*.

TweetDeck and Seesmic. Unless you control the RIA and can build monitoring into it, you'll have no visibility into the real end-user experience.

To monitor a RIA, you often need to write the code that collects events—such as a purchase or a screen refresh—into the application yourself at the time of development. Recent industry trends suggest* that we will see a stronger tie between RIA apps and traditional web analytics, and Microsoft is already demonstrating drag-and-instrument features for monitoring within its integrated development environments.

HTML5: Server-Sent Events and WebSockets

HTML5 is an update to the protocols on which the Web runs. The latest iteration of this standard—already implemented by many leading browsers—includes several features that will change how web communication happens:

- Server-sent events allow a server to initiate communication to a client when it has something to send.

- Video support will allow browsers to display video without plug-ins.

- WebSockets will establish a two-way connection between client and server that will eliminate much of the HTTP overhead and will look much more like a point-to-point TCP link than a traditional set of requests and responses.

Today, websites simulate two-way connections using long polling and nailed-up sessions—both of which have inherent inefficiencies and limitations. As HTML5 is more broadly adopted, we'll have to start monitoring different metrics, and these metrics will look a lot more like lower-level network data: round-trip time, refresh rate, and messages per second. Expect significant changes in the metrics and monitoring tools on which you rely in the coming years.

Online Communities and the Long Funnel

We've all heard of viral marketing campaigns that have been so successful that they have crippled the originators' servers. This can also happen when a particular site or page of yours is being actively talked about on a popular social media site.

On the Web, a single person can cause a network meltdown, given enough attention. Here's what British author, actor, and self-described technophile Stephen Fry had to say about becoming a human distributed denial of service (DDoS) attack:

> Perhaps justly the most havoc I've wrought has been on a site of my own. In a vain
> effort to get a revenue stream from the increasing costs of hosting my Web site I
> tweeted the arrival of a T-shirt store which carried some "I tweeted @stephenfry and
> all I got was this luxurious t-shirt" shirtings—within seconds the site was down. I didn't

* http://www.adobe.com/aboutadobe/invrelations/adobeandomniture.html

have the nerve to retweet when it was finally up and running—looked too much like
huckstering. "What a waste of time!"—as Bill Murray expostulates in *Groundhog Day*
on the subject of French poetry.

As we start to understand how online communities are linked to websites, we're
extending the conversion funnel of web analytics out into the social networks where
buzz and attention first build.

In the traditional analytics funnel we saw earlier, a successful visit might look like this:

1. Arrive at */index.html*.

2. Browse products at */shirts.html*.

3. Verify shopping cart at */cart.php*.

4. Place order at */purchase.php*.

5. See receipt and end the session at */thankyou.php*.

An analytics funnel would measure, in aggregate, how many users completed each
step successfully (conversion) and where they dropped off if they did (abandonment).
Marketing would use this data to experiment, optimizing certain steps along the
funnel (through messaging, UX tweaks, etc.) to increase overall conversion rates.

A long funnel considers the steps *before* a visitor arrives: the ecosystem of sites you
don't own where prospects are talking and market opinions are forming. The performance and availability of those sites may also have an impact on your business. You
may have to measure external sites that comprise your long funnel so that you can
identify external factors that affect your KPIs.

Monitoring for heavy spikes in mentions is one way to tell when you're about to be
Reddited or Kutchered, giving you time to move popular content into frontended
caches, bring up cloud resources, or deploy additional CDN capacity.

Tying Together Mail and Conversion Loops

If you open your inbox, you'll likely find that much of what's there isn't email. It's
password recovery messages, Facebook updates, Twitter notifications, receipts, and
more. Our inboxes have become the log for our online lives, and our email address
is the closest thing consumers have to single sign-on.

Putting aside the terrifying security implications of this for a minute, consider how
important an email is in user enrollment. To enroll in a site, a user must receive an
email, open it, and click on a link. That legitimate registration message is competing
with a deluge of spam filters and blacklists.

If you're responsible for the performance and availability of the website, you should
include the health of these external loops for enrollment, invitation, and status
updates. Email monitoring isn't strictly web ops, but it's certainly a close cousin.

You'll need to track bounce rates, open rates, and other email delivery metrics if you want a complete understanding of the user experience.

The Capacity/Cost/Revenue Equation

One aspect of cloud computing that will change capacity planning is elasticity. In the past, IT operators had to decide how much infrastructure they could afford and then measure user experience to see what latency was like. In a truly elastic model, however, infrastructure is fluid. By spending more on cloud platforms, CDN services, bandwidth, and so on, they can offer a better visitor experience. But this improved experience comes at a price. Instead of defining how much capacity there is, operators will start to decide what kind of user experience they can afford.

Now consider the research we've seen showing a relationship between user experience and revenues. We know that a faster site means more money.

Ultimately, there's a "sweet spot" where a site maximizes revenues (because of a good user experience) versus costs (of providing that experience). Call it *cost per visitor-second*—a measurement of what it costs to deliver content to a visitor in a second. In a utility computing world, this is the web ops equivalent of comparing refrigerators based on their efficiency.

In the coming years, we'll concentrate more on metrics such as these, as computing, network, and storage resources become more elastic.

Conclusion

End-user experience is a complex subject, and we've only touched on it here. Ultimately, the experience visitors have on a website is how we tie web operations to the success—or failure—of the business. As the Web becomes the primary channel for many business transactions, stakeholders throughout your organization will start to scrutinize web activity.

Web operators who embrace this increased visibility will thrive, because they're able to translate complex technical data in ways that help the rest of the company to thrive.

## CHAPTER TWELVE

Relational Database Strategy and Tactics for the Web

Baron Schwartz

I HAVE STRONG OPINIONS ON THE TOPIC OF DATABASE ARCHITECTURE, greatly influenced by my experience as a database consultant. The most common questions I'm asked, broadly speaking, are rooted in how to design a good relational database architecture for some product or application. People bring this problem to me in all sorts of different ways: they need help with an application that's currently failing; they want to choose a database for a product they are developing; their website has no redundancy, and they are worried about the risk of downtime. The questions sound different, but they're not.

There are many variations on the theme. In casual conversations, mailing list threads, and Internet forums, the same question is often there, underneath the stated topic. Many websites are partially or fully devoted to web database architectures, directly or indirectly.* Attendees rush to hear gurus from big Internet properties speak on database architectures at conferences. Anyone from a big Internet property is considered an authority, and sometimes even put on a pedestal, as though his experience with one application is the last word for every situation. (Please don't think that my experience is the last word, by the way.)

Why does the question, "How do you build a good Internet database architecture" command such attention? In my opinion, there are two reasons. One, most people have no real idea how to answer it, but they think others do. Two, people think the stakes are incredibly high. Sometimes these two beliefs are true, but as I'll explain later, neither tends to be as true as people think.

* One illustration: Highscalability.com.

There's a large portion of real-world problem domains for which it is not possible to write a simple prescription. The engineering discipline to help with much of the rest is perceived as too hard, is too little understood, is too feared, or simply is not part of the engineering culture of the organization. But in reality, there is a pretty big slice of the pie for which it *is* possible to do real engineering, and another big chunk is quite well served by heuristics and general rules of thumb. Together, I believe these cover most cases. This should make you feel hopeful!

In this chapter I'll discuss all of these points. But it's always best to begin with requirements, so let's see what requirements are important for databases that power websites.

Requirements for Web Databases

Conference attendees who speak about database architectures for large web properties are usually speaking about very large databases. They're often shy about saying exactly how big, but it's usually Really Big. I think this impression stays in people's minds and perpetuates two great untruths:

- Size is a distinguishing characteristic of web databases.

- My website's database is likely to grow very large.

These notions are not true and never have been. First, if you want to see a large database, you should be a DBA for a big traditional corporation, or better yet a scientific research project. Marketing data and purchase history, supercolliders, and telescopes generate more data than human minds are capable of grasping. Second, most websites have pretty small databases, relatively speaking. The "long tail" mostly consists of a data set that's easily handled by a single moderately sized server. Sites such as YouTube and Facebook are rare outliers. Even the most popular Facebook applications are usually hosted on just a handful of database servers.

It's much more useful to tear our eyes away from the excitement of big Internet properties and look at what is really true about them—some of which is also relatively unique—because that drives our discussion of requirements.

Always On

Web databases are usually a 24/7 operation. I almost never see a web database that sits idle overnight. This is a marked contrast to traditional applications, which are often idle when nobody is at work.

Always being on usually means that maintenance and operational tasks are harder to do. You can't simply wait until people go home for the day, and then tear down the server for a hardware upgrade or to run a backup. You have to figure out how to do these tasks without downtime, and in many cases without even adding much extra load on the application.

That being said, I rarely see databases without peak times. So, there's still a pretty good chance that you can run backups or other intrusive operations during a lull in the database activity. This gets harder as the application grows, however, because the tasks start to take longer. And as a web application gets more popular and the market begins to span time zones, you might start to experience several load peaks every day. So, you can't rely on a single daily up-and-down cycle, either.

Mostly Transactional Workload

Most web databases have what people refer to as a "highly transactional" workload. You might also hear this called OLTP (online transaction processing). The name is a bit misleading, because this usually doesn't mean financial transactions are going on. It doesn't even mean there are database transactions in the SQL sense. It usually just means the application is typically doing some mix of reading and writing rows or collections of rows. A lot of Internet applications match the following pattern:

- The application is read-mostly. The read-to-write ratio ranges from 5 or 10 reads for every write, all the way up to hundreds of reads per write.

- There is a mixture of single-row and multiple-row reads.

- Writes generally affect single rows at a time.

That's what a lot of people call a "transactional" workload. This might seem pretty normal to you, but don't assume everyone's workload is like this. For example, an analytical workload is usually bulk inserts, few to no updates, and massive reads involving whole tables at a time. Many databases are built to handle such workloads well, because businesses that need to analyze data often have a tremendous amount of data, and a lot of money to spend on proprietary databases optimized for analyzing it.

The transactional workload means that unless the application is cleverly designed, you can't make it read-only. (It's a very good idea to design for this, but that's a different topic.) From an operational standpoint, this reduces your options in the same way the always-on characteristic does.

Simple Data, Simple Queries

A related aspect is the simplicity of data and queries. Most web applications generate the transactional workload described in the preceding section because the underlying data model is usually not complex. If you diagram a typical web application's data model, you'll probably find a few central tables—usually fewer than 10. Many of these will store classes of data such as users, which are typically accessed one row at a time.

The traffic on the website mostly determines the traffic on the database. A user browses the site, which reads and writes that user's single row in the users table. Browsing the site generally causes it to read collections or ranges of data to render pages. Browsing potentially shows statistics such as the number of friends in your social network, which requires summary or aggregate queries. So, the queries usually fit the following patterns:

- Read and write user rows one at a time.

- Read the user's own data in ranges or collections.

- Read other users' data in ranges or collections.

- Read ranges of rows from tables that relate the user to other users.

- Summarize and count rows about the user's and other users' data.

Ranges and collections of rows are usually SQL queries that limit results to the top N by some criterion, such as newness. These are often paginated, so there can be an offset and a limit in combination. There are different ways to do this in different databases, so I won't show specific example queries.

The operational and architectural implications of this simplicity might not be obvious. But there are two major things to consider:

- Intra-query parallelization doesn't help much. If you were choosing a database for a supercollider project or a huge corporation's business intelligence, you'd probably pick one that can split a query into parts and run it on many CPU processors or cores (or even servers) simultaneously. Queries that just perform primary key lookups typically can't be parallelized effectively.

- If rows are accessed independently, they don't need to live together, and can be partitioned across multiple machines.

In particular, the fact that much of the data access can be partitioned is why "sharded" architectures are possible. But don't jump to the conclusion that I'm advocating for this architecture! It's relatively rare that data is truly easy to partition, even though it might be for certain types of access to the data. This is precisely due to the mixture of access patterns, such as summarizing and counting groups of rows, or reading ranges and collections of data.

Availability Trumps Consistency

Users of web applications are generally not receiving and reconciling monthly statements about their activities on the site, so most web applications don't have strict data integrity requirements. In fact, most of them probably have lots of dirty or invalid data, yet they continue running just fine. In terms of the business need, the most important thing is that the application is available for the user.

In fact, a lot of web applications deal with data that isn't even their own. Facebook applications are a great example. The Facebook terms of service limits the amount of time a user's data can be stored by third parties, so the application is supposed to throw away data that hasn't been used for a while. If the data isn't there, the application has to fetch it from Facebook. Many web applications function partially as big caches for some other service's data.

Sometimes data needs to be correct and consistent. A web application that's handling any money is an obvious example. But even then, relaxed consistency for part of the data is acceptable in many cases.

This feeds into the operational requirements for the architecture. The requirements shift from keeping things correct to keeping things online and available all the time. I have frequently assessed a crazy mess of inconsistent data, estimated the effort to solve it, and asked the client what to do. More often than not, I hear that it's acceptable to just throw away all or part of the data. Or I hear responses such as, "Losing a day's worth of data is a lesser evil than taking the site down for a few hours." A lot of web applications make money from third-party sources such as advertising, so they don't have any data that really matters; the important thing is to keep people using the service so that the source of revenue doesn't get interrupted.

Rapid Development

Traditional applications are rarely built and deployed in days or weeks. But that's the norm for a lot of web applications, which are in perpetual beta these days. I suspect the following will be familiar to many readers: you notice a bug on the site, and because your website is just a copy of your source control repository, you fix it by editing the source files online, and then you check in your changes from the web server. Maybe not all the time, but I suspect most people have developed in production once or twice, at least in extreme cases.

This is possible because a lot of web applications are built in dynamic languages, such as PHP and Ruby. Of course, it's harder to do this with compiled languages such as Java. But even Java applications are often developed and deployed daily or even more frequently.

Most of the time, this doesn't affect the database. But when developers change the database schema, it does. And an application that isn't spec'd out fully in advance, running in beta, can get schema changes pretty frequently. From an operations standpoint, this means your architecture can't assume a static schema. For example, your backup tools and routine jobs will be easiest to maintain if they discover database structures at runtime and work with whatever they find. In other words, maintenance jobs shouldn't be hardcoded to your schema, or they'll be incompatible with a rapid development cycle.

Online Deployment

A related topic is how the changes are deployed. Ruby on Rails has a wonderful concept called *migrations*. Schema and data changes are created as code artifacts, and there's a framework for applying them and rolling them back easily. This is as nice as any system I've seen. Still, even with Rails migrations, you have to build the database architecture to handle the schema changes.

Ideally, table changes should be done online without blocking the application, to meet the always-online requirement. Much depends on your backend database, and MySQL in particular isn't great at this. Most schema changes will lock the table in question, and no schema changes can be done transactionally in MySQL. Some other databases are better at this, but no database is perfect.

Meeting this challenge can be difficult, but it's possible to do. The typical solution I've seen is to have a hot standby server on which you can perform the changes. You then swap the standby and the currently active server and repeat the changes.

Built by Developers

My experience is that there are a lot of phenomenally talented developers, but somewhat fewer people who understand databases well. Perhaps I'm basing that observation on a biased selection—after all, I'm a database consultant, and I'm called in when database expertise isn't available in-house. But I really think this is a typical pattern. A lot of applications are built by developers, without access to a good DBA—sometimes without even a good system administrator.

My experience of working with these people is that they can do magic with their code, but they don't think the way the database thinks. I'm from developer roots myself. I crossed the chasm, and I know how hard it is. Good coding paradigms are so fundamentally different from good database paradigms that the interface between the two systems is often ugly. A lot of smart people know this, so they built frameworks that isolate the developers from the database. After all, why should a person have to think about CREATE TABLE syntax, when the application framework can determine the table structure by inspecting the application's data structures?

And that's the origin of a pattern that frequently becomes a serious problem as an application grows: the database's design and workload are driven by the framework, not by the application. It's often possible to look at the database server and know which framework the application uses—just from the schema or workload characteristics, mind you, without seeing a single query the application is running.

In practical terms, this means the application's database architecture is semidetermined by the choice of application framework. Many of the frameworks aren't particularly flexible, and they impose their designers' choices on the application. These choices are often geared toward making the coding easy and "database independent." For example, Rails wants to add DATETIME columns named updated_at and created_at to every table. In MySQL, there's a more efficient data type, TIMESTAMP, which uses half the space on disk and in memory. But Rails doesn't like to use that data type. Some frameworks like to create GUID (a.k.a. UUID) primary keys for every row. It doesn't matter what database you use, GUIDs are cross-platform database-independent ugly badness!

Another typical pattern I see is that applications built by developers don't have some of the things a good database or system administrator uses to perform work such as capacity planning, troubleshooting, and analysis. In particular, historical performance metrics are often lacking, and the applications are almost never instrumented for performance analysis. Both of these should be requirements when you're architecting your application.

How Typical Web Databases Grow

Most web databases grow through a relatively predictable set of architectural choices in the typical application life cycle. At some point, a growing application just gets bigger than the architecture can support, and the next step is usually determined by the constraints on the system and the depth of understanding of the people who work on it. It's useful to talk about this progression, but I don't want you to peek too far ahead. Sometimes people decide that they're eventually going to be playing a certain end game, and they become determined to skip the intervening steps. This doesn't always go well.

One of the reasons the progression is predictable is that it's logical. Smart people, when presented with the same situation, will often think of and try a relatively small set of solutions.

Single Server

A typical application starts its life on a single database server. (Some even start their lives on a single server, period.) This is actually a really nice situation to be in, if you can pull it off. Having a single server has a lot of benefits:

- There's only a single copy of the data. There's no question about whether you're working with incorrect or different data.

- Configuration is easy. You hardcode your database's hostname into your configuration file, or even the application code, and you're done. (I know that none of you has ever done that, of course.)

- It's cheap. There are no costs for redundant hardware and no extra networking equipment. And the hardware is fully utilized. The moment you have more than one server, one of them will be working harder than the other. Not so with one server.

Figure 12-1 shows a diagram of the typical single-database-server setup.

Figure 12-1. *A typical application that begins its life on a single database server*

The downside, of course, is that you have only a single server! You have no redundancy if something fails. You have to take backups in the middle of the night. Your long-running cron jobs and your application conflict, and once every hour your users experience slow site load times as you recompute summary statistics and search indexes.

Master and Replication Slaves

The next typical step is to add one or more replication slaves. Replication technologies vary among databases, but in general a slave database repeats data modifications that take place on the master, so it has a read-only copy of the master's data. The slave might not be fully up-to-date with the master's changes at all times, depending on the database, the load on the systems, and the types of queries executed.

Figure 12-2 shows a diagram of a master, a single-slave database, and an application server.

Adding a replication slave has a lot of nice benefits. You can divide the read traffic between the master and the slave, which is known as *read/write splitting*. You can use the slave to handle inefficient queries, backups, and other potentially disruptive tasks. This method of adding servers to add capacity is commonly known as *scaling out*. That name distinguishes this technique from *scaling up*, which is what you're doing if you buy more powerful servers. You might also hear these referred to as *horizontal* and *vertical scaling*.

The next logical step is to add multiple replication slaves, as shown in Figure 12-3. Most replication technologies work fine with two or more replication slaves, although some are limited to just a handful before performance becomes a problem. Many also support further slaves—slaves of slaves, two or more levels deep.

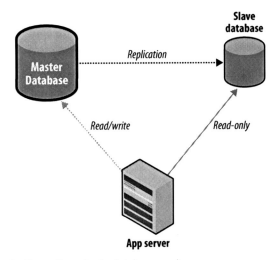

Figure 12-2. *An application with a single database replica*

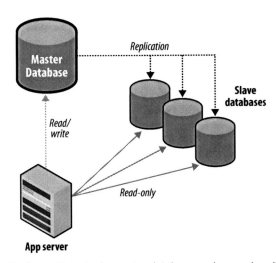

Figure 12-3. *An application with a single master database and several replication slaves*

You can get really fancy with this. And as you add more and more slaves, you add more and more read capacity into your system. But there is a point of diminishing returns in several dimensions.

The first dimension is related to your application's ratio of reads to writes. Applications that are mostly reading data from the database tend to scale out better. There is a continuum between fully reads, which scales out linearly (with each new server you get a new server's worth of read capacity) and fully writes, which doesn't scale out at all, because adding replication slaves only means you're duplicating the master's write queries on a bunch of machines. In general, read queries can be scaled through replication because a read is executed on only one machine, but writes can't because they must be executed on every machine for replication to work.

The second way in which you'll see a diminishing return is by how busy the master is with writes. In a perfect system the master's writes are repeated exactly on the slaves, so if the master is 50% busy with writes, the slaves are, too. (For various reasons, this perfect system doesn't exist, but let's pretend.) As the application grows and the number of writes in the system increases, the master's write workload squeezes its read capacity more and more. And exactly the same thing happens on the slaves; they spend all their time writing and have no spare energy for read queries. As the master reaches its limits, the effectiveness of scaling out with replication drops sharply.

The third limitation is operational cost and complexity. Managing a collection of servers is much harder and more expensive than managing one server. Even with nice tools to help you automate system administration tasks across the many servers, the cost and effort are significant. One of the most important things to think about is the number of places your system can fail. It's a pretty simple calculation. Suppose the mean time between failures on your servers is a year. If you have 12 servers, you can expect a failure every month; with 24 servers, you're going to be dealing with failures every two weeks. And in a replication scheme, slave servers are dependent on their masters. If the master fails, you can choose to promote a slave into its place, but this is far from a seamless operation in most replication systems. And when your replication tree is more than one level deep, a master can be responsible for the failure of all the slaves below it, which can be considerable.

The final drawback I'll mention is application complexity. Going from one to two sources of data is a significant shift for most applications. The application has to connect to potentially many places to run queries. Connection pools, load balancers, and similar technologies can shield you from this to an extent, but ultimately the application is still exposed to at least some of the complexity.

One of the biggest sources of complexity is asynchronous replication, which is a hall-mark of MySQL in particular.* *Asynchronous* means the writes complete on the master and are then sent to the slave to execute sometime later. As a result, the slaves always lag the master by some amount, even if it's tiny. And this matters a lot. The typical scenario is that the application performs some write on the master and then reads from the slave, expecting to see the same data, and it's not there yet. The result can range from an inconsistent user experience to data integrity problems.

There generally just isn't a magical solution to fix this problem. The application has to be built to handle delayed replication. There are many techniques for managing read/write splitting. Some are simple, some are complex. The simplest one that I've

---

* This is not uniquely true of MySQL. I've seen problems with asynchronous replication on other platforms, too, such as Microsoft SQL Server.

seen actually work is just checking the replication delay on the slaves and not using the slave if the delay is too high. But this is very clumsy. The simplest technique that works well in my opinion is session-based splitting. After a user makes a change, all of that user's queries are directed to the master for some period of time afterward. The timestamp at which it's considered safe to query the slave again is usually stored in the session.

There are a number of other ways in which replication is a difficult or inefficient approach. For example, having multiple copies of your data on disk and in memory is wasteful. But I think the preceding points illustrate the most common things I've seen people stumble over.

Functional Partitioning

I mentioned that replication can scale only reads, not writes. As an application gets bigger, the write workload eventually gets too intensive for some part of the system to handle. What fails first depends on the technology you're using. In MySQL, the typical symptom of scaling past your limits is that the replication slaves can't keep up with the master anymore. This is characteristic of asynchronous replication. In databases with synchronous replication or trigger-based replication, the master can be subjected to significant extra load because of replication, or the master can spend a lot of time waiting for slaves to execute the changes it sends to them, and so the master can show the strain first. In all cases, however, there is a weakest link.

At this point, a lot of people I've worked with choose what I call *functional partitioning*. They know their application intimately, and they realize that if they separate some parts of it from others, they could grow those independently. This is often accomplished through some combination of replication slaves and entirely separate servers. For example, on a blogging service, you might segregate the commenting functionality into its own servers.

Functional partitioning can work extremely well, especially when combined with replication slaves. Many applications grow very large indeed, without doing anything more complex than judiciously moving parts of the system onto separate servers and then scaling those independently. Special-purpose servers can also be more efficient than servers that are expected to handle a mixed workload, so sometimes there is less waste.

From the operations side, the application's functionality can also be treated independently when pieces of it live in different places. For example, if you want to take the comment servers down for a hardware upgrade, it's much easier if you can simply switch a configuration variable that puts comments into read-only mode for a bit. Users are less likely to get upset about comments being read-only than they are about the entire site being in degraded or offline mode.

The downside is the added complexity. Now the application has more places to get its data, and the operations team has to keep those servers running right. Backup jobs, server deployment scripts, documentation, and many other things can be more complex and costly to maintain. And ultimately, the architecture is still not infinitely scalable, because any one piece of a major application can grow larger than a single master and slaves can handle. For those applications, the most popular choice is sharding.

Sharding, or Horizontal Partitioning

Sharding—the dreaded *S* word! Actually, in my experience a lot of people don't dread sharding, but they should. In recent years, *sharding* has become a buzzword. Everyone seems to think it's the ultimate way to build an application, and that's just not true. I will treat this topic rather lightly, for two reasons. One, I will venture a guess that you're already more familiar with sharding than you are with functional partitioning! Two, all things considered it's just not the best architecture for a lot of web applications.

Sharding, or horizontal partitioning, is a way of breaking a single logical data set into many pieces and distributing it across more than one server. All the pieces are logically and functionally the same, even though they contain different subsets of the data.

The primary design goals and advantages of a sharded architecture are twofold. One, it enables write scaling. Because replication doesn't help you scale writes, if your application gets more writes than any single server can perform, you'll have to shard to reduce that write workload. The write workload must be divided onto completely segregated sets of servers; the writes from the servers in one shard can't be replicated to the servers in another. The second goal and advantage is the ability to add more capacity as the data set grows. A properly designed sharded architecture can scale linearly with added servers, if you're lucky. There's ideally no interaction between servers in different partitions of the data set, and thus you don't add overhead when you add servers.

Some applications lend themselves well to this paradigm, and if yours does, you should consider yourself fortunate. A typical example is a multitenanted application, where each client's data is completely separate. You can assign data to shards by assigning a client to a given shard. The client's ID becomes the "sharding key." To find out where to query, all you need is the client's ID and some way to find out what server(s) that maps to.

Unfortunately, it's not always that easy. Many applications don't have a single clear sharding key upon which the data set can be partitioned. Mixed sharding schemes often becomes necessary in this mode. Sometimes the data has to be divided into different logical subsets that are sharded on different keys. Some data duplication and denormalization is often required.

A lot of queries also become hard or impossible in a sharded architecture, too. For example, queries that need to access data about all clients typically have to be run separately on each shard, and then aggregated together in the application code.

Sharding is also tough to add into your application unless it's built in from the start. From the operations point of view, complex and often difficult jobs become necessary, such as moving data from one shard to another to rebalance the load. Taking part of the data offline and moving it is hard.

There are many other shortcomings and complications in a sharded architecture. Even things such as choosing primary key values can be tough. If you're relying on an automatically increasing number generated by the database, for example, that usually won't just work seamlessly across multiple servers. All of these problems are solvable, but it can be complex, difficult, and expensive. And the solutions that look easy can turn out to be riddled with gotchas.

Caching Layer

Caching isn't strictly a relational database architecture, but it's a natural addition. The goal of a caching layer is to prevent queries from reaching the database. Most caches are dumb, fast, simple key-value data stores. There's usually no authentication or other complexity. You can add a caching layer to your application architecture at any stage in its life cycle, and the sooner the better, really.

The canonical example is memcached. If you haven't heard of memcached, just think "big distributed in-memory hash table that's reachable through the network." (If you're a Python programmer substitute "dictionary" for "hash table.")

There are different kinds of caches. The typical idiom is to use memcached as a passive cache: you look in the cache for the data you want, and if it's not there you fetch it from the database and store it into the cache for next time.

The primary advantages of a caching layer are that it's super-easy and simple. For example, memcached has only a handful of configuration options. It's not really tunable because there isn't much to tune! It's also quite fast.* Operationally speaking, memcached is almost a no-brainer.

As a developer, you should think about two main complexities. One is the thundering herd problem. Suppose a busy application has a heavily used value in the cache, and it expires. All of a sudden, a whole bunch of application requests notice it's not there and send queries to the database to regenerate it. In reality, only one of those requests was necessary. There are a few ways to mitigate this; you can get some ideas from *http:// highscalability.com/strategy-break-memcache-dog-pile*. The other common gotcha is what happens when you add or subtract memcached servers. It's possible for a change to the list of servers to cause requests to go to different servers than they previously did; causing a sudden spike of cache misses. To avoid this, use a consistent caching algorithm.

---

* But not so fast that you don't have to think about how you're using it; that's a common myth.

From the operational standpoint, you need to think about redundancy and availability of your cache servers, just as you do with any other servers. But memcached is significantly simpler to administer than a database server.

The Yearning for a Cluster

At this point, you are probably wondering if I'll ever get around to helping you understand how to choose a good database architecture for your application, or if I'm just going to keep telling you about more and more choices and explaining why they are all complex and there's no simple answer. Well, yes. I'll do both. I have one more thing to cover—and it's very important—and then I'll tell you about some database architectures that I consider to be reasonably good bets.

The topic of clustering is absolutely vital to cover, for two reasons:

- Right now no good clustering option is available for most web database use cases, and I am not sure that'll change anytime soon.

- Everyone goes through a phase of pinning her hopes on something with the word *cluster* in its name. I did it myself, and I've seen a lot of others do it, too.

When applications start to have trouble of one kind or another, or when managers start to ask hard questions about high availability or scalability, people's thoughts turn to clustering like a young man's thoughts turn to love in springtime. Everyone has a vague notion of the word *cluster* in the beginning. People dream of some amorphous, magical system that takes a whole bunch of servers and makes them look and act like a single server. This works fine for web servers, but not for databases.

The fundamental reason people hope for a cluster to solve their problems is that things are so easy when you have just one server. When you add in more than one server, you have to think about all sorts of hard problems. Splitting reads and writes, how to deal with the bigger and bigger problem of failed servers, and all sorts of other things rear their heads. Why can't life stay simple?

The CAP Theorem and ACID Versus BASE

Let's define *simple* before we begin. Applications that have a single database server are simple in three ways that really matter:

- There is only one copy of the data. Everything looking at the data has a completely consistent view of the world.

- The data is available if the database server is available.

- All of the data is in one place, so you don't have to think about where to find it.

Now why can't there be a simple system that lets you have these three properties and store your data on a cluster of servers? Alas, it's been proven impossible. There's a principle called CAP, which stands for Consistency, Availability, and Partition Tolerance. The principle states that you can have any two, but not all three.* So, as soon as you distribute your data across multiple machines, you run the risk that there'll be some kind of problem, and at least one of your desired properties will no longer be true.

CAP is related to ACID. Database users are probably familiar with this acronym, which stands for Atomicity, Consistency, Isolation, and Durability. An ACID database is reliable and comforting to work with. You can just take for granted that the database is going to protect you from weird things, such as incorrect outcomes from two users manipulating a bank account balance at the same time, or your changes being destroyed after the database says they're complete. Databases typically provide these nice guarantees through transactions, locking, and redo logs. But the moment you distribute your data across a bunch of servers, the guarantees go out the window. Even distributed transactions can't really be proven to work—the failure scenarios are still there, they're just less likely.†

So, if a clustered database can't deliver ACID properties, what can we get? The answer is the cleverly named BASE, a more recent acronym that stands for basically available, soft state, and eventual consistency. You can read more about this at *http://queue.acm .org/detail.cfm?id=1394128*. The key takeaway is that ACID is about consistency foremost, whereas BASE is more concerned with availability. Wait a minute, that sounds familiar, doesn't it? Didn't we talk earlier about how availability trumps consistency for web applications?

At this point, we need to stop using the word *cluster* loosely, because there is a problem with it. The problem is that people mean different things when they say "cluster." They have different requirements in mind.

Some people think a cluster is a means to improve performance by distributing work across servers. Others want a cluster to provide redundancy and high availability by having standby machines to replace servers that fail. There are literally about 10 different major clustering paradigms, all with different properties, so the belief that "a cluster" will solve all problems is not grounded in reality. The unqualified use of the word *cluster* is one of the biggest communication problems in databases today.‡

* See *http://citeseer.ist.psu.edu/544596.html* for the proof.
† Distributed transactions rely on a transaction coordinator and a multistep commit protocol, which is susceptible to communication failures that can't be eliminated. See *http://en.wikipedia.org/wiki/ Byzantine_fault_tolerance*.
‡ Hmm, everything is a freakin' communication problem, isn't it?

I never was able to clarify this, but Josh Berkus, one of the PostgreSQL core team members, did it for me. He defined the use for cases for clusters in terms of the users, rather than the types of clusters.* Josh posits that there are exactly three different types of cluster users: the Transactional User, the Analytical User, and the Online User. His description of the Online User is almost a perfect match for the requirements we've been discussing for web database architectures. To quote and paraphrase a bit:

> Some data loss is tolerable. Online User needs very predictable response times for very simple queries. Each node, whether the second or the 900th, needs to add the same amount of throughput to the cluster. Online User also needs his cluster to support easy deployment of schema and application changes.

With that in mind, let's look at the clustering options available for MySQL, the database with which I'm most familiar, and arguably the most popular database for web applications.

State of MySQL Clustering

When MySQL users start to think about clustering, they find out that there's something called, naturally, MySQL Cluster. They experience a surge of hope. Hey! This thing must take MySQL servers and cluster them together! Unfortunately, that's not exactly what it does. What it really does is use the MySQL server as a frontend to a completely unrelated piece of software called NDB. NDB stands for Network Database. It is a very fast, distributed, shared-nothing, highly available database. And it has completely different properties and limitations from MySQL. In the broadest sense, it doesn't perform well for joins and GROUP BY queries, and web applications need those.

From an operations standpoint, NDB is complex, and the skills and knowledge to run it well are hard to find and expensive. I work with Yves Trudeau, one of the foremost NDB experts in the world. There are literally only a few people with that level of expertise. You can't hire one for 60 grand a year.

In my opinion, it's actually kind of a shame that there is a product called MySQL Cluster. People waste a lot of time and money trying to make it solve problems it can't solve. Most of the time when people call us up for consulting advice on MySQL Cluster, it's simply the wrong product for them.

Given that MySQL Cluster is not what's needed for most web applications, let's look at what else is available.

DRBD and Heartbeat

DRBD replicates block devices between servers. It copies modified blocks over the network to a standby server. If the active server fails, Heartbeat activates the standby

---

* You can read Josh's article at *http://it.toolbox.com/blogs/database-soup/the-three-database-clustering-users-35473*.

server. This typically involves running filesystem recovery to get the filesystem into a consistent state, and then starting the database server.

From an operations standpoint, DRBD is very nice. It "just works." But it doesn't satisfy the needs of a typical Online User. It is not designed for the kind of high-availability requirements a typical web application has. Instead, it's best suited for ensuring that you don't lose data—it's focused on consistency, not availability. In particular, if you're using it with MySQL, you need to use a transactional storage engine for your tables, such as InnoDB or XtraDB. The failover process looks like this: you start MySQL, and the storage engine has to run its recovery process to bring the data into a consistent state. This takes some amount of time. But even worse, then the database server has to warm up. A big database with a large buffer pool can take many hours to warm up fully and is really unusable for production traffic in the meantime.*

The other problem is that a DRBD-based cluster doesn't improve performance. Web applications need uptime and performance; DRBD-based clusters deliver consistency instead, with a performance cost and a long downtime upon failover.

Master-Master Replication Manager (MMM)

MMM is a set of Perl scripts that manage replication and virtual IP addresses to provide a pseudocluster for MySQL. They are hosted at *http://mysql-mmm.org/*.

The application servers connect to the virtual IP addresses, rather than to the server's permanent IP address. When there is a problem with a server, MMM moves the virtual IP address to a server that is healthy. It also moves replication slaves away from a failed master, to a master that is working. It lets you take servers offline manually for operational tasks such as maintenance.

In theory, this system is a reasonable fit for the requirements of a web application. It's essentially just a lightweight, best-effort helper tool that tries to keep the application connected to servers that are functioning well. It lets you design for high performance by scaling out with multiple replication slaves, and you get high availability by having hot standby servers—servers that are up and running, serving queries, warmed up and ready for production traffic. There are minimal efforts to avoid some common scenarios that can make the data inconsistent: standby servers are in read-only mode, for example.

The downsides are several. There is a fairly broad set of failures it can't handle gracefully, because MySQL's replication is not very robust itself. In these cases, replication is likely to fail and/or the data is likely to become inconsistent. The tools themselves aren't very resilient to failures in their environment. There are architectural shortcomings such as the use of agents, which introduce points of failure, and the tools have

---

* At the time of this writing, XtraDB has just gained the ability to save and restore the state of its buffer pool.

a history of being buggy in ways that show up at inopportune times, such as when there's a problem with the network. The tools are also a bit hard to configure and use correctly. If you'd like to form your own opinion about MMM, I suggest browsing the mailing list and looking at what types of questions and problems people write about.

Heartbeat with replication

If MMM can't manage replication and virtual IP addresses perfectly, what about Heartbeat? Heartbeat is nothing if not tested and reliable. It seems that it should be well suited for this task.

There are actually two versions of Heartbeat. The old version lacked the flexibility required to manage a best-effort high-availability cluster. For example, it didn't have statefulness, which is needed to avoid problems such as flipping back and forth between failed servers. Unsupervised failback is a recipe for disaster. A MySQL server with a replication problem is in a delicate state that could be rescued by an astute human, but there's almost zero chance that a tool can successfully handle all of MySQL's replication failure scenarios. Thus, for high availability, you need a system that never automatically fails back to a server once it has failed away from it.

The newer version of Heartbeat, which is called Pacemaker, is said to be flexible enough that it should be a good platform to build scripts for managing replication. To tell the truth, I was intimidated by its complexity although I've been assured it's not that bad once you learn it. Still, as far as I know no one has yet written the scripts to make Pacemaker perform the kinds of tasks that MMM can, so at the time of this writing I believe you're on your own if you want to go this route. You'll have to build the functionality to move IP addresses around in response to failures and replication delay, toggle servers from read-only to read/write and back, move slaves from one master to another (potentially after their master has failed and you can't find out information about its replication state), and handle a large variety of special cases. The task is much more complex than it might seem.

Replication delay is still a complex problem to handle, regardless. It must be handled at least partially at the application layer unless you have no consistency requirements, which is very rare and probably not true of your application.

Proxy-based solutions

There's a selection of proxy-based, man-in-the-middle solutions, with MySQL Proxy foremost among them. HAProxy is another popular one. These tools introduce a piece of software that your application connects to as though it's the MySQL server itself. This is fundamentally different from Heartbeat and MMM, which merely manipulate IP addresses from the sidelines.

Some proxies, such as MySQL Proxy, actually understand the MySQL protocol itself and intercept, interpret, and pass along messages. This gives the opportunity to rewrite the messages and inspect the responses, which can be handy in a lot of cases. For example, it lets you write rules about which server the query should go to, based on whether it modifies data or whether the connection is inside a transaction. Other tools might just pass along the TCP traffic without peeking inside it. HAProxy is an example of this.

A not-so-obvious proxying solution is a traditional load balancer. I've seen people pin their hopes on load balancers that promise to be super-smart and solve all problems magically. Unfortunately, no matter how smart it is or how many tens of thousands of dollars it costs, a load balancer is functionally the same as a proxy, and in fact most load balancers provide little to no functionality that's specific to database traffic.

Proxy-based solutions still don't solve the replication delay problem as optimally as needed. They also introduce a single point of failure and can affect performance, although perhaps not unacceptably much.

InfiniDB, Galera, Tungsten, and ScaleDB

There's an emerging breed of clustering systems that might be of interest. However, none of these is a magical, transparent solution for every problem. Most of them are special purpose. Some are not at all suitable for our Online User. If I knew any of them was a really promising solution, I'd say so, but at this time I'm not sure of that.

Summary

The short version of all of the preceding information is that there just isn't a perfect one-size-fits-all answer. Some systems solve specific problems very well; others are mediocre at a broad range of use cases; others are just not much good, period. It's not a completely unsolvable problem, and there's much room for improvement and lots of opportunities for someone to develop a killer app for at least some use cases, but it's much harder than you'd think it is.

As an example, Amazon RDS is trying to build a system that just scales, in a way that's relatively transparent to the user. Even in this controlled environment, where Amazon has so much ability to limit or exclude things that make generic clustering really hard, it's not a solved problem.

I'd also like to point out that there is a lot that I don't know—a lot of technologies whose capabilities I'm not familiar with. No one can be an expert in everything. But in my experience, the best database architectures are purpose-built for the application they must serve, and the responsibilities that a cluster is expected to fulfill are distributed throughout the database, network, and application layers, with a healthy dose of operations involvement and glue software to bind the pieces together.

Database Strategy

I've been writing a lot about generalities, trying to lay the groundwork for a good architecture. Let's shift gears. Let's move from the abstract into the concrete and see how to choose an architecture that serves well for a lot of Internet architectures. I'll start with what I think are realistic requirements for a database architecture (remember, you can't have it all), and then tell you what I think are some reasonable and safe options to pursue.

Architecture Requirements

As always, you're much better off to define your requirements, and specifically, to document what's out of scope and therefore someone else's problem. If you have this clear, you'll do everyone a big favor. The sooner you decide who should focus on solving issues the sooner this person can budget and plan for it. So, let's create an imaginary web application as an illustration and list the requirements for it informally.

Our mythical application will be always-on, 24 hours a day. There will be spikes and peaks in the traffic. There'll be two daily peaks as the East and West coasts of the United States wake up. We will have high enough peaks that we'll be able to do maintenance operations in the slow periods, but we won't be able to go offline. We'll only be able to reduce our capacity to perform these operations. Downtime will directly affect the bottom line. In the future, we'll expand into Europe and Asia, thus making it even less feasible to take downtime. We'll have seasonal spikes, and we might even get mentioned on the front page of some popular website and slammed with traffic. That's OK—we'll degrade our functionality rather than crashing.

We'll have 95% reads and 5% writes. Most writes will be single-row, but we're going to have to do some complex queries. These will be costly enough that we'll be forced to precompute some summaries or denormalize some data, which will be an intensive process. We'll amortize the cost of those slow analytical jobs across an entire day and deal with the slightly stale data. Sometimes it'll be OK to use the stale data, and sometimes we'll have to build incremental updates to it as the day passes.

The schema is not fixed; the application is immature and there'll be rapid development, including schema changes. As a result, online deployment is a must. We're going to have to run ALTER TABLE in production routinely, and it can't affect availability. We know that our data will get big, and ALTER is going to take much longer than we can tolerate.

Growing load will push us past the capacity of a single server. How far doesn't matter, because only three numbers matter: zero, one, and many. However, we don't think this application will grow to Internet scale. We're probably looking at somewhere between a handful and a few dozen servers, tops.

Data loss is acceptable, up to a point. If we lose a server for a while, we'll lose a small amount of money, but we won't face any regulatory agencies. However, we strongly desire the database servers to be highly available. We want no more than a day of combined downtime each year. Five minutes of downtime is more expensive than losing five minutes of data.

For disaster recovery purposes, we want the ability to recover to yesterday's data in the worst case, and in most cases we much prefer to be able to recover to something pretty recent, hopefully losing no more than a few seconds' worth of data. We'd like the recovery process to take no more than an hour in the common case; in the worst case, such as catastrophic loss of data or servers, we certainly want recovery to take less than a day.

There is general competency with databases on the team, but the team is really Ruby on Rails experts, so advanced database topics will need outside help. The system administration team is also very good but again not very specialized in databases.

With that in mind, let's see how to achieve these requirements.

Easy wins

Before beginning to look at specific architectures, I'd like to point out a few things to plan for, regardless of the eventual architecture:

- The first thing you should do is add a caching layer. Memcached is so easy to use, and makes it possible to offload so much work from the database, that it's silly not to use it.

- Don't let users create outlier situations, such as having 10,000 friends or 100,000 photos. Restrict the size of key areas you expect to be expensive by disallowing unlimited functionality, and you'll keep things much saner without angering anyone who matters. Do this in advance, so there are no surprises and it just becomes part of the user's experience.

- Be careful with requirements. Don't hold yourself to higher standards than your users expect. Don't build expensive functionality into the application. Showing the exact number of search results and the precise pages within them is a classic mistake. Google doesn't do it, so you don't need to either.

Safe-Bet Architectures

The following are some database architectures that in my experience are relatively safe bets:

One master and many slaves
> The classic way to scale a read-heavy application is to make copies—sometimes many copies—of your data, and it works very well. Use the replication slaves to offload the master and perform intensive operations.

> Add one more slave than you think you need for your routine operations, and specialize it. Take backups from it, and restore those backups back onto it to test them. Use it to run intensive cron jobs that summarize the data as needed for analytical queries, and then export the results and bulk import them to the master. Use a session-based read/write splitting strategy to offload SELECT queries from the

master, and do this as early as possible in your application's life. If a slave fails, you simply perform its work on another slave, because slaves should be identical. You can use a variety of load balancers for this simple type of failover.

Although this architecture is great, it still has some pain points: there's no easy way to perform offline schema changes, because they'll generally have to be done on the master, which will block access to the table that's being altered. And when the ALTER TABLE command replicates to the slaves, they'll become delayed in replication, and jobs you've offloaded from the master will become stale or delayed. Master failover is hard to automate in a master-slave architecture, because the master and slaves are not identically configured, so you can look forward to manual failover if the master fails. However, this is really not such a bad single point of failure. As you get more slaves, it'll be much more common for slaves to fail than for the master to fail.

Master-master replication, plus slaves

This is really just the same as using a master and slaves, but the master also happens to be a slave itself. The major advantage of this architecture is that you can build easy failover and failback between the co-masters. This solves irritating pain points such as the need to make schema changes online. The major disadvantage of this architecture is the risk of writing to both masters and causing some kind of inconsistency in the data, which is hard to prevent and hard to solve. Unless you're really careful and strict with privileges, you can almost count on a mistake causing this to happen someday.

Functional partitioning

As the application grows, this is a good idea. Move off the costliest parts of your application to specialized servers or clusters of specialized servers. For example, get session storage off the master; I frequently see the "session" table consuming a disproportionate amount of time. Create a different cluster for the analytical queries, and use the same export-import strategy to load summarized results back onto the main application cluster if needed. Use Sphinx or Solr clusters for search. Time and good instrumentation will tell you what the costliest parts of your application are, so it's fine to delay if you're not clear on that in advance. This architectural choice can come later in the application's life.

In addition to the basic safe-bet architectures in the preceding list, I consider the following suggestions to be very safe. As in anything, once you learn the rules you can often find cases where they should be broken, but I think these ideas shouldn't be disregarded without a very good reason.

Failover and load balancing

Use a load balancer or floating virtual IP addresses. Failover is hard, as you know. Use your expensive load balancer if you have one, or just use a peer-based solution that moves IP addresses around among the servers—it'll work just as well if done properly and is less expensive.

Don't use DNS or application logic. These practices can seem like a good idea at first but quickly turn into a nightmare. It's usually OK to use DNS to look up IP addresses, but don't use DNS itself as a way to build failover—in other words, treat DNS as static, and don't build a system that relies on changing DNS, configuration files, code in your application, or anything like that.

Don't automate too much. Read-only servers are easy to fail over; writable servers are hard. Don't try to build automatic failback. Some things should be done by humans. It's better to be paged at 3:00 a.m. to do a failover than to be paged at 6:00 a.m. and spend the next three days without sleep, trying to recover data.

ACID is still relevant

Use all-transactional systems from the start. The assumptions of nontransactional systems can become deeply embedded in your application code and can be very difficult to find and solve. Switching to a transactional system later causes trouble with deadlocks, lock wait timeouts, and other unexpected behavior.

High availability requires fast and reliable crash recovery, so in MySQL, use InnoDB as your storage engine, but don't use foreign keys, triggers, views, or stored procedures because they cause various problems with replication, performance, backups, and a host of other things. Don't use MyISAM for any read/write data, because it's not crash-safe and takes ages to recover.

Use the right tool

The database can become the hammer for every nail. This is not a great idea. Keep the database out of the critical path. Don't use it for a queue, for example. (A queue just doesn't map well onto a database, and it's one of the most common trouble spots I've seen.) Don't make your application depend on the database for things such as configuration information, static lookups that ought to be cached or stored in your application code, or storing images. The database should store the data, not the application itself.

Treat the database simply, because it's your hardest-to-scale and most expensive resource. Do as much with files and cron jobs as you can. For example, presummarize data before you put it into the database. Simple scripts or GNU command-line utilities can be orders of magnitude faster than using a database! Learn your core utilities, such as sed, awk, sort, and uniq. This attitude is fundamentally opposed to what you may have learned in the world of Oracle or SQL Server, where the application is just a bit of presentation logic on top of a massive database full of tables, views, triggers, stored procedures, and every iota of business logic. This centralization is sometimes appropriate in complex businesses, and I've worked in that environment myself. But I'll defend my view in the realm of web applications: separate the application and the database, and use the database only to store and retrieve data.

Risky Architectures

Here are architecture and design patterns that I have seen a lot of problems with. Some are useful in very limited circumstances, if you really know what you're doing. If so, you probably don't need to read this chapter. But to the extent that it's safe to make blanket statements, I'd advise you not to use these architectures.

Sharding

It's pretty common to hear someone give the advice to "shard early, shard often." My advice is quite different: I say don't shard unless you have to. If you have enough experience to know that you'll have to shard, prepare for it, but still defer it until you need it. Here are some of the problems with sharding.

The main problem with sharding is that it's become popular, and people are doing it way too early and often. Most of the systems I've seen where sharding was either in use or being considered didn't need it at all—they simply needed to take full advantage of the power of the commodity hardware available these days. In my opinion, it is very foolish to decide that a mid-size application has to be infinitely scalable, and attempt to build it on a sharded architecture across hundreds of low-performance machines, instead of just buying a few decent commodity machines and thinking a bit about the engineering. For every wide-eyed person pointing to a sharding success story (and I've been one of those myself), I can show you large applications built without sharding by a handful of smart people. My colleagues and I have also seen behind the scenes of a lot of the most popular sharded applications and witnessed tremendous wasted resources.

Sharding also tends to create an architecture that can be significantly more expensive than you expect, even in the short-to-near term, and definitely in the long term. Examples of this include failing to build for rebalancing, or taking too-simple approaches such as using a simple modulus for the sharding function. It's rather shortsighted to build a sharded architecture that is hobbled by poor engineering and thus fundamentally unscalable. It's also hard to think about and engineer for the really important things, such as common failure scenarios. If you're going to distribute your application across many machines, or even just a handful, you need to really nail failover and failback, for example. You also probably need your application to be very failure tolerant so that it can run in degraded mode if part of the data set is unavailable.

A third problem with sharding concerns a risk of overengineering. Most things are hard to do just right. People tend to do them either too much or barely at all. Fear of an architecture that is not flexible enough, or fear of not knowing how to do it right, can easily lead to overengineering. This can cause endless trouble with too much complexity.

Writing to more than one master

One of the most seductive traps to fall into is to believe that you gain anything by making more than one server in a replication topology writable. The usual thought traps are, "I'll get more write performance" or, "All nodes will be equal and failover will be easier." Both are false.

You do not gain performance by writing to both masters in a master-master setup. All writes are sent through replication and must be repeated on every node, so it doesn't matter where they originate.

Because replication is asynchronous,* writing in more than one location is very brittle and is almost guaranteed to cause trouble in failover, application mistakes, programmer mistakes, and a host of other common circumstances. The usual result is lost data and long, sleepless nights trying to get the system back to a reasonably consistent state. You might have a hard time convincing your boss or coworkers that this is a bad idea, but try anyway.

Multilevel replication

Try to stay away from multilevel replication if you can. Your architecture will be much simpler with one master and N slaves, rather than slaves of slaves of slaves. Daisy-chaining slaves has advantages sometimes, but it's best to avoid this if possible. The grand-slaves and great-grand-slaves will be troublesome to manage if anything happens to the intermediate levels between them and the ultimate master at the top of the pyramid. Common problems include replication delay, server crashes, bugs, and network problems.

Ring replication (beyond two nodes)

Avoid it like the plague. The number and complexity of failure scenarios is too much to contemplate. Just a few days ago I got a support call from someone with five servers in a ring. He tried to remove one of the servers and replace it with another, and ended up with a statement going in an infinite loop around the ring. This is just a brittle architecture—a disaster waiting to happen.

Reliance on DNS

I already said this, but it's worth repeating. DNS is flaky and will ultimately bite you. It's OK to rely on DNS for name lookups, but DNS should be regarded as something that stays the same even during a failover. Don't play games with round-robin DNS for load balancing. Similarly, don't use /etc/hosts; it's just another thing you have to version, manage, and deploy atomically.

---

* So-called semisynchronous replication in newer versions of MySQL doesn't solve this.

The so-called Entity-Attribute-Value (EAV) design pattern

Whenever someone calls me and says, "I have a hosted multitenanting SaaS application..." I can finish the person's sentence with "...that uses EAV and is having performance problems." EAV is tempting when you don't know what your final schema is, or when there simply is no final schema. This often happens with "hosted, multitenanting SaaS applications" precisely because the business wants to sell something flexible. They want to tell their customers, "Your data fits into our system, no matter what shape it is." This isn't how relational databases work. You end up with 100-table self-joins very quickly, and the resultant query plans do nothing but random I/O as they seek all over the disk, finding tiny bits of data in indexes and assembling these atomic values into rows—at a snail's pace. You won't even get as far as 100 joins in MySQL, which has a 61-table join limit per query, and actually starts running into trouble before it reaches 20 tables in a join due to the complexity of computing an execution plan.

Database Tactics

Now that we've covered a variety of strategic approaches to create a robust database architecture and seen some things to avoid, let's talk about database tactics. These are day-to-day operational tasks you'll perform to keep that database infrastructure reliable.

This section will focus on getting things done. In contrast to the previous discussion of architecture, where almost everyone reaches intuitively for a handful of obvious and sometimes wrong solutions, there are lots of different ways to do things—so many that I won't spend any time urging you away from long lists of particular tactics. I'll concentrate instead on a few specific things that I think are good to do.

Taking Backups on a Slave

I haven't talked much about backups, so I hope you'll let me lecture just a bit before I go on to the real topic:

- Stop procrastinating on backups. They're not that hard.

- Don't build something awesome; just build something recoverable.

- Document at least the following: acceptable data loss, acceptable downtime, retention policy, and security requirements.

- Practice and document the recovery process. Recovery is more important than backing up!

- You need external verification of a backup job's success or failure. Don't rely on the job itself to notify you.

With the formalities out of the way, let's look at how to use a replication slave for backups.

The first and most obvious thing is to use the slave itself as a backup. Unfortunately, this isn't a real backup. A real backup protects you against problems such as losing a server or part thereof, a malicious attack that corrupts data, and an accidental DROP TABLE. A replication slave doesn't help with the latter two, because it'll merrily replicate the offending changes and duplicate the corruption or loss on its own copy of the data.

So, how do you make a real backup? If you have one replication slave that acts as spare capacity for cron jobs and so on, just stop the database server when you're not using it, and back up its data. I'll be MySQL-specific again here: don't copy InnoDB's files while the MySQL process is running. It doesn't work. If you can shut down MySQL and copy away its data, that's the safest bet for most cases.

If you don't want to stop the server, another option is XtraBackup, a free and open source nonblocking backup program for InnoDB and XtraDB tables. If you have MyISAM tables, there'll be some locking while it copies those. XtraBackup is based on the same principles as InnoDB's own hot backup tool, but it's open source and has additional features.

I used to advise people to use filesystem snapshots, LVM snapshots in particular. They let you create backups without interrupting the database's operation, too. But after more benchmarking, my colleagues and I have drifted away from this recommendation a bit. The problem with LVM is the performance impact, which has turned out to be much higher than we used to believe it was. There are other snapshot-capable filesystems, and one of those is ZFS, but it's relatively new and I am not expert in it, so I have not finished forming my opinion of it. I have some clients who are using Solaris and ZFS, and although it's hard to isolate variables or compare performance directly, I can't say the performance is so obviously good that everyone is thrilled. And the copy-on-write behavior of ZFS brings up a number of complex considerations about how the data is physically organized, which again I haven't had time to really understand well enough to make a responsible recommendation. So, in my mind, the jury's still out on ZFS as a filesystem for databases, and as a result I just don't know of a killer solution for snapshot-based backups in the open source arena.

Lots of databases have a hot-backup capability built in. If yours does, use it. The preceding discussions are mostly about MySQL, which doesn't have this capability and is thus a bit more complex to back up.

In the MySQL world, and possibly in other databases, too, there's another thing you can do with a replication slave: delay it by some amount of time, such as an hour. You can use the mk-slave-delay tool from Maatkit for this purpose. A server that's delayed gives you a "backup" that has two interesting properties:

- It's continually fetching updates from the master but not applying them, which means you have a pretty low chance of losing your data as compared to last night's backup, which could be 24 hours old at the time of a crash. You can simply tell it to finish applying the updates it has fetched.

- It gives you a grace period if something bad happens. That accidental DROP TABLE won't get replayed on your slave for an hour, so you can skip the DROP and switch to using the slave as the primary server while you recover the table on the master, or similar. The extra time gives you lots more options for recovery.

Use a delayed slave in addition to backups, not instead of them. You still need actual backups!

Online Schema Changes

One of the more difficult operational tasks is to roll out schema changes. There are several common scenarios: syncing schema with other changes during a deployment, doing rapid development, and optimizing performance by changing indexes and other structures. If a schema change is a blocking operation, which it generally is in MySQL, this becomes a real problem.

Keeping your tables small is a big help. Archiving or purging data is a good tactic for that, but there are other ways to do this, too. For example, if your application is going to be sharded, you can keep each shard small enough that the individual tables don't get huge. It's also possible to separate data into different tables naturally, such as creating a new table every day for date-based data. Most of these suggestions apply in edge cases, and I'm not suggesting them everywhere, but a little creativity goes a long way.

The newer version of InnoDB (called the InnoDB plug-in), and hence XtraDB as well, offer the ability to add and drop indexes online—and quickly. This is really nice. I still remember the first time I calculated how much production downtime an index change would take, got approval from my client for an hour, ran the command and it took 30 seconds instead—and then I remembered they were using the InnoDB plug-in. I think the InnoDB plug-in version (or XtraDB) is a pretty compelling upgrade, if you're not using it yet.

If your tables aren't small enough that these types of operations are possible, you'll have to do something else. Although it's theoretically possible to use external tools to help by creating a "shadow table" with the desired new structure, and then doing a swap-and-rename at the last instant, I don't think these are really a solution for every possible scenario yet.* So, there are still a lot of cases where swapping servers is the preferred route.

The general idea is to set up a master-master replication pair. Only one of the servers should be writable, of course. Go to the read-only server and execute the change, but prevent it from going through replication to the writable server. You can do this by disabling logging of the change, or simply by stopping the replication process on the writable server. Once the change is complete, make the application fail over in the

---

* Maatkit's mk-table-sync has a --lock-and-rename option, and there's oak-online-alter-table from the openark toolkit.

usual manner so that the reader and writer roles are reversed. Then repeat the change on the other server—perhaps just by restarting replication. In this fashion, you can hide the downtime from the application.

Monitoring, Graphing, and Instrumentation

Building systems for metrics (graphing, application instrumentation) and monitoring (alerting) is a high-value activity. These are very important core bits of infrastructure, and they're not that hard to create, but they are among the most commonly neglected things I see. It's very difficult to be proactive about managing a system that you can't measure. Historical metrics are particularly useful for capacity planning and troubleshooting.

Monitoring and metrics technologies fall into three categories: those that inspect systems and notify when something doesn't look right, those that record metrics and draw graphs of them, and those that try to combine the two functions and end up doing them both badly. I prefer to use two single-purpose systems instead of one that tries to do everything and ends up not being very good at it.

In my opinion, Nagios is good enough for monitoring, even though it has a steep learning curve. RRDtool-based systems such as Cacti, Munin, and Ganglia are good enough for keeping historical metrics. I am a bit biased toward Cacti, not because I think it's great but because I have written some Cacti graphing templates. They are available at *http://code.google.com/p/mysql-cacti-templates/*. I think the MySQL templates are arguably the best available for any graphing system. Regardless, I think it's wise to use a system that's in wide use, so you can find people who can help when you get a little stuck. You might chafe at the limitations of any given technology, but I assure you it's a much harder problem to solve than it appears to be—reinventing the wheel is a favorite pastime of system administrators.

Instrumentation is another topic. Just as MySQL is hard to optimize precisely because it's hard to get detailed diagnostic data about what it's doing, your application's performance can be a tough nut to crack for the same reason. You really need information about the tasks your application does, how many times it does them, and how long that takes. In some cases you don't need to do it yourself. New Relic builds a great product for Rails developers, and most programming languages have profilers that are easy to use. But even simple instrumentation that's targeted toward your specific application's critical activities can be highly beneficial.

Analyzing Performance

You'll almost surely face some performance problems with your database server at some point. I'd like to be able to explain an entire performance-optimization method here, but that's a subject for another book. *Optimizing Oracle Performance* (*http://oreilly.com/catalog/9780596005276/*) by Cary Millsap (O'Reilly) is the best I've seen on that topic.

Analyzing MySQL's performance can be a difficult exercise, but a lot of performance problems will yield pretty quickly to a relatively simple approach that almost anyone with a little aptitude at troubleshooting can follow. The general process is to gather detailed diagnostic data during the time of the trouble, eliminate possible causes, and focus on what appears to be the problem. Often the problem is simply too much load on the server, and that's usually caused by bad queries.

MySQL's so-called *slow query log* is the answer here, not because it collects slow queries but because it has timing information on the queries. You want a version of the server that has microsecond timing granularity. You can get this level of detail only in MySQL 5.1 and later, or in third-party builds of 5.0 such as those provided by Percona or OurDelta (the latter two also include much more information in the log than the standard builds of MySQL do). Configure the log to capture all queries by setting the time threshold to 0. Collect enough data to analyze; during your busy periods a few minutes to a half hour might be enough. Then aggregate the log with Maatkit's mk-query-digest and examine the queries that the default report shows.

If you can't do this, a useful alternative is to capture the queries from the TCP traffic. You can achieve this with mk-query-digest and tcpdump—take a look at the documentation. It's quite simple. You can also use mk-query-digest to analyze your HTTP and memcached "queries" in a similar way, making it very useful for a variety of performance analysis tasks.

If the performance problem can't be blamed on queries, you might need to profile MySQL itself. One of my favorite tools for this is OProfile. To use OProfile, simply initialize and start the profiling daemon with the opcontrol tool. After it runs for a while, you can get a report of any application on the system, or the kernel itself. Here's a sample session, in which I'll ignore the kernel and profile only the MySQL binary:

```
# opcontrol --init
# opcontrol --start --no-vmlinux
# ... time passes ...
# opreport --demangle=smart --symbols --merge tgid `which mysqld`
```

The resultant report can look something like the following, although I have formatted it for readability:

```
samples   %         image name    app name      symbol name
893793    31.1273   /no-vmlinux   /no-vmlinux   (no symbols)
325733    11.3440   mysqld        mysqld        Query_cache::free_memory_block()
102349     3.5644   mysqld        mysqld        my_hash_sort_bin()
76977      2.6808   mysqld        mysqld        MYSQLparse()
52203      1.8180   mysqld        mysqld        read_view_open_now()
46516      1.6200   mysqld        mysqld Query_cache::invalidate_query_block_list()
```

This report is from a real server. A customer called me for help with a strange increase in server load. I was able to determine that all the queries were highly optimized, and there were no problems with I/O or other resources. I could not find a place to optimize the application itself. It just seemed as though MySQL was using too much CPU suddenly. I used OProfile and was able to point to the MySQL query cache very quickly as a source of inefficiency, and indeed disabling it improved performance nicely.

You can use OProfile to find out where any binary spends its time, not just MySQL. There are other tools, including DTrace, but this is what I use most often.

Archiving and Purging Data

Plan to archive and purge your inactive or obsolete data from the very beginning. This helps reduce the size of your "working set." The working set is the data that the database needs often. You could think of it as the data that's accessed 95% of the time. In most applications, this is probably only a fraction of the total data set. I'll use myself as an example. I have an account on Facebook, but I don't use it. I created it only so that I can see my clients' applications in action when I need to help them, and I've probably logged in to it only a few times. I am definitely not in Facebook's working set! Similarly, I think I might have an account on SmugMug somewhere...and FeedBurner...and lots of other services. I never use them.

If you're smart, you can archive users like me. Move us off to slower servers, or just expire our accounts altogether. That way, we don't bloat the size of your working set by being located adjacent to celebrities and teens, whose data your application accesses constantly. Or put our data into separate tables, and bring it back to the regular tables when we log in.

Another category of data you can archive or purge is old historical data. My order history, my old messages, and everything else that is old can be moved off. I used to work at a firm that manages online advertisements. Statistical data about advertisements, such as clicks and cost, was rolled up into daily tables for a while and then expired out. It remained in weekly tables for a longer period. This way, the working set—the most recent data—stayed small.

It's a good idea to move this historical data to another server, especially if your boss doesn't like the idea of just burning it to a CD and deleting it, or if you need it for analytical purposes such as year-over-year reports. You can build a data warehouse server on the cheap with big, slow disks and move it there.

Run those archiving jobs routinely so that your systems don't get "too fat to exercise." Maatkit has a tool for this as well: it's called mk-archiver.

Conclusion

I'd like to conclude this chapter by refocusing your thoughts on what matters most in my opinion: make database architecture decisions based on logic as much as you can, instead of basing them on keeping up with the Joneses or doing something that feels good or cool. A while back, David Fetter and I were having a conversation on IRC. He's a PostgreSQL user and consultant, just as I'm a MySQL user and consultant. Can you see where this is going? I'll paraphrase a bit, to avoid the holy war: we decided that most people choose one database or another based on how they feel about it, rather than on its technical merits.

Similarly, I believe most people make choices about programming languages, database architectures, and other technologies based on what makes them feel happy and safe and productive, or even what makes them feel cool.

We do this because we're human. I am not here to make your life less fun, really. But I encourage you to build your own application, and don't chase after coolness or reinvent the wheel.

Try to build small, not big—go only as big as you're forced to. Determine the application's true requirements, and try to match those as well as possible. Stay away from things that seem clever, in favor of things that have proven to work well. Don't rely on unreliable things, such as DNS. Accept that the state of the art is sometimes lagging, and databases have a long way to go before you'll have a perfectly scalable cluster that just makes all your problems disappear. Cache early and often, but don't shard early and often.

Above all, remember this: take backups. The long-term benefits of backups have been proved by scientists, whereas the rest of my advice has no basis more reliable than my own meandering experience.

CHAPTER THIRTEEN

How to Make Failure Beautiful: The Art and Science of Postmortems

Jake Loomis

AS AN ENGINEER AT YAHOO! DURING THE EARLY DAYS OF THE DOT-COM BOOM,
I lived in a world where features were king and eyeballs were gold. Engineers could do
whatever they wanted with the production site, and the customers were often the first
line of QA. Customers didn't expect the Internet to always work, and they joked about
the *World Wide Wait*. It wasn't until real revenue started to flow in that Internet sites
were forced to grow up. Downtime meant actual dollars being lost, and things such as
email became critical to people's everyday lives.

But like a newly graduated teenager, just knowing you needed to grow up didn't tell
you how to do it. Sites such as Twitter, with a history of downtime, know they need
better uptime if they are going to continue to succeed after their initial burst of new
users. Could a "fast-moving" Internet site really have uptime similar to "slow-moving"
utilities such as power, phone, or cable? Change was the riskiest thing you could do
to a system, and Internet sites often changed production daily. In addition to that,
many of the successful sites were growing at an unprecedented rate, and the Internet
technologies they were built with were new and unproven. Whether it was hardware
solutions continually chasing Moore's Law or novel software solutions bludgeoned
into handling millions more customers than they were ever designed for, sites were
built on unstable ground.

Regardless of the obstacles, customers demanded reliability. The Internet had become
essential and outages were costly. I received my wake-up call years ago when one of
our key business partners was threatening to cancel their highly lucrative partnership
with Yahoo! due to a pattern of outages. We knew we had to get them under control,

and we started by gathering for a postmortem. It was one of the worst postmortems I ever attended. Gladly, we've learned a lot since then.

The Worst Postmortem

The VP started by yelling, "Whose fault is it?!" The room full of engineers stayed silent. Most of them had been up all night trying to fix the most recent incident. The VP started again. "Someone said we had network problems. Why is the network always breaking, and why does it take them so long to fix it? Don't they know how important this partnership is?!" No one from the network team had been invited to the postmortem, so again the room was silent. Finally, one of the managers from another team spoke up and said, "I heard they don't monitor the network very well." The VP and manager then spent the first half of the meeting talking about all the possible problems with the network team. Meanwhile, the engineer who finally fixed the issue by rolling back the most recent code push stayed silent, happy that the heat wasn't on his team for the bad push. The first on-call engineer had initially thought the issue was network related, an easy scapegoat, until they tracked it down to the code push. In the end, the postmortem discussed many ideas for improving everything but the bad code push. Some of the corrective actions were good, some were worthless, but it didn't matter, because none of them were recorded, tracked, or had owners, and they were forgotten the following week when a new issue popped up.

Over my past eight years at Yahoo!, I have been in many postmortems. Luckily, few were as bad as the one I just described. Since then, we have learned to turn our failures into a learning experience. We have developed a rigorous postmortem and operability process, and now, as VP of Service Engineering, I have applied it to applications as large and diverse as Yahoo! Mail, Flickr, Yahoo! Answers, Yahoo! Messenger, and our backend platform systems. As a result, we have dramatically decreased the number of incidents we experience.

Whether it was Yahoo! in its early days or a hot, new startup today, the lessons learned are still the same. The first thing you want to do to make sure your site is stable is to establish a systematic postmortem process. Postmortems allow you to fully understand the nature of the incident after the outage has been stabilized with the primary purpose of preventing reoccurrence and improving the way your organization handles incidents.

In this chapter, I will cover how to run a postmortem, what information you need to cover, and what to do after the postmortem is over, and I'll provide a few examples along the way. These lessons come from attending many postmortems involving numerous applications and very different teams. I've witnessed postmortems that ranged from incredibly effective to dangerously destructive.

Regular postmortems are the closest thing you have to employing a scientific method to the complicated problem of web operations. By gathering real evidence, you can focus your limited resources on solving the issues that are actually causing you problems.

What Is a Postmortem?

A postmortem needs to cover these essentials at a minimum:

1. A description of the incident

2. A description of the root cause

3. How the incident was stabilized and/or fixed

4. A timeline of actions taken to resolve the incident

5. How the incident affected customers

6. Remediations or corrective actions

The first five items make sure everyone involved has a common understanding of the facts. Many incidents reoccur because people do not understand what really happened and how the problem was fixed. Different teams and different layers of management arrive at the postmortem with different understandings of what happened. During a postmortem, everyone with significant involvement in the incident should be present at the same time to document a common description of the facts of the incident. Without an accurate account of the facts, it will be impossible to determine and prioritize the corrective actions that are the biggest benefit of a postmortem.

Determining the root cause should go without saying, but I can't tell you the number of times I have been in a postmortem where participants spent tons of time debating each possible remediation item or the number of customers affected, only to find that they had wasted their time because they didn't have the root cause right.

The same goes for the stabilizing steps. Often during the chaos of a major incident, multiple people attempt multiple fixes. Determine the true root cause and the step that brought it to stable before moving on. Note that an incident might be stable without actually being fixed. You can eliminate customer impact without fixing an issue like when you reboot servers to address a memory leak. Although it will be stable for a short period, the servers are just going to run out of memory again if the root cause is not addressed.

A timeline will be important for determining how the incident could have been fixed more quickly. Again, multiple people may have a different understanding of the timeline. Allow each participant to contribute the items they are aware of before moving to remediation items around decreasing Time to Resolve (TTR). Make sure to answer the following questions:

- When did the incident begin to affect customers? (Note: Not all incidents affect customers.)

- When did someone in the organization first become aware that there was a problem?

- How did this person become aware? Through monitoring? The Customer Care team? A personal report?

- How long did it take for the knowledge of the incident to get to the person who ultimately resolved it?

- What would have allowed someone to diagnose the fault earlier? (For example, better monitoring, more comprehensive troubleshooting guides, etc.)

- Did the stabilizing steps take a long time to implement? Could they be automated or simplified to speed them up?

Reducing the TTR of an incident is every bit as important as eliminating incidents themselves. Ultimately, total customer impact minutes (TTR × Number of Customers Affected) is what counts. Some outages may be unavoidable, but if you can ensure quick recovery, your customers will benefit.

After determining the customer impact, you may want to assign a severity level to the incident. You can develop your own severity categories, or use this example:

Severity 1: site outages affecting a significant number of customers

Severity 2: site degradation, performance issues, or broken features which are difficult to work around

Severity 3: other service issues that have minimal customer impact or easy workarounds

Assigning a severity level will help you to prioritize completion of your remediation items and is also useful during the triage stage of an active incident. You may have already assigned a severity level while attempting to resolve the issue so that you could determine whether it is a five-alarm fire requiring all hands on deck or a minor blip.

When to Conduct a Postmortem

You should conduct a postmortem after every major outage that affects customers, preferably within 24 hours. This is a little more difficult than it sounds. Teams are usually busy. They are especially busy right after an incident occurs, because they probably spent unplanned cycles on firefighting. Some of the firefighters may have been up all night resolving the incident. Once an incident is stable, people have a tendency to get back to whatever they were doing before they were interrupted to try to make up for lost time.

The important thing to note is that until a postmortem is conducted and corrective actions are identified, your site is at risk of repeating the incident. If you can't conduct the postmortem within 24 hours, don't wait any longer than a week. After a week, incident participants will start to forget key details; you may be missing key logfiles; and of course, you remain at risk for reoccurrence.

Although it's good to complete a postmortem within 24 hours, you should not conduct a postmortem while the incident is still open. Trying to determine preventive actions or assign blame is a distraction that teams don't need while they are attempting to stabilize the service. Remember, this process is ultimately intended to benefit your customers, and the process should never directly get in the way of restoring service to them.

Who to Invite to a Postmortem

Make sure the people who know the facts are at the postmortem. That usually means you need the on-call engineers to be present for a postmortem to be useful. If managers are there instead, they need to have the facts at their fingertips and not be there to hide internal problems.

Running a Postmortem

The first thing you need to do when you start a postmortem is to lay down the ground rules. Make sure you tell the participants that the postmortem is not about assigning blame, but rather that the primary purpose is to prevent the incident or similar incidents from reoccurring. Incidents will occur in fast-moving Internet sites. What is important is that we learn from our mistakes.

Start by getting the facts concerning root cause, stabilizing steps, and timeline. This is necessary for a productive discussion of corrective actions and will hopefully calm the nerves of people who might be afraid that the meeting will turn into a witch hunt.

Once the facts are straight, start to discuss what can be done to keep the incident from happening again. Make sure you address the root cause, but also look for ways to fix it faster (lower the TTR). The remediation stage should also consider potential similar incidents. If you ran out of capacity on one set of servers, for example, have remediation in place to add capacity to those servers but also to investigate other servers for similar weaknesses.

Avoid personal attacks. Humans make mistakes, and if that's what caused the incident, move on and look at how the human element can be made more failsafe. Look for automation opportunities, better planning, or simplification of the process.

Make sure participants are coming up with remediations for their own areas. Sometimes people will try to blame other groups or individuals. Ask what they can do to make it not happen again. If someone is providing a trivial response or hiding issues within her area don't be afraid to ask probing questions when the story doesn't quite add up. The remediations should be meaningful and worth spending effort on.

One last piece of advice: sometimes teams that take a postmortem to heart will overcorrect. Avoid the recency effect and make sure your remediations make sense to the overall business. For instance, don't make new software changes so painful and process heavy that the business grinds to a halt just because of a fear of outages. Strive for speed and stability.

Once you have a set of remediations, record them as well as the owner and the date that they will be completed. Too many times I have seen teams devise bundles of great ideas, only to leave them undone when the next bright and shiny object comes up. As a result, they are bitten by the original problem again and again.

Teams can be great at firefighting. But that same ability to quickly jump onto something new can keep them from fixing the items they know need to be fixed. The core of a postmortem is the remediations, and they are worthwhile only if time is taken to implement them.

Postmortem Follow-Up

Remediations should be tracked to completion. Remember that you are at risk for reoccurrence until your remediations have been completed. Make sure owners and due dates are assigned and that owners are held accountable even after the originating event has faded into the past. Marking them as high-priority items in a bug-tracking system or other similar tool will help to ensure that the right information is recorded and not lost.

Often, corrective actions will compete with development resources for prioritization. It is important to have an executive advocate who will make sure site stability is treated with the same level of importance as site features. As an organization, declaring that site stability is a top priority can go a long way toward ensuring that corrective actions are completed. Remediations should be prioritized based on the potential number of likely incidents they can prevent. If one remediation will stop only the exact incident that just occurred whereas another will fix a number of similar possible incidents, the latter should receive higher prioritization and be the focus of engineering efforts.

Additionally, make sure you enter your postmortem data into a tracking tool. Assign a root-cause category to your incidents to allow for data mining and the ability for management to identify long-term trends. We use incident categories such as Hardware Failure, Change Related, Capacity/Traffic Incident, and Preexisting Software Bug to identify buckets of incidents. Then we use the historical data to make wise decisions about how to apply resources and which tools and automation projects to kick off. Apply your resources to the categories with the most incidents to try to drive them down systematically across the organization. Having data with historical outage counts is particularly useful in justifying difficult, resource-intensive projects.

After many years of postmortems, I've found a few areas that you will likely want to consider for corrective actions. I call this *site operability*.

Eliminate single points of failure

Hardware can and will fail. Utilize redundancy to protect yourself. Don't let hardware failure be a cause of a customer-impacting incident.

Capacity planning

Understand your site and its future capacity needs. Base your capacity planning on total utilization of primary constraints such as CPU, memory, I/O, and storage, not on secondary constraints such as number of users. Provision in the areas you need, before you need them.

Monitoring

This is essential for detecting and diagnosing incidents. Other chapters in this book provide great recommendations for monitoring techniques.

Release management

Change is historically the most likely cause of incidents. Make sure your release process has the right quality controls in place. Consider implementing concepts such as automated testing, staging environments, limited production deployments, dark launches (rolling out code without activating functionality for customers until the code is proven stable), and the ability to roll back immediately.

Operational architecture reviews

Hold an architecture review that is entirely focused on how the new release or product will perform in the production environment before rolling it out to customers. Consider maintainability, failure scenarios, and incident response as well as architectural reliability and scalability.

Configuration management

As your systems grow, production configurations become increasingly complicated. The inability to understand the implications of changes to production configurations often leads to incidents attributed to human error. Having a configuration management system that is straightforward and logical will help engineers avoid unintended issues. Read Chapter 5 in this book for more recommendations.

On-call and escalation process

Identify the issue and get it to the person who can resolve it as quickly as possible.

Unstable components

Identify and fix software components with a history of crashing and unintended behavior. Make it a priority even when there is an easy manual fix. Those manual fixes add up to become a drag on customer experience and your ability to scale and be effective.

By proactively ensuring that your site is operable, you will be able to avoid many painful postmortems before they are even necessary.

Conclusion

In the end, postmortems are the most useful way to avoid repeats of incidents. It's understandable for an incident to happen once in a fast-paced environment, but there should be no excuses for it to repeat. By taking the time to clearly understand the facts of the issue and then deciding on, recording, and implementing high-impact remediation items, you can avoid repeat incidents.

Here's how the "worst postmortem" example might have played out if these guidelines were followed:

> The VP starts by saying, "Thank you for resolving the incident last night. The point of this postmortem is to understand exactly what happened and identify the best ways to make sure it doesn't happen again. In our business, incidents will occasionally occur, but it is our job to make sure they don't repeat." The manager then starts by piecing together a detailed timeline based on the actions of each participant in the incident. The group discovers that the incident was originally thought to have been caused by a network issue, but the cause was later identified as a bad code push, which was fixed by rolling back. Once all the facts are straight, the team spends its time brainstorming remediations to both prevent the incident from repeating and reduce the TTR of future incidents. Then remediations are prioritized based on their ability to reduce the likelihood of future incidents versus the level of effort. High-priority remediations are then assigned owners who are responsible for allocating resources and determining due dates for completion. Finally, the results of the postmortem are documented and tracked as part of a global program. The data can be further mined for systemic patterns across the organization, and management can rearrange resources and initiatives to have the greatest impact on outage numbers.

## CHAPTER FOURTEEN

Storage

Anoop Nagwani

ONE OF THE THINGS YOU NEED TO KNOW AS A STORAGE PROFESSIONAL is that data is your single most important, irreplaceable business asset. Your data may consist of piles of financial transactions that flow through your trading systems, the source code repository that your company uses to build its killer app, the photos, videos, and email messages of hundreds of millions of users, or the state of the Internet's virtual farms and mafias. No matter what industry you find yourself in, your users and your company have entrusted you as the guardian of this precious asset.

These days, the ability to access data effectively and instantly is almost certainly the lifeline of your business. It's how your business satisfies the demands for its products, makes money, pays its employees, and gives value to its shareholders. The loss of this data could very well cause your business to go off the air completely in the worst case, or tarnish its brand in the best case. Whether your data lives in the cloud, in your company's datacenters, or some combination thereof, it is your respect for this data, your mastery of storage concepts, your attention to detail—and at times your natural paranoia—that will help you ensure that a sound data infrastructure is in place, that information keeps flowing, and that your business continues to operate.

Data Asset Inventory

The first thing you should do when you start a new storage job is to make sure you know where all your data is. Usually, it's everywhere. It's on the refrigerator-sized managed storage systems that are typically easy to find. It's on the local disks of servers that may or may not be backed up. It's on external drives under people's desks; on that stack of tapes sitting on your datacenter floor that should have been sent off-site weeks ago; and anywhere in between.

This next statement may seem pretty obvious, but it's a very important thing to keep in mind every day: you can't protect data that you don't know about. New sources of data have a knack for cropping up spontaneously in most environments, and are usually the product of developers and engineers releasing new features and functionalities. It will be hard for you to make sure your data is stored and protected effectively if you don't have a good handle on where all of your data is located. If you're reading this and think your environment may house data you don't know about, or you aren't entirely sure what some of your data is used for, it sounds like you need to perform a complete and thorough data asset inventory right about now.

What exactly is a data asset inventory? It's a list of all your databases, network shares, LUNs, virtual and physical tape pools, and any server filesystems that store information that you need to keep around. The inventory should include important information about the data, such as where the data is physically located, the name of the system on which it's stored, the type of system on which it's stored, the service or product that uses it, what kind of data it is, and the size of the data set. I'm going to illustrate how to perform a data asset inventory by using the following example infrastructure.

Let's say you just started working for a company that owns and manages virtual farms. The company uses a database to keep track of which crops are planted on each of its farms. The database is stored on a managed storage system and is backed up nightly to a virtual tape library. All of these devices are located in the company's San Diego datacenter.

We plug all of this information into a table or database to create a data asset inventory for our company. So far, it should look something like Table 14-1.

Table 14-1. *Data asset inventory*

Location	System	System type	Data type	Data size	Service
San Diego	database1.sd	Storage system	Crops database	500 GB	Crops
San Diego	vtl1.sd	VTL	Crops database backups	10 TB	Crops

Now that you have your list of data assets, you need to figure out how important each one is to your business. The fancy phrase for this step is "business impact analysis." Basically, you want to understand what's going to happen to your company if any of these data assets become inaccessible or disappear. Talk to the people who create, use, maintain, or manage each data asset. In your search to answer these questions, you'll likely be in touch with developers, DBAs, application engineers, data analytics and reporting people, as well as folks responsible for product and business operations.

You'll also want to ask if any formal or informal expectations around data and application availability are in place. These expectations, commonly referred to as service-level agreements (SLAs) or operating-level agreements (OLAs), can cover a broad range of criteria regarding the minimum availability, performance, time for incident response, and other measures that a service provider and its customer have agreed upon. Unless you are at a company with relatively mature service and data management practices, odds are good that you won't find any formal SLAs or OLAs in place. This is where you come in.

You need to develop, socialize, and ultimately nail down the recovery-time objectives (RTOs) and recovery-point objectives (RPOs) for each data asset you've identified. Generally, RTOs and RPOs apply to an entire application or infrastructure, but in this case we are looking at them only on the storage layer. I'll talk about what each of these recovery objectives are and how I would define them for my company.

RTOs define the maximum length of time it should take to recover from any sort of disruption of service. Let's say your expensive NAS appliance goes down, and part of your site depends on it. You'll need to know how long the system can reasonably be unavailable before it has a serious negative impact on your product or users. It's important that you talk with your product people to figure out how long the system can be down (and data inaccessible) before the business side of things starts to unravel. This is something you'll want to know and agree upon before something bad happens.

RPOs describe the maximum amount of data loss that is acceptable after a disruption of service. The amount of data loss is usually measured in time. Let's say the crops database I described earlier is backed up nightly at 10:00. If the storage system melts down and loses all its data at 9:00 p.m., the only backup you have is from 10:00 the night before, and you will have lost about a day's worth of data if you restore from that backup. This means the maximum RPO for this system is about 24 hours, the time elapsed between nightly backups.

Just like with RTOs, you should chat with the right people at your company to determine what an acceptable RPO is for each data asset. If the business expects no more than a few minutes of lost data on this server due to a failure event, and all you have are nightly backups, you will be in pretty bad shape if your database gets corrupted or destroyed. On the other hand, if you had set up this storage system to mirror its data to another location every few minutes, your RPO will be significantly shorter, and you'll lose much less data if something goes wrong. As you identify RTOs and RPOs for each data asset, you should add them to your data asset inventory.

OK, back to our example infrastructure. After talking with the DBAs and product managers at your company, you learn that although it's important for the crops database to always be available, an outage of up to 15 minutes can be tolerated. Anything longer than that would seriously affect the ability of users to harvest their crops and plant new crops. You also learn that the company can tolerate about a 10-minute window of data loss in the event of a system failure, but anything beyond that would be tough to handle. You know that the RTO for the crops database is 15 minutes and that the RPO is 10 minutes, and you know the impact to the business if the database were to be inaccessible. You also do the same exercise for the VTL (see Table 14-2).

Table 14-2. *Data asset inventory with RTO, RPO, and business impact*

Location	System	System type	Data type	Data size	Service	RTO	RPO	Business impact
San Diego	database1.sd	Storage system	Database	500 GB	Crops	15 minutes	10 minutes	Users can't harvest crops or plant new crops
San Diego	vtl1.sd	VTL	Database backups	10 TB	Crops	12 hours	24 hours	DBAs can't back up or recover the crops database

Once you've completed your data asset inventory, you can start to figure out whether the way each data asset is currently protected is acceptable. If your current backup and data replication policies allow for you to meet or exceed your RTO and RPO targets for each data asset, you are in good shape. If this isn't the case, well, I'm afraid you've got some work to do. And this work involves taking your first steps toward ensuring that you have good data protection strategies in place.

As you saw in Table 14-2, the following items should be on your data asset inventory checklist:

- Location
- System name
- System type
- Data type
- Data size
- Service

- RTO

- RPO

- Business impact

Data Protection

Data protection is important for all systems. Good data protection practices can help your business deal with scenarios ranging from restoring a file that was accidentally deleted by a user, to recovering from catastrophic events such as datacenter fires and floods. When your systems and storage are operating smoothly, the importance of having effective data protection strategies in place may not always be apparent to your users or your business. But when things go wrong, and data can't be accessed or is destroyed, a deliberate and effective data protection response is essential. You will rely heavily on the tools and policies that were put in place before an event that destroys or corrupts your data. And you'll be glad those tools and policies were there.

The range of data protection options available today is vast. The minimum, yet timeless, standard of data protection is backing up systems and storage devices to virtual or physical tape with some level of frequency. The virtual or physical tapes are then securely sent or transmitted off-site to another datacenter or vaulting facility to make sure your data is safe should something bad happen to your primary location. This level of protection is much better than not having any copies of your data outside of your primary location but will probably not be sufficient to address the data availability requirements of many applications today. The amount of time it would take to retrieve and then restore the data, coupled with the data being only as recent as the last backup, will result in greatly extended RTOs and RPOs.

In our example, our crops database is backed up nightly. We identified the desired RPO for the database to be 10 minutes, but currently we can lose as much as 24 hours' worth of data because we take only one backup per day. We have a few choices to remedy this situation. We can take a backup more than once a day—in this case, every 10 minutes if we want to reach our target RPO. Taking backups at this frequency would be unsustainable, especially with a large data set. Or we can continuously replicate this data to another storage system and also run our regularly scheduled nightly backups to the virtual tape library. If we were to lose the primary system, we have a replica storage system in our datacenter that has the entire data set ready to go. It sounds like we found a solution to reach our RPO, right? Well, maybe.

This is a great solution for protecting against catastrophic server or disk failures, but it's an inadequate solution if we want to protect against data corruption. Once bad data is written to the primary database, it would get replicated to the replica database server almost immediately. Now we have two copies of the data, and both copies are bad. To recover from this situation, we'd have to revert to the previous night's backups, which would put your recovery point back to losing 24 hours' worth of data.

A better solution is to continue with the nightly backups, implement a replica for the database server as described earlier, but also continuously copy the database transaction logs from the primary database server to another system. In the event of a server failure, you would switch to using the replica database server as I described earlier. In the event of data corruption, now you can restore from a nightly backup and replay transaction logs to the point at which the database corruption was introduced. You can also examine the transaction logs to better understand the point at which the corruption was introduced, see which objects were affected, and perform other kinds of necessary forensics.

Let's go back to our data asset inventory and add a column that describes the data protection strategies we've implemented. So far, we've talked about the importance of protecting our data and how a mixture of backups, snapshots, and replication can be powerful tools to achieve this. For the crops database, we are doing nightly backups, have a local database replica, and are continuously moving transaction logs from the master to our virtual tape library for safekeeping. Our data asset inventory now looks like Table 14-3.

Table 14-3. *Data asset inventory, updated with data protection information*

Location	System	System type	Data type	RTO	RPO	Business impact	Data protection
San Diego	database1.sd	Storage system	Database	15 minutes	10 minutes	Users can't harvest crops or plant new crops	Nightly backups; local replication; continuously back up transaction logs from master to VTL
San Diego	database2.sd	Storage system	Database	4 hours	2 hours	No replica for primary crops database	None
San Diego	vtl1.sd	VTL	Database backups and transaction logs	12 hours	24 hours	DBAs can't back up or recover the crops database	None

Another way to enhance data protection is to use *snapshots*. Simply put, a snapshot is a point-in-time version of your data. Most modern managed storage systems and operating systems have snapshot technology available. Depending on the snapshot technology you use, there can be very little overhead in maintaining multiple snapshots of your data. You can take snapshots on a daily basis, every few hours, or as often as every hour or less if you need to, in order to ensure a high granularity of recoverability of your data.

When you take a snapshot, both the snapshot and the data the snapshot was taken of are exactly the same. The data can continue to accept reads, writes, and deletes while the snapshot exists. When you change any part of the data, the snapshot remembers the way the data looked when the snapshot was taken. For the snapshot to do this, it needs to be able to store what the data looked like previously. This requires extra storage space that is proportional to the amount of change the data undergoes. So, when you first take a snapshot, it doesn't use any storage space because the snapshot and data are identical. If you take a snapshot and then delete a few files, the snapshot will need to have enough space available to save those deleted files until the snapshot is removed. Snapshots are a great way of undoing situations where a file was accidentally deleted or modified. They can also help revert from database corruption.

If you think about it, backups are also a point-in-time version of your data. So, what makes a snapshot different from a backup? A proper backup copies the contents of your data to virtual or physical tapes, or to another storage system entirely. A snapshot, on the other hand, uses the same disk subsystem as the primary data itself. Although snapshots are a good addition to data protection, they won't protect you against the failure of the storage device or its disk subsystem underneath. In this way, a snapshot is not like a backup because a backup exists on separate storage.

For some applications and databases, snapshots may help you back up your data in a smarter way. Typically, applications are almost always performing some amount of data or metadata changes to a filesystem, LUN, or database. If a backup is taken while these data operations are happening, your backup will likely have data that has been partially written to. We call this an *inconsistent backup* because it contains a mixture of old and new data for the data operations that were in progress when the backup occurred. A backup that doesn't contain this type of in-flight data is called *application consistent*, or simply *consistent*. Recovering from an inconsistent backup may or may not work, depending upon your application. If your application isn't designed to recover from an inconsistent backup and your recovery doesn't work, you will definitely be in a bad situation.

If your application or database is designed to successfully recover from an inconsistent backup, any inconsistent backup taken is usually termed *crash consistent*. Applications that have the ability to recover from a crash-consistent backup generally need to verify the recovered data in some way to make sure it's in a usable state. This process can take a while to finish. Even if your application has the ability to recover from a crash-consistent backup, it is best to make sure you always have application-consistent backups for a few reasons.

First, there is no guarantee that recovery from a crash-consistent backup will work 100% of the time. If your recovery doesn't work, you will need a crash-consistent backup to get yourself out of this situation anyway. Second, even if your application is able to successfully recover from a crash-consistent backup, the checks it has to perform to confirm that the data is in a usable state will extend your time to recovery. For these reasons, it's best that you don't rely solely on crash-consistent backups, but it's good to know that you should be able to recover from them if you really need to. As long as you have regular application-consistent backups in place, it's not a bad idea to take more frequent crash-consistent backups by using snapshots. This way, you will have a recent crash-consistent snapshot to recover from and also a more reliable application-consistent backup in case you can't recover from the crash-consistent backup.

One way to ensure that all of your backups are in a consistent state is to pause all data operations for the duration of your backup operation. This will result in a consistent copy of your data, but it usually isn't a practical solution because your backup may take minutes or hours, and you won't be able to write to your database or data set while the backup is in progress.

A clever way to create a consistent backup with minimal impact to your application is to use snapshots. Many applications today can use snapshots to help take consistent backups by momentarily pausing data operations, asking the storage system to create a snapshot, and then resuming data operations once the snapshot has been successfully created. Since it usually takes just a few seconds to create the snapshot, this will help you take a consistent backup with minimal impact to your application. Not all applications and databases include the ability to perform snapshot backups out-of-the-box, so you may need to ask around and find out how others have implemented this for your specific application, or you may have to just roll your own.

Snapshots have saved the day many times at the companies I've worked for. Usually when data is accidentally deleted or corrupted by a user or application, recovering the data from snapshots is pretty easy. We either recover individual files or objects from a snapshot, or rewind the entire data set to a snapshot where the data is in a known-good state. Snapshots can be extremely helpful in these situations. Here's an example where they didn't help us at all, and how we learned a lesson in a very hard way.

I had just started working for a company that ran several multiterabyte MySQL databases housing lots of important information for our users. The databases stored their data and logfiles on a popular NFS appliance that had built-in snapshot capabilities, and the entire system had been in production for about a year without incident. The storage system had no disaster recovery replica, and the databases were not being backed up. There was only one copy of this data set, and if something were to happen to it, the data would be lost forever. Additionally, the storage system was running out of capacity, and there was no additional physical space in the existing datacenter to expand the system. Basically, we were operating without a data protection net, and we were also about to hit the ceiling of available storage capacity. Things were not good.

I sat down with the DBA responsible for this data set, and we decided it was important to replicate this data to a system at an alternate site and to also take snapshots of the database at regular intervals. Having a replica system at another site would allow us to recover from a situation where the primary storage system was destroyed or became inaccessible for an extended period. Implementing regular snapshots of the data would help us recover from data corruption caused by application or user error. And just to be extra careful, we would back up the database regularly and also copy and retain the transaction logs on a different storage system. Together, these changes would provide a good amount of protection for this data set. The new setup was definitely better than the risks we were exposed to with the old one.

We ordered database servers and a pair of storage systems with enough capacity to allow this data set to comfortably grow for the next 12 to 18 months. We deployed the primary storage system and database servers at a datacenter we recently provisioned, and the replica storage system and database servers at a site located several thousand miles away. We set up snapshots on the new storage systems and configured replication between the storage systems located at different sites. We were ready for the DBA to start the data migration of the few dozen MySQL tables that housed the data set.

The data migration proceeded as planned, and the new systems were able to keep up with the migration workload as well as the production workload of serving data. We were about halfway done with the data migration when the DBA accidentally deleted a few tables from the old system before they were copied to the new system. This was a simple administrator error, and something that should typically be straightforward to recover from. I checked to see when the last snapshot had been taken of the affected data set and was shocked to find that snapshots had been disabled. Because we didn't have any snapshots to recover from, we were not able to revert the database to a point before the tables were removed. The data was lost forever.

During my root-cause analysis of this event, I found that snapshots had been intentionally disabled sometime during the lifespan of the system. I'm not sure exactly why this happened or who decided to do this, but it definitely hurt the company's ability to recover from this simple administrator error. This resulted in a huge black eye for the entire storage team and resulted in some complaints from our users. The lesson to learn from this story is that, with very little exception, you should always have snapshots enabled on your managed storage systems. The next time a developer or administrator tells you that snapshots are not required and asks you to disable them the alarm bells in your head should start ringing loudly. People don't think they need snapshots until they lose data. Make sure you have the snapshots they need.

Let's add hourly application-consistent snapshots to our primary database server, and update our data asset inventory. It should look like Table 14-4.

Table 14-4. *Data asset inventory, updated with hourly application-consistent snapshots*

Location	System	System type	Data type	RTO	RPO	Business impact	Data protection
San Diego	data-base1.sd	Storage system	Database	15 minutes	10 minutes	Users can't harvest crops or plant new crops	Nightly backups; local replication; application-consistent snapshots every hour; con-tinuously back up transaction logs from master to VTL
San Diego	data-base2.sd	Storage system	Database	4 hours	2 hours	No replica for primary crops database	None
San Diego	vtl1.sd	VTL	Database backups and transac-tion logs	12 hours	24 hours	Can't back up or recover the crops database or transac-tion logs	None

Although catastrophic datacenter events are rare, they do happen. Events ranging from downed network links or power outages to datacenter fires and other unex-pected events can make your datacenter or systems unrecoverable. Over time, I've witnessed quite a few serious datacenter problems. I've seen datacenter cooling systems fail, battery backup systems fail, and datacenter roofs leak water onto critical infrastructure. In all of these situations, these failures were never supposed to occur, but somehow they did. You should not be of the mindset that these things will never happen. Rather, you should be of the mindset that when they do happen, you will be prepared to handle and recover from them. That's where good disaster recovery planning comes in.

To provide full protection against datacenter issues, it is important to replicate your critical data to a different   site. You'll want to replicate your data to a site that is far enough away that any localized or geographic events such as natural disasters or large-scale power failures won't affect the ability of your business to access important data. Even if you choose to replicate to a site that doesn't meet this distance requirement, you should at least replicate your data out of your datacenter to another site even if it's not that far from your primary site.

Most storage systems today have some type of replication technology available, and usually it's a fairly simple process to get it set up and running. Replication between storage systems is typically available in two flavors: synchronous and asynchronous. *Synchronous replication* ensures that your data is sent from the primary storage system to the replica storage system before the primary storage system acknowledges any write operations back to the client. This manner of replication ensures that either both systems have accepted and committed the write to stable storage, or the write has failed for both systems. *Asynchronous replication* allows for the primary system to accept and acknowledge write operations to the client, and then to send the written data to the replica storage system at some later point.

Both types of replication are effective, but each has its limitations. Because synchronous replication guarantees that your data is committed to the replica storage system before acknowledging the write, it makes sure your data is up-to-date on both systems and gives you the peace of mind that you can lose either system and your data up to that point is still safely stored. Synchronous replication should not allow for a write to be committed to the primary system, without being written to the secondary system. This is a good thing. Unfortunately, the amount of time it takes the primary system to synchronously transmit the data to the replica system will increase overall response time. And this latency is proportional to the physical distance separating the storage systems. If the distance between the systems is beyond a couple hundred miles, the latency between the systems will increase to the point where synchronous replication will degrade the performance of both storage systems to an unacceptable level.

Asynchronous replication isn't affected by the performance limitations caused by latency and physical distance because it allows data to be immediately committed to the primary storage system, and then later it sends it to the replica storage system at some regular interval. Unfortunately, this mode of replication will increase the risk of data loss if your primary system fails before newly written data is transmitted to the replica storage system, or if the link between the two systems goes offline for an extended period.

The type of replication that you should implement is dependent upon your RTOs and RPOs. If your business has an aggressive policy that does not allow for any data loss, you will likely need to implement synchronous replication to protect your data set. On the other hand, if it's OK to lose minutes' or hours' worth of data without much of an impact on your business, asynchronous replication should work just fine. You can also combine both types of replication to ensure that your data gets replicated to another nearby site synchronously, and then also gets replicated to a site that is located farther away in an asynchronous manner. Let's do this for our example environment and update our data asset inventory (see Table 14-5).

Table 14-5. *Data asset inventory, updated with remote replication*

Location	System	System type	Data type	RTO	RPO	Business impact	Data protection
San Diego	database1.sd	Storage system	Database	10 minutes	15 minutes	Users can't harvest crops or plant new crops	Nightly back-ups; local replication; application-consistent snapshots every hour; continuously back up transaction logs from master to VTL
San Diego	database2.sd	Storage system	Database	4 hours	2 hours	No local replica for primary crops database	Remote replica
New York	database3.ny	Storage system	Database	4 hours	2 hours	No remote replica for primary crops database	None
San Diego	vtl1.sd	VTL	Database backups and transaction logs	12 hours	24 hours	Can't back up or recover the crops database or transaction logs	None

A few years ago, I was working at a company that had a critical application running on storage systems set up in replicated pairs between datacenters in London and Dublin. The storage systems in London were set up as the primary systems at the time and were accepting writes that they then sent asynchronously to the replica systems in Dublin. The thought was that if something were to happen to the London facility, the service could be failed over to Dublin and brought online. Asynchronous replication was used because the physical distance between the systems was too great to support synchronous replication.

Now, London is usually known for its moderate to cold temperatures year-round and definitely not known for having heat waves. So, it came as a surprise to folks during that summer when a heat wave sent temperatures soaring for part of Europe and scorched London with high temperatures near 100°F. The heat wave caused one of the London datacenter facility's dozen or so cooling systems to fail. The interesting thing about datacenter cooling failures is that if one unit fails, it puts more stress on the other units to continue cooling the facility. This additional stress can increase the probability that another cooling unit will fail if weather conditions are severe enough. This is exactly what happened to the London facility. The site was not designed to handle the unexpectedly high temperatures of the heat wave that summer, and after one cooling system failed, the others started to fail one after another, resulting in a complete cascading failure of the entire cooling system.

The storage systems in the datacenter had an array of temperature sensors located in different parts of their chassis and components, and began to send alerts that temperature conditions were outside the range in which they were designed to operate. As the datacenter's temperatures continued to increase, the storage systems began to shut themselves down automatically to prevent damage to their internal components and to minimize the possibility of potential data corruption. The London datacenter personnel quickly began an emergency procedure to shut down the thousands of servers and other devices in the facility in an effort to reduce datacenter temperatures and save the servers from permanent harm caused by the rising temperatures.

The application engineers were ready to fail over the critical application to the replicated storage systems in Dublin when the temperatures in the London datacenter cooled significantly as nighttime approached. Because the storage systems were using asynchronous replication between the sites, it meant there was a high probability that data that was committed to the London systems had not yet been replicated to the systems in Dublin. If the engineers performed the failover to Dublin, unfortunately there was no easy way for them to merge the nonreplicated data on the London systems with the data on the Dublin systems. Because the temperatures in the London datacenter were now approaching normal conditions, the decision was made to turn on only the network and storage systems in order to perform a final replication sync between the London and Dublin storage systems, and then turn up the application in Dublin.

We learned a few interesting lessons from this event. First, we never would have anticipated the extreme temperatures that the heat wave produced in London, because we generally predict possible failure scenarios based upon past events. Second, the application engineers were not prepared to, in a timely manner, merge and reconcile the two disparate data sets that would have resulted from doing a failover without a final sync.

The data protection practices I outlined here are of no value to you if they can't produce a readable, correct, and working data set. This means that verifying the recoverability and validity of your backups is just as important as making sure your backups complete successfully. The same is true for recovering from snapshots as well as from replication targets. Scheduling regular data recovery drills will confirm that your data is protected correctly and that it will be available when you need it. Now that we've talked about the importance of enumerating our data assets, defining our recovery objectives, and implementing good data protection practices, let's talk a little bit about capacity planning.

Capacity Planning

After ensuring that your data is effectively protected, capacity planning is the second most important responsibility you have as a storage professional. Planning ahead and ensuring that your applications and services have enough resources to operate and grow without hitting the ceiling is not only critical, but also mandatory. The benefits of scaling capacity and headroom ahead of demand are enormous. It reduces stress both for you and for the application, allows for unexpected spikes in utilization, and helps avoid unplanned capital expenditures.

I always try to maintain at least six months' worth of headroom in my storage environments. Having a proper capacity planning regimen in place makes forecasting capital and operational expenditures predicable, and also allows for planning datacenter space, power, and supply-chain logistics more effectively. The last thing you want is to receive that phone call in the wee hours of the morning letting you know that your production workload has overrun the performance or capacity capabilities of your infrastructure. Here's a situation where capacity planning went very wrong.

I worked at a company where we used NAS appliances to store files that users would upload and later view. The NAS appliances were correctly sized for their workload and were also capable of replicating the files asynchronously to a secondary NAS appliance at a site located several thousand miles away. The systems could comfortably store and serve files, the asynchronous replication lag didn't exceed our target RPO, and we were able to sustain things such as disk failures and reconstructions. We maintained six months' worth of headroom nonetheless to ensure that we had a nice cushion of capacity to help us absorb spikes, as well as the organic growth we projected.

The appliances worked well, but they were expensive. Buying more of them was something the company didn't like doing because of their cost, and the company knew it could devise a more economical solution by creating its own storage engine.

The new storage engine was an exciting technology that would help the application's storage infrastructure scale in a much more economical way. It ran on much cheaper storage devices and was designed specifically for the workload of storing and serving files in a very efficient way. It took more than a year to finish, but the storage engine was now code complete and had been tested under several synthetic workloads. The only thing left to do was to make sure it would operate under our real application workload and also confirm that it would correctly store and serve all the files at this scale. We decided the safest way to proceed was to save the files to both the new storage engine and the NAS appliances during the final stages of testing the storage engine. Once we were confident that it was operating correctly and could be completely trusted to hold incoming file content, we would discontinue writing the files to the NAS appliances.

Right around this time, the company's site became extremely popular and experienced explosive growth in all areas. As more people used the site, the number of files they uploaded increased at a steep clip. This was very good for business, especially because the new storage engine that we were testing would allow us to store the files at a much cheaper cost than the NAS solution. We had already discontinued purchasing new NAS appliances in anticipation of the storage engine being ready soon. Unfortunately, several bugs delayed confirmation that the new storage engine could be trusted, and the site's growth in popularity caused us to quickly reach the point where we had passed the workload and replication capabilities of the remaining NAS appliances dedicated for the application's storage needs. Because we had no new NAS appliance purchases in the pipeline, we had to rebalance the workload on the appliances by reducing the frequency of the asynchronous replication in order to increase the resources available to the storing and serving of files. This unfortunately resulted in a breach of our RPO. We were in a situation where the NAS appliances were running much hotter than we were comfortable running them at, and the increased demands on the appliances were very heavy. We had already stopped buying more NAS appliances, expecting to switch fully to the new storage engine. And the storage engine still wasn't ready.

Then, a disk failed. The NAS appliance's utilization subsequently spiked due to the RAID reconstruction, and the storage system could not keep up with the production and replication workloads. We disabled writes to the appliance with the failed disk and had the other systems shoulder the write workload. Even after doing this, the read performance was still affected. Unfortunately, because we scaled back the asynchronous replication schedule, we didn't have the entire data set available at our secondary site. So, we had to disable reads for the data on the affected RAID group for several days while it was reconstructing. The RAID group reconstructed successfully, and no data was lost. But we learned a valuable lesson here. Always make sure you have enough capacity to survive spikes in growth, as well as delays in the timeline of software development. Had we insisted on maintaining our standard six-month headroom until the production-testing phase of the new storage engine was complete, we would have easily weathered this event.

Storage Sizing

Storage is expensive. It is one of the most costly components of any modern infrastructure today. This is especially the case in data-intensive environments that house the user-generated content and data of millions of users. For this reason, it is important to plan and spend capital on storage wisely. I've been responsible for some large budgets during my time operating large-scale storage deployments. I've learned that it is key to have a concrete understanding of exactly why the applications you support need storage, how they intend to use it, and how it can be designed and implemented as efficiently as possible.

Engineers and application groups will oftentimes come to us with exact, well-vetted storage requirements in hand. They've researched the workload, growth projections, and capacity requirements they anticipate their application will need, and they have already compiled details and answers to many of the questions they believe we will ask. They've done their homework, and more importantly, they've shown their work. At other times, we've been approached by groups that know very little about the storage they require, other than the fact that their application needs storage. They can't fully identify how much storage they need or what type, and in many cases they have little understanding about storage and how it works. Their initial requirements are fuzzy, but they are eager to work with us and to learn and understand how to design and size a storage solution.

At one of my previous companies, I was a member of a committee that reviewed requests to purchase hardware and software. The committee consisted of one of the tech-savvy co-founders of the company, several executives, as well as some technical experts of various core infrastructure areas. The committee served as an exhaustive and methodical checkpoint where engineers requesting hardware or software would present their case to the committee, questions would be asked, the requests would be discussed openly, and sometimes a request would be approved. By and large, the most common outcome was that requests were denied because they lacked the proper data to support them.

When it came to requesting storage, many times engineers didn't fully understand the requirements of their applications, and there was no clear definition of what was needed or why a managed storage system was necessary to service their storage needs instead of simply using a server's internal disks. At times, they didn't have sound capacity projections, or a model of how storage capacity would need to scale over time. Almost always, very little attention would be paid to a disaster recovery or data replication strategy, or to what the big picture of business continuity would look like. Basically, engineers would ask for too much or too little, and usually without the appropriate evidence to support their request.

The committee served to ensure that engineers, by the end of the review process, had sound reasoning for every piece of hardware, software, and storage they requested. The outcome of this was that every purchase was deliberate, necessary, and backed by data describing exactly what the requirements were, and the reasoning behind the solution. I've carried the spirit of this committee with me to the companies I subsequently worked at, and have used it to make sure all storage purchases were data driven, had an effective business continuity plan, and had a proper capacity plan.

Whether you're an engineer requesting storage, or a storage professional reviewing storage requests from engineers, the following list of questions and discussion points is good to keep in mind:

- What is the application?

- Where is it located?

- What types of data are stored?

- Is shared storage needed?

- Is a particular access protocol required?

- What are the typical file sizes?

- Is data compressed?

- How would you describe the workload?

- Are batch operations required?

- Is the workload mostly reads, mostly writes, or a combination of both?

- Is the workload mostly sequential, mostly random, or a combination of both?

- What is the snapshot schedule?

- Are snapshots application consistent, crash consistent, or inconsistent?

- What is the storage capacity requested in 6-month, 12-month, and 18-month projections?

- What are the workload requirements in 6-month, 12-month, and 18-month projections?

- What is the replication strategy?

- What is the business continuity plan?

- What are the availability requirements?

- What is the frequency of backups?

- What is the backup retention plan?

- What is the archiving strategy?

- What are the compliance requirements?

- What are the encryption requirements?

Operations

In the inherently always-on web operations environments of today, there is little time for planned outages, maintenance, and other common operations that affect site availability and revenue generation. Essentially, no time is a good time to be down or to have your workload affected, ever. Tasks such as regular backups, disk failures, replication, and software and firmware upgrades must not disrupt your workload, and you must take these factors into account when designing your storage infrastructure.

There are a few best practices I'd like to point out that are essential for big storage shops to operate with much less pain. These same things can help smaller shops as well. Here are a handful of the things I make sure to always do at the companies I work for. They are common sense, but I'm listing them here because I think they are very helpful.

Make sure to lock down and document your escalation paths and points of contact into your storage suppliers so that you know who to contact and how to contact them in emergency situations. This means making sure you have a list of phone numbers and email addresses for everyone on your account. This includes your account manager, your systems engineer, and your primary support contact. Do the same thing in reverse—include the escalation path, phone numbers, and email addresses for the members of the storage team, the storage manager, and the manager of the storage manager so that the supplier can easily contact your company if it needs to.

Hold regular operations meetings with your suppliers. Use these meetings to review open cases, cases that were recently closed, and their resolution. Use this forum to ensure that root-cause analyses are requested and completed by the supplier and discuss any failure or operation trends that may be cropping up.

Make sure you have agreed-upon software and firmware releases, as well as the software and firmware road maps for future releases. Generally, we do up to two major software releases each year. In the larger environments I've worked in, it is usually about once a year. Make sure you upgrade a pilot set of systems first to reduce the risk associated with the upgrades. Once you are comfortable that the pilot systems are operating correctly after the upgrade go ahead and upgrade the rest of the fleet in phases. Usually I make sure to operate the pilot release for anywhere from one to three months, unless there is a critical bug or issue that is addressed by the upgrade.

For large storage fleets, making sure there is an ample supply of frequently used replacement parts at each of your sites can be invaluable. Instead of waiting for a part to ship from the supplier and arrive at your site, you can immediately replace the faulty part. This isn't as critical for parts such as failed disks, but it can be huge if there are issues that affect the components that interconnect shelves or storage nodes. It's always best to fix problems as soon as you discover them. This also allows you to schedule repairs around your business needs and when your datacenter personnel are available, rather than around how soon the replacement parts can arrive at your site.

Another thing to make sure you have a good process around is the returning of parts received under your maintenance contracts. Suppliers will send you replacement parts as soon as you request them, and it's great that your on-site cache of replacement parts will allow you to swap a faulty component as soon as you discover there is a problem. However, you need to make sure faulty components are tracked as soon as they are pulled out of the storage system and that they make it back to the supplier.

Conclusion

Data is your most precious business asset, and it is irreplaceable. I cannot overemphasize to you how important it is to continuously be on the lookout for risks in your environment. Are any of your backup jobs not completing successfully? Is replication lagging? Are you regularly breaching your RPOs and RTOs? Have you just discovered a critical single point of failure in your infrastructure? When it comes to situations that could compromise your data protection and data availability, if you see something wrong, you need to address it immediately.

## CHAPTER FIFTEEN

Nonrelational Databases

Eric Florenzano

SCALING THE DATA STORAGE LAYER OF YOUR APPLICATION IS HARD. It seems that
no matter what database technology you use, as the volume of data and the number
of transactions increases, changes need to be made to accommodate that new load.
With some databases, it's as simple as buying more hardware; more nodes to add to
the cluster. For most of the open source SQL databases on the market right now, however, that's simply not the case. Queries, schemas, and application logic all need to be
changed to make the data access faster and more scalable.

SQL database scalability usually boils down to four main things: caching, query optimization, buying new hardware, and sharding the database. Caching is a bit beyond
the scope of this chapter, but it can help to alleviate some of the read load on the database. Unfortunately, it adds complexity to your application and has an upper bound on
how much load it can reduce. Query optimization, like caching, can do only so much.
Caching and query optimization are good practices, but they can go only so far.

Buying new hardware is always a valid choice when it comes to scaling SQL databases.
It's fairly simple to do, and it is proven to work. As database load increases, simply buy
better and faster hardware. The problems with this are twofold: it's expensive, and
once you've bought the best hardware, there's nothing more you can do. In practice,
expensive hardware, caching, and efficient queries can carry a single SQL database
node quite a long way. But they do have their limit.

After having done all of that work, if you're still having issues it's time to shard the
database. Some applications lend themselves very well to sharding. The canonical
example is that of geography—run two database servers, one for users in the United

States and another one for users in Europe. Then, based on their IP or some other identifier, ensure that each query is going to the correct database. Some applications, however, present a much more difficult path to sharding. What happens if a user from Europe interacts with content produced by someone in the United States? Now every time you want to render the content item, you have to do a query on both databases—which can actually be worse than having a single database, owing to the additional connection and transaction overhead costs. Sharding can be done, and thousands of applications do it successfully every day, but it's difficult to do, and it's difficult to do properly.

How can this scaling process be easier? How can we avoid this painful rearchitecture of our applications? How can we store data closer to the way it's represented in our applications? These are the questions that some newer developers are trying to answer in the creation of a new class of databases, dubbed NoSQL. Of course, not everything has to do with scalability. Sometimes the data that needs to be persisted simply doesn't fit well into a relational database.

Take HTTP sessions, for instance. In most cases it works like this: given some session cookie, a bundle of key/value pairs is retrieved from the database. HTTP sessions can surely be mapped to an SQL database—one column can be the key and another column can be the serialized bundle of keys and values. When examining this HTTP session use case, however, two things are clear: it's not relational, and it's not structured. This type of use case is an excellent candidate for being written into a database that deals better with its unstructured, nonrelational nature.

NoSQL Database Overview

The term *NoSQL* encompasses a broad range of databases, each with its own strengths and weaknesses, and most with wildly different goals and use cases. When looking at the NoSQL ecosystem today, the databases tend to break down into five broad categories: pure key/value, data structure, graph, document oriented, and highly distributed. Each of these categories of databases has a slightly different use case, and each category makes different trade-offs. We're going to go through them and take a look at those trade-offs.

Pure Key/Value

Pure key/value databases have actually been around for a very long time. Even before SQL databases had risen in popularity, dbm (a pure key/value database) was in use on many Unix systems around the world. After that, there was Berkeley DB, which is still a maintained and viable database solution. Today these pure key/value stores are seeing a resurgence in popularity, thanks in part to the resurgence in popularity of all NoSQL databases but also because of the development of some faster and more modern implementations such as Tokyo Cabinet, Kyoto Cabinet, and MemcacheDB.

It's their simplicity that defines this family of databases. Give the database a key and a value, and then subsequently when you give it that same key you'll get the same value back. There's no structure or type system—usually they just deal with bytes or strings. Because of this simplicity, these databases have little overhead and can be extremely fast. In fact, they're usually implemented as an on-disk B-tree or hash table.

Sharding a pure key/value database is straightforward—you can simply choose a hashing algorithm, run the key through that algorithm, and the output will be the database node to query or write. Doing complex queries, on the other hand, is not straightforward at all. Instead of being able to query for "users whose age is greater than 50," you would have to maintain a separate key/value pair whose value was a serialized list of keys to users whose age was greater than 50. This list would need to be updated every time a user was created or updated.

Possible applications for pure key/value stores are HTTP sessions, user preferences, and URL shorteners. I described HTTP sessions earlier, and they could be implemented in a very direct way on a key/value store. The key would be the user's session key, and the value would be a serialized object containing the user's session. For user preferences, it could work like this: the key is the user's ID concatenated with a preference name, and the value is the user's actual preference. For a URL shortener, the URL path would be the key, and the value would be the location to redirect to.

Data Structure

Data structure databases are a slight modification of key/value databases. Whereas pure key/value databases typically store only keys and values as strings or bytes, data structure databases store their values as specific data structures such as lists, sets, or hashes. With this added structure comes the ability to perform atomic operations on the values. For lists, you can push or pop values. For sets, you can do unions and intersections. You can perform the kinds of operations you would expect to be able to perform on data structures in your applications. Essentially, these are the data structures your application already uses, but they're maintained in an external process.

At the time of this book's publication, the only real contender in this space is Redis. Some of Redis's implementation details are the things that make it so interesting. By default, Redis stores the entirety of its content in memory and only periodically snapshots its contents to disk. This means it's insanely fast, but if the database crashes, there will be some loss of data. It also means you must have enough RAM to store the entire database. It's worth noting that these defaults can be changed—durability can be increased at the cost of speed, and a virtual memory scheme can be enabled, meaning you can store much more data than you have memory (although there is still a limit).

Because Redis is so fast and it can operate on data structures, it is perfect for things with many fast and small operations such as pageview counters, task queues, or trend analysis. Imagine giving each logged-in user a unique key that maps to an empty list and every URL for every page that the user visits is pushed to the end of that list. You could then pull up any user's information and see his browsing path, and do analysis on that path. By taking the length of that list, you can see how active the user is. This is one contrived example, but it illustrates the types of things that can be done when you're working with extremely fast in-memory operations and rich data structures.

Graph

Graph databases are almost a specialization of data structure databases, as graphs are data structures themselves. The difference is that graph databases are no longer key/value based; data is stored as nodes and edges in a graph. Instead of querying values by key, you're given a handle to the root node, and you're able to traverse the graph to find the nodes or edges you're looking for. This can be extremely valuable, because so many applications make extensive use of graphs already, and mapping those data structures into operations on a graph database is trivial. Like data structure databases, the database's graph is just like the one your application already uses, except it's maintained in an external process.

The main contender in this space is Neo4j, which is an embedded Java graph database, but can be accessed from several languages. In addition to Neo4j, other open source graph databases include HyperGraphDB, InfoGrid, and VertexDB. HyperGraphDB focuses on a more generalized graph representation where (among other things) an edge can point to more than one node. VertexDB is interesting in that it exposes a RESTful HTTP API with which to access the database, whereas the others are accessed primarily via Java methods.

Graph databases are good at what you would expect them to be good at: storing graph- or tree-like data. If your website wants to maintain a social graph, for example, a graph database can enable some interesting applications. Finding and recommending new friends to users goes from something that's complicated and slow, to something that's easy and efficient—just run a breadth-first search or a shortest path traversal and you're set.

Document Oriented

Document-oriented databases are again similar to key/value databases, except instead of the values being bytes, strings, lists, or sets, the values are "documents." What's a document? In the two document-oriented databases we'll cover here, CouchDB and MongoDB, documents are stored as JSON (or JSON-like) objects, which is essentially a hash or dictionary. That these values all share the same structure means it's possible to write queries that inspect that structure and return only the documents you want. Keep in mind that this ability to query is in addition to the ability to look up documents by their key.

CouchDB is one document-oriented database, which is written in Erlang and has several interesting implementation details, such as an append-only data structure and the ability to serve applications directly from the database. MongoDB is another document-oriented database, which (written in C++) is more optimized for speed and exposes a more traditional query layer. Although these two systems look similar on paper, they do tend to target different audiences. At the time of this writing, CouchDB is trending toward being installed by consumers onto the desktop and into the browser, and MongoDB is trending toward being used more in the datacenter.

Document-oriented databases are great for when you don't know exactly what data you're going to get, as in a lifestreaming application. In such an app, a document retrieved from a popular photo site will have certain photo properties, a document from a microblogging site might have some geographic properties, and a document from a blog will likely have neither. Another good application for document-oriented databases is a content management system. In such a system, each document could represent a page, or a part of a page.

Highly Distributed

Highly distributed databases come in a few different forms—some are closer in nature to key/value stores, and others are like very large multidimensional hash maps. One thing they all have in common is that they're optimized for multinode deployments. In these systems, adding more capacity involves simply adding a new node to the cluster. The failure of one node doesn't result in a loss of data but simply a loss of capacity. Most of these systems allow the user to choose to sacrifice some consistency to guarantee high availability and partition tolerance.

HBase is a highly distributed database that grew out of the Hadoop project, and it was very directly influenced by BigTable (Google's proprietary highly distributed database). Cassandra is another highly distributed database that was originally developed at Facebook and, although its data model is very similar to HBase, it focuses on having no single points of failure and on write performance. Both HBase and Cassandra store their data essentially as large multidimensional hash maps. Riak is another highly distributed database by the Basho corporation, written in Erlang, which is accessible over a RESTful HTTP API, and is more of a straightforward key/value model than HBase or Cassandra. Project Voldemort and Hypertable are other highly distributed databases worth mentioning as well.

Why would you use a highly distributed database? Well, usually because you have no other choice. These databases are typically used once another database, SQL based or otherwise, cannot handle either the amount of data or the number of queries you have. Almost every problem domain can be modeled with these database systems, but it can sometimes be trickier than with more traditional databases.

Some Systems in Detail

Now that we've briefly overviewed the different categories of NoSQL databases, we can begin to explore some individual databases in depth. Although we can't cover each and every database out there today, we can certainly cover those that have been getting the most attention lately. It's interesting to note some of the similarities between the databases and how the decisions they make affect system operability. For example, several of the databases choose an append-only data structure, which means backup can be as simple as an `rsync`. Let's dive in and take a look.

Cassandra

Cassandra is a highly distributed database that is used in production by Digg, Twitter, Facebook, Rackspace, and Reddit, to name a few. Cassandra has a few key philosophies that inform some of its basic design decisions. Cassandra takes the stance that writes are harder to scale than reads, so it's heavily optimized for writes. In fact, the hard drive disk head never has to seek on a write operation, because the only immediate write that's needed is to a log, which is append-only.

Another of Cassandra's philosophies is that there should be no single point of failure. It's for this reason that there's no "coordination" server, or "elected master" or anything of that kind. Cassandra servers know about each other via a gossip protocol that lets them relatively quickly propagate information across a cluster. Writes for any piece of data can happen to any node in a cluster, and reads can do so, too. Whichever node receives the request can, and will, forward the request to the proper nodes.

The other philosophies that Cassandra adopts largely coincide with the philosophies of the Dynamo paper, a seminal paper released by Amazon describing a proprietary data store that Amazon developed for its own data storage needs. That is, consistent hashing to determine where to store data, read repair to ensure that all replicas have correct data, and hinted handoff to ensure that downed nodes don't cause a loss in database availability.

Cassandra's data model itself can be thought of as a huge multidimensional hash map. First there's a KeySpace, which logically separates different applications and acts, essentially, as the database name. Then there's a ColumnFamily, which contains Column objects, which have a name and a value. Put directly, you can access a column's value given a key, a ColumnFamily, and a Column name. Cassandra can provide two indexes automatically: one based on the column name and another based on the key. This means you can get an ordered list of all columns given a key and a ColumnFamily. Cassandra also has the concept of a SuperColumnFamily, which instead of holding Column objects directly, holds ColumnFamily objects which, in turn, hold Column objects.

Operationally, there are a lot of things to consider when running Cassandra. Because the system tries so hard to avoid disk head seeks on writes, it can be a substantial performance boost to buy a completely separate and speedy disk just to hold the commit logs. The commit logs are purged periodically, so that disk needn't be large, but it should be fast enough to receive each write.

It's important to note that Cassandra periodically runs a compaction process, which compacts the datafiles and detects any data that has fallen out of sync. During this major compaction step, the datafiles can temporarily double in size, so it's important to have enough free space on that disk to handle the temporary extra data. With Cassandra, the more RAM you can get the better. It stores a large working set of data in memory so that it's fast to access. Additionally, the more memory your operating system can use as a disk cache, the better read performance Cassandra will see as a result.

Cassandra's operational interface is a command-line tool called nodetool. Using nodetool you can add new nodes to the cluster, decommission nodes, force a compaction or a cleanup, force a flush to disk, or export a backup. In fact, backups in Cassandra are usually performed by using nodetool's flush command followed by its backup command, on each node in the cluster.

Monitoring for Cassandra happens via Java's management extensions, or JMX. Helpfully, the Java community has also produced an open source project called PolarRose, which exposes JMX metrics via HTTP and a RESTful interface. Using JMX and/or PolarRose, you can access just about every important metric about each Cassandra node, such as the read or write latency, the read or write count, or the number of pending tasks.

In the Wild

Asked why Digg chose Cassandra over MySQL, the company's Chris Goffinet said that it came down to five key points:

- Digg's application has a high write-to-read ratio.
- They needed multidatacenter support.
- Within the datacenter, the needed rack awareness.
- They found eventual consistency to be acceptable.
- They wanted load balancing of data to be automatic.

Regarding how Cassandra operates:

- Redundancy and failover are done automatically.
- Digg's application handles failovers across datacenters.

He adds:

> With Cassandra, Digg isn't limited by CPU, but rather by disk size, I/O throughput, and network bandwidth.

According to Chris, Digg's setup currently handles multiple terabytes of data and is the primary datastore for the new version of Digg.

HBase

HBase is a project that started at PowerSet and builds upon Hadoop technologies such as HDFS. It's an open source implementation of Google's proprietary BigTable architecture, which differs in some slight ways from Amazon's Dynamo. For one thing, it chooses consistency and availability as its core values, and as a result there can be certain network partitions in which the cluster doesn't gracefully recover. In return for this sacrifice, HBase has a stronger consistency guarantee which means that immediately after a write finishes, its value can be read back. This can be extremely convenient from the application developer's perspective.

HBase has quite a few companies using it in production, including StumbleUpon, Meetup, Yahoo!, Mahalo, Adobe, and WorldLingo, to name a few. Its data model is ColumnFamily based, and can be thought of as a large multidimensional hash map. Each row in HBase has a key, and then given a ColumnFamily, a column qualifier, and a column name, you can set or get the column value. With HBase you can also access a cursor-like connection to the database where you can walk all or part of the database, pulling out only the values you care about.

Access to HBase can be done through a Thrift interface which is cross-platform and cross-language, or you can directly access the database from Java, or you can use a RESTful interface if that's easier. HBase also uses a project called ZooKeeper to coordinate certain things such as master election, bootstrap location storage, and region server discovery. Google has an analogous system named Chubby, and in addition to handling these things, it also handles schema information and access control lists, but HBase does not use ZooKeeper for those purposes.

Operationally, HBase exposes its monitoring metrics via JMX in a similar way as Cassandra, and therefore PolarRose will work just as well here. It's important to give HBase lots of RAM, as it will make use of as much as it can. Performance will suffer quite a bit if the JVM ever needs to swap, so in addition to giving the JVM lots of that RAM, it's important to also turn down the swappiness on the machines on which HBase is running. By simply having more hard drives on each HBase node, Hadoop will stripe the data and increase I/O throughput, so generally the more disks per node the better.

Backup of HBase clusters can be done using a tool called distcp, which expands a list of files into a series of map/reduce jobs, where each job copies one file from the source to the destination. This won't copy any of the database values that are still in memory, so it's important to force a flush of the database before initiating the distcp command. There are a few tickets in the project's ticket tracker at the time of publication that aim to make this process easier to do on a live cluster. Thankfully, the architecture of HBase is such that losing a node or two doesn't necessarily result in data loss, so the urgency of backing up the data is mitigated in that regard.

Gary Helmling at Meetup.com had this to say about Meetup's deployment of HBase, which has been in production since June 2009:

> With its semistructured data model it's easy (and there's no cost) to store different types of activity, each with their own set of associated fields, into the same table. We were able to come up with our own approach to member-level queries, building a per-member index of the most recent activity items applying to them specifically. Scaling and sharding are built-in. As your data grows, it automatically and transparently gets split out to multiple servers. If we need to add more capacity (for load or storage), we just plug in more servers, and they're dynamically added to the cluster, with the data load being rebalanced.

Regarding the size of the company's data set:

> The overall data footprint is not very large at the moment—maybe 600 GB raw, though a lot of that compresses well.

Regarding its scaling plans:

> We can easily scale horizontally by just plugging in more servers and adding them to the cluster. We're actually in the process of doing this now. The additional servers can be added dynamically, and the HBase master process will reassign some regions to the new servers to balance load.

According to Gary, their cluster peaks at around 5,000 requests per second and serves data for display on roughly 28% of pageviews.

Riak

Riak was open sourced by the Basho corporation in 2009, but it had been used by Basho for several years as its internal data store. Now Riak is in production use by Mochi Media (disclaimer, I work there), Collecta, Comcast, and EA. Riak is a fairly faithful implementation of the set of technologies described in the Dynamo paper I mentioned earlier. In fact, Riak even implements vector clocks, which is something that several other highly distributed databases have not chosen to implement—opting instead to rely on simpler timestamp-based techniques.

Vector clocks are a mechanism in distributed systems to generate a partial ordering of events. With vector clocks, it can be much simpler to resolve conflicts that happen on the same value on two different nodes independently. From the perspective of a Riak client, each client instance should have a unique token that it includes (along with the vector clock that it received) when it performs an action on the Riak cluster. Then, when a client reads data, it can see both vector clocks and their values, use the information contained to merge the two results, and save the corrected version back to the database.

Riak also has no single point of failure. It uses a gossip protocol to communicate failures and coordinate requests. As with some of the other highly distributed databases, any query can be sent to any node in the cluster, and that node will redirect the request to the proper node. Erlang was used as an implementation language, and it provides some of these networking facilities out of the box, allowing the Riak developers to focus on the core of their database.

Data in Riak is straightforward key/value pairs, which is accessed over a RESTful HTTP interface. It can also be accessed directly from Erlang, if your application backend is written in Erlang. One interesting feature of Riak is that it has the notion of links, which can add some graph-like capabilities on top of those key/value pairs. Riak also lets you upload functions (currently in JavaScript) that are scattered across the cluster and run right where the data lives.

One significant choice that Riak has made is to provide a pluggable storage backend layer. This means different clusters can use different storage backends, each of which makes its own set of trade-offs. Right now the options that ship with Riak itself are filesystem, dets (a disk-based Erlang term storage), ets (in-memory Erlang term storage), and osmos. That being said, arguably the most powerful backend storage engine is actually developed as an external project by Basho, and it's called innostore. Innostore uses an embedded version of InnoDB, which is one of MySQL's storage backends as well.

Operationally, it's important to make sure to choose the storage backend that matches your problem domain best, and also that you configure that storage backend properly. For most applications, the innostore backend is probably the one to consider. Innostore does a similar thing to Cassandra in that it allows you to store the logfiles in a different location from the datafiles, so a similar tip applies—a separate disk for the log directory can substantially improve performance. Unlike Cassandra, innostore's log directory is never reaped, so the hard disk will need to be large enough to store all of the data (or rotated regularly).

Backups for Riak are achieved in an interesting way: you run a command which creates a virtual node in the cluster, and then drains all of the data from the cluster onto disk. Monitoring is available via SNMP, but at the moment that's available only for customers of Basho's EnterpriseDS product, along with some improved management tools and multidatacenter support.

In the Wild

At the time of this writing, Mochi Media has four Riak clusters that each serve different purposes: to provide a user data API that game developers can use to store information for players of their game, to maintain session state for the Mochigames.com web frontend, to store a social graph, and to store metadata for a URL shortener. The session Riak cluster needs to have stronger consistency, whereas the URL shortening Riak cluster can have slightly more relaxed consistency. Mochi chose to use Riak because of these kinds of tunable trade-offs, as well as the ability to easily add capacity or handle node failure. The availability of enterprise support through Basho played a large role in the choice as well.

CouchDB

CouchDB is a project that was first started by Damien Katz, who actually worked on some portions of Lotus Notes. CouchDB now is supported by a company called CouchIO, which employs many of the core developers of the project (including Damien himself). Cloudant is another company that has built itself around CouchDB and CouchDB support. Companies that are using CouchDB in production include the BBC, Engine Yard, Meebo, and Sauce Labs. In fact, Canonical is working on integrating CouchDB with all of its desktop applications, in an initiative it's calling DesktopCouch, with the slogan "A CouchDB on every desktop, and the code to make it happen."

CouchDB has a very consistent view of the world: everything should be a document, and everything should be RESTful HTTP. In CouchDB, like in Riak, you can upload JavaScript map/reduce functions, called "views," that execute in the database where the data lives. In CouchDB, however, these map/reduce functions must be stored as documents in the database. This gives them the advantage that their results can be persisted to disk as an index, and then the next time these views are run, they need to be run only on data that's been added or modified since the last time they were run.

CouchDB can also host static media directly from the database. This seemingly innocent feature, in addition to its RESTful interface, actually allows for entire applications to be hosted directly from the database. These are called CouchApps, and there's a lot of development going into making these more prevalent and easy to build. CouchDB tends to be very good at creating applications or scenarios where you go offline for longer periods of time, and then come back later and sync up with any changes that have happened in the meantime. In fact, CouchDB's included administration application (lovingly named Futon) is constructed in exactly this way.

The CouchDB data model is a novel one, in that it's stored as an append-only B-tree. Many databases are represented as B-trees on disk, and many databases have append-only disk representations. The novel thing about CouchDB's data format is that it's a B-tree, it's append only, and it interleaves its indexes in the very same data structure—all at the same time. This means backup is as easy as rsync, an unclean shutdown of CouchDB can't corrupt data, and it can have many concurrent lock-free reading processes.

Because CouchDB is append only, anytime a document is updated or deleted, there are spots in the file that are unused but cannot be reclaimed by the filesystem. To combat this, CouchDB has developed a process called "compaction." Compaction in CouchDB essentially does a dump of all of the data in the database, and a load into a new database, cleaning out any unused or old documents in the old database. This can be an I/O-intensive process, so that's an important thing to be aware of, from an operational perspective.

Monitoring of CouchDB can be achieved by polling a special URL provided by the database. This URL will return JSON that has all kinds of information about a running CouchDB node, and plug-ins are available for popular monitoring tools that can parse that output and keep track of it over time. Interestingly enough, one thing CouchDB won't consume a lot of is RAM. Obviously, RAM is helpful to have for other reasons such as OS disk cache, but CouchDB itself will consume well under a few hundred megabytes—even under periods of high load.

CouchDB's replication tools are arguably one of its most interesting features. They're triggered, like everything else in CouchDB, by sending an HTTP request to a node telling it to replicate its contents to another node. In recent versions of CouchDB, replicas can actually be filtered so that only a subset of the data is replicated. Also new in recent versions of CouchDB is continuous replication, which means the replication will continue to happen in the background as new documents are inserted. Using this setup, it takes only a few HTTP requests to set up master-master replication, or to reverse the roles in a master-slave setup.

In the Wild

The BBC's Enda Farrell had this to say about why the BBC chose CouchDB over MySQL:

> We run a "platform" for the rest of the BBC—but we don't want to have a large set of DBAs, nor do we want to have to have large "traditional" DB servers. So, something from what is now called "NoSQL" is what we need. Given that we also have (now) two and (before long) three datacenters, we needed something that could run master-master and/or master-master-master. The "platform" demanded that we put a lightweight authorization API over CouchDB—so we added sharding/partitioning there, too.

Currently, the BBC stores 1 TB of information in CouchDB, but it expects that to (at least) triple in the next year. The cluster accepts 6 million writes per day and 200 million read requests per day.

MongoDB

MongoDB is a document-oriented database that is developed primarily by a company called 10gen. It's currently being used in production by SourceForge, Urban Airship, Disqus, GitHub, and Justin.TV, among others. MongoDB's document format is very similar to JSON and is a format that 10gen is calling "BSON"—a binary-encoded specification of JSON-like objects. MongoDB is written in C++ and tuned for high speed.

MongoDB's querying facilities are much more traditional than some of the other databases represented in this chapter. Instead of uploading a JavaScript map/reduce function, specifying a key range, or doing anything nontraditional like that, MongoDB supports an almost object-oriented query layer. You build up a query expression object where you can do ad hoc queries for things such as "all users whose age is less than 30 and whose first name is Tom." Most of the same kinds of things you can do with SQL, you can do with MongoDB's query expressions.

MongoDB also supports indexes, in the same vein as you would expect from an SQL database, and those indexes can also enforce uniqueness. MongoDB can be set up in one of many replication strategies: a master-slave strategy, a replica pair strategy, and a (limited) master-master strategy. The master-slave strategy works exactly as most SQL databases do—writes to the master are asynchronously shipped over to the slave. Replica pairs are interesting in that they are master-slave but on a node failure, the slave can become a new master. MongoDB clients know they should write only to the master, and as such they automatically transition to the new master. Master-master is not recommended, but it is possible. In that setup, both nodes asynchronously ship data to the other.

Monitoring a MongoDB cluster can happen in one of several ways. The database itself can be queried from one of its drivers, logs can be analyzed, but most importantly, MongoDB comes with a command-line utility called mongostat. The output of this utility can be consumed by many of the popular monitoring tools. There is even a scout plug-in that will report slow queries based upon a specified threshold.

Backups to MongoDB can happen in several different ways. The simplest and most straightforward approach is to shut down the database and copy the datafiles to a backup location. Of course, then the database will be down for a period of time. Another way is to temporarily lock the database from writing, copy the datafiles, and then unlock the database. If the database is small enough, this can be a viable solution. A third way to back up is to run the mongodump utility, which dumps an entire database into a binary file. Finally, you can simply set up a database slave and do any of the aforementioned operations on that slave database, instead of on the master.

In the Wild

Michael Richardson of Urban Airship said that the company moved over to MongoDB because of scale problems it was facing with PostgreSQL:

> We were using PostgreSQL for everything; however, our growth and usage patterns became such that Postgres wasn't the most efficient solution. MongoDB hit several sweet spots, so after a long period of testing we migrated over several very write-heavy sections. In our tests (again with our usage profile and requirements), MongoDB was able to handle what we were throwing at it more easily than Postgres.

Asked about the configuration, he provided these details:

> We currently have MongoDB in a replica pair, which provides for automatic failover; this has worked extremely well for us. We're considering moving to a master-multiple slave model, however, with more manual failover.

Urban Airship aims to make use of some of the new MongoDB scaling features on the horizon, such as auto-sharding and replica sets.

Redis

Redis was originally started by Salvatore Sanfilippo, and its name is a shortened version of the phrase "remote dictionary server." I mentioned Redis earlier, but it deserves a bit more depth here. It's currently in production at GitHub, where it's being used primarily as a task queue, and at Superfeedr. It's also used at LLOOGG, which is a sort of real-time website analytics website, and is developed by Salvatore himself.

What I didn't mention earlier is that Redis can be set up in a master-slave configuration. The way that works is that you can start a new Redis node as a slave of some other Redis node. It will negotiate and determine which documents to send, and send them in bulk. Then, any new writes are automatically and asynchronously streamed from the master server to the replica.

There are a few important decisions to make with regard to durability when choosing to use Redis. Depending on your application, you may want to opt out of the periodic snapshots in favor of an append-only datafile. With this, you get a much better durability guarantee—in fact, as writes happen, they are written instantly to disk. But just writing to disk isn't necessarily enough of a durability guarantee, as the filesystem may not actually physically write to disk when you tell it to. Because of this, Redis allows you to tune the times at which an fsync call is made to the operating system. This can be set to never, letting the OS choose when to fsync, periodic (e.g., every second), or on every write for maximum durability. Note that every increase in durability comes at the expense of speed.

Whether you're running Redis in snapshot mode or append-only file mode, backups can be made by simple rsync. Snapshots are done atomically, and the append-only format is inherently able to be rsynced. An interesting tip about Redis is that it actually matters a lot whether the binary is built for 32-bit versus 64-bit; 64-bit builds have quite a bit more overhead, so if your dataset will be less than 2 GB in size, it's best to build Redis in 32-bit mode so that it can be slightly more space efficient. In fact, a neat trick is to run multiple instances of 32-bit Redis on the same node, with each instance holding less than 2 GB of data.

Finally, monitoring can be done by issuing a simple plaintext command over TCP (the INFO command). The results of this command come back as a newline-delimited list of properties, such as connected_clients, connected_slaves, used_memory, and so forth. Again, like for CouchDB, plug-ins are available for popular monitoring tools that can parse that output and keep track of it over time.

Conclusion

These are really the very early days in the NoSQL space. It's amazing how many of these databases simply did not exist even just two or three years back! For each category of databases, there are several nascent databases that all seem viable. Over the coming years, some of these databases will probably fade away, and new ones will probably crop up to replace them. The maturity of all of the different databases will increase, though, especially as real-world use continues to define and evolve the feature sets that each database provides.

Right now, though, the best thing you can do is think about your data and operations team. What does your data look like? Does it fit well into an SQL database, and if not, what category of database best suits it? Does your team have any experience with any of the prospective databases? Once you have the answers to these questions, you have only to prototype the database and try it out for yourself. Hopefully, this chapter has given you the knowledge and the tools you need to evaluate each NoSQL database's viability for your problem.

## CHAPTER SIXTEEN

Agile Infrastructure

Andrew Clay Shafer

Agile *adj.* quick and well coordinated

IF YOU ARE BUILDING AND MANAGING WEB INFRASTRUCTURE, chances are
good that you have heard of Agile software methods. Perhaps you have been supporting the application produced by an Agile team. Maybe these software developers
and managers use words such as *stories* and *iterations* and then talk passionately about
"people over process" and "responding to change over following a plan." Agile popularized these ideas within development organizations, but all too often that is where
Agile starts and ends. No amount of unit tests, continuous integration, stand-ups, story
cards, or jargon can fix the problem of code tossed from developers to operations with
ceremony but without communication. Agile might seem like a living hell if you are
the one with the pager. Hopefully, we're going to change that together.

Agile means change, and lots of it. Our experience tells us change causes outages.
Changes also enable the organization. That poses a dilemma that creates tension
between ops and dev in many organizations. One problem is that both teams optimize
for their worldview. The tension is an opportunity to optimize for the whole organization, but that requires recognizing and validating each other's concerns. No technology
can do that for us.

Agile ostensibly focuses on improving communication and the flow of ideas, but when
that focus is lost, Agile can become a ritualized excuse for failing to communicate,
especially at the perceived process boundaries. If operations is outside the Agile "circle
of us," the tension between dev and ops can become an open conflict. That boundary

is often defined in both directions, and in the worst cases it may be an institutionalized wall of confusion and antagonism with totally separate management structures. The boundary may predate any notions of Agile, but Agile adoption likely intensified the relationship. If Agile isn't a thing your organization has adopted, let's not focus on the label. Let's focus on what we want to enable and how to get those results, and let's tear down the figurative walls.

Before we discuss web operations, if we are being honest we must recognize that in most organizations technical standards are embarrassingly low. If you have spent time working in web technology, you feel that truth in the pit of your stomach, unless you have been extremely lucky, have been extremely sheltered, or are extremely clueless. So, what's the problem? All technology problems are people problems. People are also the solution. Every bug, every failure, every outage, every recovery was set in motion by people.

Controlling and manipulating machines is easy, compared to controlling and manipulating people. People have feelings and egos. They have needs and desires. People are fallible and relatively error-prone, but people are also amazing and creative.

Technologists have a tendency to focus on technology when looking for solutions, but tools are only as good as the people who use them and solutions can be only as good as the people's level of understanding of their problems. Web operations, in theory and in practice, is enabling value at the intersection of computation, networking, storage, software, sys admins, programmers, and last but not least, a business. This is an oversimplification. The best technology will never explain what a business needs, justify what a programmer wants, stop someone from making a mess with it, or figure out what went wrong when the pager is getting alerts.

Most people are solving similar problems. Unless your environment and business are pushing the threshold of some technical boundary, chances are good that an open source library, framework, or system is available that can solve many or all of your problems. When this isn't the case, understanding the ecosystem of frameworks with their assumptions, conventions, principles, and trade-offs will almost always result in better decisions. A lot of smart people have solved similar problems before and you probably won't stumble on an optimal solution in isolation. A lot of those same people are willing to share their ideas and solutions with you.

There are also frameworks for people, but you can't just download and install them. You can't just push out new config files to your team and expect new behaviors, regardless of the details in the pages of the new policy, and adding another layer of managers is hardly effective. Mandate is rarely effective as an agent of change. If you want to ensure that a policy is ignored, I suggest you document it thoroughly.

> If you want to build a ship, don't drum up people together to collect wood and don't assign them tasks and work, but rather teach them to long for the endless immensity of the sea.
>
> —Antoine Jean-Baptiste Marie Roger de Saint Exupéry

Technologists often tune out when hearing words such as *synergy* and *symbiotic*. We are rightfully skeptical of those peddling silver bullets, rainbows, and unicorns. Although I am generally optimistic about what organizations can accomplish, I'm not talking about silver bullets. Sometimes the first step toward healing is to recognize and feel the pain, and then to rebreak the bones that are set incorrectly. I believe that people generally perform when working on something they take pride in, when they feel their work matters, when they feel quality is appreciated and rewarded, and when they understand how they add value. If this doesn't match your experience and beliefs, perhaps these ideas aren't for you. Maybe you can get more from the other chapters in this book. Best of luck.

My hope is that you can take these anecdotes and principles and apply the ideas to your unique goals and constraints. Where the insights and action you should take are clear and the results you get are good, I credit you, my teachers, and the people I have worked for, I have worked with, and who have worked for me. Any points that are too abstract or confusing for you to put into action are entirely my failing.

Agile Infrastructure

The tao that can be told is not the eternal Tao.

Agile as a word and concept often has a polarizing effect on people working in technology based on their experiences and biases. Just like anything riding the hype cycle, success attracts attention and inevitably dilutes understanding. The process often results in a group of true believers exhibiting cult-like behaviors and those soured by the experience. For many Agile adoptions, the only change is that people start to have a daily meeting and stop writing documentation, expecting unicorns to magically deliver high-quality products faster than the speed of light. That might be hyperbolic, but people are involved and people have different levels of understanding, different abilities, and different motives.

"Agile" started with a manifesto in February 2001 as a loose federation of methodologies coming together in reaction to the heavyweight methods popularized by tool vendors and considered prudent at the time. Agile delivered software, largely by streamlining the process so that people could actually focus on the software instead of on reams of checklists and documentation. The Agile manifesto shielded the programmer from the mythic evil beast "Waterfall" and armed her with test-driven development (TDD). The Agile movement has continued to evolve since the signing of the manifesto. Significant progress has been made; for example, the influence of "Lean" thought and the advancement of TDD and continuous integration in theory and in practice have made profound impacts on the way teams deliver software.

Finally, after all the hand waving and marketing documents, what is Agile? My understanding of Agile past, present, and future breaks down all the methods into two categories: first, technical best practices; and second, techniques for coordinating the results of our work and the business. Another way to outline these two categories is: techniques for people to interact with technology and techniques for people to interact with each other. Balancing both of these concerns is required to get benefits, and you ignore either technology or people at your peril.

The techniques of web operations will change. The principles and properties driving the most effective teams that build these infrastructures will change much less. Agile Infrastructure, DevOps, LeanOps, Extreme System Administration, Infrastructure 2.0—the labels we choose are less important than the results. My goal is not to give you better answers, not to sell you back your own hopes and dreams of a better way, but to illustrate what is possible, to leave you asking better questions and let you solve your own problems.

But Agile Is Not the Only Thing That Has Evolved

Somewhere along the way, software changed. When was the last time you bought software off a shelf? Software used to be something bought mostly in a shrink-wrapped box. More and more applications are delivered on a nearly ubiquitous high-speed network. The Agile manifesto was probably signed at the inflection point in the transition to domination of client/server architectures. Servers are the backbone of the applications that connect us together to both simplify and complicate our lives. Video, buying, selling, sports scores, chatting, billions of bits—none of which would be possible without the backplane of supporting networks, storage, and systems.

This transition traded the headaches of testing and supporting an application on operating systems in the wild for the proper care and feeding of massively scaled infrastructures (plus the headaches of testing the application in every browser; can someone please kill off IE 6?). The server-backed application makes those systems and the admins who care for them a critical link in the value chain, but you already know that, or you probably wouldn't be reading this book.

Some People Are Born to Web Operations, Some People Have Web Operations Thrust upon Them...

I came to web operations in theory and in practice from a developer perspective. In many organizations, there exists a standoffish antagonism between the developers and the system administrators. The problem is that developers always want to change things, and the admins always suffer the consequences. This relationship probably originated before the rise of the Web, back in the days when the admins' main respon-sibilities were network security and keeping the mail server up. The two groups have different burdens to bear, different worldviews, and in many cases different manage-ment with an institutionalized wall of confusion separating them.

As I alluded earlier, an already antagonistic relationship did not improve when the developers went from throwing code over the wall every couple of months to shoveling it over every two weeks (see Figure 16-1). The developers tried to explain: "Now we're Agile, which means we are going to be delivering the software in short iterations. We've got a good thing going over here, and it's all about people and communication, except we're not going to really talk to you, because you don't really speak our language, so we'll go back to writing code and you can go back to whatever you do in the dark recesses of the datacenter. We're cool, right?"

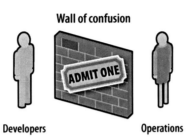

Figure 16-1. *Wall of confusion between development and operations*

> Any problem in computer science can be solved with another layer of indirection (/wiki/Indirection). But that usually will create another problem.—David Wheeler
> (In other words, a ticketing system is no substitute for a conversation.)

I've seen these scenarios played out over and over. In an extreme case, an infrastructure team of half a dozen was responsible for supporting nearly 60 different "Agile" development teams. Institutional imbalances in allocating resources aside, the relationships between the ops and dev teams ranged from cooperative to hostile. With the worst cases, the hostility was created by the developers steamrolling deployments over to operations with a works-at-my-desk, holier-than-thou attitude justified with Agile rituals and incantations.

Agile was born a developer's movement, but if the goal is really to deliver software, and software is delivered on servers, talk about "people over process" without recognizing the role those systems and the people who care from them play is disingenuous at best and potentially counter to the stated goals of "working software."

Working Software Is the Primary Measure of Progress

The ostensible aim of any team of technologists is to enable an organization to meet business goals. For the team of people responsible for web operations this means making sure the fabric underlying the applications is a strategic combination of available, stable, performant, and flexible.

People in operations are fond of saying, "You own your availability," which is a true but potentially misleading statement. Just like most other things that can be "owned," availability isn't free. The cost of availability is an initial down payment of time and resources, and then perpetual ongoing costs that must be paid in time and money. Every "nine" costs approximately 10 times more than the last one. I think of this as an "availability tax." You also own your stability, performance, and flexibility.

From my experience, a critical success factor in delivering any software is the fidelity of the delivered service with the vision of the organization. A mismatch between that vision and what is produced results in all manner of dysfunction, ranging from blame game hot potato to a smoldering distrust between every person involved. Agile approaches attempt to provide transparency while balancing the perspectives of different personas with changes in the functionality as the business learns more about what it needs and wants.

The job of the operations team is not just to keep the site up, or just to provide the highest level of service at the lowest possible cost. Their job is to enable the business, which additionally means providing relevant information and advocating proportional investment in the infrastructure, while understanding how the organization creates and captures value.

Nothing you know to be a problem should go unattended or unnoticed just because it is not your job. Many IT organizations create an ongoing crisis of conscience as important details are left unmentioned because they are not yet causing pain. Change your organization or change your *organization*.

The Application Is the Infrastructure, the Infrastructure Is the Application

If an application is delivered as a web service, there is no application without the infrastructure. The business value of the organization depends on those systems. All the features, 3x5 cards, and unit tests in the world do not matter when the site is down.

The choices the developers make can have profound impacts on the quality of life of the ops team. The converse is also true. The implementation of a new feature that works great on a single workstation or when tested in isolation can and will bring the production environment to a crawl once it is introduced to the users at large. This will likely (hopefully!) result in pager notifications, but the most effective solutions require an understanding of the application, the infrastructure, and the needs of the business. Communication such as this can't happen through a wall of confusion. No technology exists that can solve this.

Operations is also changing. In 2010, we are in the midst of an infrastructure renaissance of technology and tools. Provisioning, configuration, deployment, and monitoring can all be driven with APIs, and these tools should only be getting better. For most organizations, the days of racking servers and pulling cables are quickly becoming a thing of the past and are the most commoditized operational concern. The future is manipulating compute, storage, and network resources with code. The infrastructure isn't just something that supports an application. *The infrastructure is an application!*

Managing that infrastructure is writing software. Why not leverage lessons, tools, and techniques from the software development domain?

So, What's the Problem?

The sys admin subculture almost prides itself on firefighting and reliance on secret knowledge. Several years ago, I would prepare for deployments at an e-commerce start-up I was working for by picking up an energy drink on the way into the office for the late-night ceremony. (I was partial to the 24-ounce Rockstar Juiced Pomegranate at the time but have since moved on to the 180 Açai Berry, but I digress.) The ritual began with reciting incantations and starting some scripts. Files were moved, processes were restarted, sometimes schemas were changed or new systems were added. The process was an unpredictable mix of running scripts, babysitting the results, tailing logs, and watching the monitoring. "Operations" wasn't part of my title or official duties, but I knew my alternative was to go to bed and chance an outage. If things went well, I never had to pop the top on my cylinder of sugar and caffeine; but my desk was decorated with a platoon of empty cans. The production infrastructure was roughly two dozen eight-core machines with all the RAM they could handle, smallish by web scale standards but complex enough to manifest pathology. A major source of problems was the inconsistent configuration between machines and between environments, which meant the same code might behave or perform differently from one machine to the next. Another source of problems was the inconsistent deployment process introducing the opportunity for human error with a lot of manual steps. Finally, the monitoring was largely useless from the perspective of the service. CPU and I/O are meaningless if people can't buy stuff. Through a series of choices and circumstances, and armed with my trusty energy drink, I became a human shield with flawless reasoned decisions amped up at 3:47 a.m. As fun as that sounds, don't be that guy…

Sadly, problems that could have easily been addressed with small investments in time and resources were allowed to persist and were protected with political turf wars. Pain can be the best teacher, but I can't recommend it. If you have been in this business for a while, you have probably heard of worse.

For many organizations, their operational failings are not entirely the systems team's fault. Developers are adding shiny new functionality all the time, while the ops team is viewed as a cost center that doesn't even exist unless there is an outage. As a result, operations is often resource starved, managing a patchwork of heterogeneous systems, which can lead to a vicious cycle of stability problems. There is never an opportunity to get ahead of the storm, and even if there is such an opportunity, there is little incentive to remove the little recognition the sys admin gets for her heroism. Realizing something is not your fault is not useful if that prevents you from doing something to correct the problem.

With traditional approaches and attitudes, and a team of well-intentioned admins managing an environment with two or more systems providing a service, the probability that the systems are configured the same is low. Every time work is performed on those systems, the probability gets lower. As those services begin to scale, the probability quickly approaches zero. The inconsistency leads to confusion, delay, and mistakes, resulting in long hours of troubleshooting and throwing the sprawling directory of scripts at the brightest fire. And just when things seem to be quiet, the developers want to change a bunch of stuff, and if you are really lucky you also happen to be responsible for the VoIP phones and keeping the printers working. (Any resemblance to real events is purely coincidental.)

I started out by asserting that the standards in this industry are embarrassingly low, but that's not telling the whole story. Like most things there is a distribution that ranges from awesome to subdismal. I'm not going to point fingers, but I hope we can collectively raise the bar above "suck."

Talk Does Not Cook Rice

Here I will outline what I believe are guideline principles and practices for providing high service levels to an organization. The rest of the chapters in this book should give you details and particular techniques. These practices have emerged from the necessity of providing highly scalable, performant infrastructure with pressure for unprecedented uptime. One thing is certain: the scale of web applications is not going to get smaller anytime soon, and I believe that will drive even more innovation. If you are familiar with the language and practices of Agile software development, you will recognize that some of the ideas have been borrowed and reapplied. I think reapplying principles in novel domains often leads to insight, but I want to avoid the thought that every idea from software development can or should be mapped onto system administration. I don't intend this to be comprehensive so much as thought provoking, and I hope you will take these ideas, make them your own, and improve them. These are technical principles, but they will never be any better than the people who are implementing them.

The infrastructure is an application

If you take away just one idea, let it be this: the infrastructure is an application. If everything in the infrastructure is managed with an API, the management process is software development. The application domain is "system administration." This mindset enables and empowers goodness. Try it, you'll like it.

Version control: The foundation of sanity

In software development, version control is the foundation of every other Agile technical practice. Without version control, there is no build, no TDD, no continuous integration. We can apply that same basic idea to managing systems, starting with just versioning the sprawling "scripts" that are being used to manage systems now. You should never again have the problem of making a mistake editing a file and not being able to recover the original. The next step is to version *everything* and to extend the notion of "building from source" to systems. You should version the network configurations, the system configurations, the application configurations, the monitoring configurations, the database schema, everything you don't want to lose, you want to be able to restore, and you want to be able to track.

In modern operations, systems can (and should) be provisioned from bare metal to running and monitored services in a fully automated fashion. (If you leverage virtualization, the provisioning step is just an API call and the rest can be handled with the same configuration and deployment strategies. The nice thing about virtual machines is that for most purposes, they behave the same as real machines, which is sort of the whole point.) You have no good reason not to use version control. None. Version control is a prerequisite enabling consistency, flexibility, correlating change, rolling back, disaster recovery, and everything beautiful.

Configuration management and automated deployments

To really leverage versioning and accomplish the goal of automated builds from source, you should commit to a configuration management strategy. There are different philosophies about how to do this and tools available to fit whichever philosophy resonates with you. The difference between the current approaches is relatively small when compared to the difference between committing to a solution and not doing so. At a high level, good configuration management allows you to create policies about how different classes of the systems need to be configured—for example, web servers, databases, or whatever specific services the systems need to provide. The configuration management then audits and enforces the desired states of your systems. Modern tools will reliably put systems into a consistent state without the need for any human guidance or intervention. Managing hundreds of systems is almost as easy as managing one of each type, and there is added benefit to modeling and reasoning about the complexity of the services.

Where configuration management ends and deployment begins is unresolved in my opinion. Most people draw some line between managing the configuration of the host systems and the applications. People draw the line in different places depending on their backgrounds, the operating systems and technology they have chosen, and the scale of the services. The spectrum ranges from deploying using package managers to blasting files about with BitTorrent. This division is somewhat arbitrary, and I believe the line will blur even more as the tools evolve. Regardless, the result should always be a fully automated pushbutton deploy that moves new versions of code to production.

Monitoring

People I respect a lot have compared monitoring systems to testing in software development. I don't think of them as totally equivalent, but there is value to recognizing similarities and differences. Extreme programming evangelized and popularized TDD; no code should be written without a test. The argument is that you don't know code works unless the tests prove it does. How do you know your systems are up? People are experimenting with ways to approach test-driven system administration, and I'm sure those experiments will refine the practice, but sometimes I feel like people are trying too hard to find one-to-one mappings with the development techniques. I suggest you follow the evolution and perhaps get involved. What I will strongly advocate is that no service gets deployed without monitoring that the service is functional.

If a service isn't worth monitoring, it isn't worth deploying. Full books are written on monitoring, with all sorts of substrategies on alerting and trending. Do you need to know the state of fans on individual servers? Maybe, maybe not. Do you know a service is functional just because the host will still ping? Can you ping it from outside the firewall? I've been the guy on the phone reporting that the systems are down and being told they are still up because they were pinging from inside the firewall. Needless to say, hilarity ensued. Hopefully, I can convince you that nothing is up unless services can fulfill their requests. For me, this is about a mindset that seeks to enable the business and making proportional investments toward an easier life for the people who have to reason about both the state and the intended state of the infrastructure. If you sell widgets, you should probably monitor trends on widget sales.

Dev-test-prod life cycle, continuous integration, and disaster recovery

Have you ever witnessed strange behavior in production because the systems were configured differently than the test environment? System changes blur with application changes. Making changes directly to production is heroic but is rarely the responsible choice. (Although sometimes that responsible choice needed to be made weeks ago and things have to be fixed *now*.) Having configuration management that enforces the configuration means the small mistake a sys admin could make on a console which prevents the service from restarting gets propagated to all your systems as part of the new configuration policy. I'm amazed at how many people I've seen implement configuration management with only one environment. Sometimes these same people balk at the thought of developers making code changes directly in production. The changes to the configurations and the application should be deployed as part of the same process, while putting the infrastructure through the full dev-test-prod cycle like any other code changes. "Fail happens"; protect your production environment from the mistakes and bad assumptions that will get committed.

Continuous integration is the process of testing small changes to code against a battery of tests. Several popular open source choices with nice dashboards are available, but the main idea is to take a build through a set of tests. Most people build and test the application and then call it good, but we want to push that boundary in both directions and apply it to the infrastructure. The continuous integration process can provision a new machine, configure it, deploy the new build of the application, run all the tests and monitoring, and store the results. When the new features pass all the tests, the build can be promoted to production.

Not everyone is in a business that can justify building highly available fault-tolerant systems. I decided to mention disaster recovery here because in my opinion applying continuous integration to systems can provide a new level of confidence in a team's ability to rebuild the infrastructure, largely because they rebuild it and verify that it works every day. I'm simplifying a bit, and continuous integration is only as good as the foundation of automation and monitoring underneath. Obviously, there are other considerations besides the systems that may need special care to be recovered (like maybe the data), but I guarantee you will sleep better the day you know you can automatically restore all of your infrastructure and services from scratch.

Radiate information

Starting with version control and moving to monitoring the dev, test, and production environments in conjunction with continuous integration, there is an amazing amount of information, almost an overwhelming amount. Choosing what to see and how to see it will have profound impacts on how teams discover and decipher issues in the application and infrastructure. The goal is to detect issues, correlated with deployments, usage patterns, and network or hardware problems, as quickly as possible (see Figure 16-2). The ideal solution is a dashboard that provides a high-level summary with some reasonable ability to drill down and allows different metrics to be seen, correlated in time and overlaid with known events—for example, deployments tagged with the revision and the name of the person who pushed the button. In my opinion, you should try to make this information available and understood by as many people in the organization as possible. Having a shared reference and context will save lots of hair pulling and miscommunication on the occasions when time is most critical.

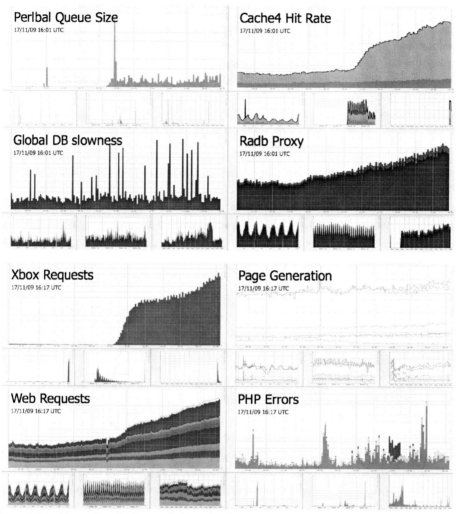

Figure 16-2. *Examples of information radiators (http://www.flickr.com/photos/ davidsingleton/4112671768/in/pool-webopsviz and http://www.flickr.com/photos/ davidsingleton/4112659086/in/pool-webopsviz)*

Reflective process improvement

If you treat your infrastructure as an application and have everything in version control, with configuration management and fully automated deployments building fully monitored systems that everyone can access and understand already, pat yourself on the back. If you don't, start making proportional investments in the improvements that will give you the most impact. Start with version control. Setting up a version control system will take almost no time; you probably have one for the application code. Getting your team in the habit of using version control all the time is another story. If you would like a new process to be ignored, document every detail; if you would like a new process to be adopted, start doing it. A mandated process that causes more pain than it solves is not the path to take. When inconsistency causes failure, or you seem to be repeating the same work, invest in configuration management and automation. The next time you fail, try to add the step of preemptively detecting the root cause to the monitoring. Step by step by step, improve the application that is your infrastructure.

Incremental changes and refactoring

When a new system required a purchase order and weeks of waiting, sometimes it made sense to create a big design upfront and deploy it with concern and ceremony, but not anymore. Virtualization makes rapid experimentation with the infrastructure accessible. When you have a question about how something will work, test it. Fire up some virtual machines and see. Protecting the production infrastructure with a development and testing process makes changing safer. The impact of small, data-driven changes to the infrastructure can be readily correlated and interpreted while the changes are still fresh in the mind. (Especially because you can see the change set in your version control and the effect of the deployment in the monitoring, right?)

The simplest thing that could work

Simple is almost always better. Agile developers are fond of saying "the simplest thing that could possibly work." Often this idea is used to justify "the stupidest thing that will probably work which I happened to think of first." When several years of these solutions are built on top of each other, small changes can have unpredictable and far-reaching effects. In systems or software, build complexity from simple, loosely coupled primitives. Complexity has an ongoing cost in difficultly reasoning about cause and effect. The system domain and application stacks have enough inherent complexity; don't make your job harder by being clever. Many before you have overengineered highly distributed, redundant, single points of failure. Don't be the one to push that boundary. When you are making changes, don't just look for solutions that add to the system; also look for opportunities to remove and simplify the system. (My favorite organizational antipattern is the prima donna architect who mandates clever solutions but never has to build or deal with any of the consequences.)

Separation of concerns

This used to be more of a problem, before the advent of inexpensive, reliable, and performant virtualization, if people didn't have the luxury of a budget for dedicated hardware. A system should ideally be responsible for providing one service. That service can have inherent complexity, but separating the different components will pay dividends when you are trying to reason about failures and performance. A collection of simple decoupled services is generally much easier to manage because people don't have to worry about the configurations colliding or interacting in strange ways.

Technical debt

Some of you might point out that separating concerns seems to violate simplicity. What could be simpler than just running everything on one system? First, there is often some tension between different idealized principles, and our job is to balance them with reason. Second, I don't believe this is the case in the sense that each individual system is much simpler, and that really pays off in troubleshooting and maintenance. Making decisions that will cost more to maintain later incurs a technical debt. There is a difference between the simplest system that delivers value and the simplest thing I could do to solve a problem. People in operations are always deciding between doing things right and doing things right now, often moment by moment. If an organization always chooses solutions that are quick but superficial, eventually servicing the technical debt becomes overwhelming. The simplest examples are upgrades and patches are that put off or key processes that aren't automated. The extra work that comes from not being up-to-date and repeatedly doing the same task is paying interest on the technical debt. That doesn't mean incurring debt is always the wrong answer in the short term, but quite often it is.

Continuous deployment

Deployment is often a ceremonial handoff from development to operations. I've touched on the benefits of incremental change, and I like to think of this as the idea of turning "incremental change" up to 11. Assuming all the systems are relatively stable, automated, monitored, and continuously integrated, the next step is to deploy after a change set passes the automated testing. That doesn't mean you are flapping in the wind because the code passed all the tests and you are monitoring the new feature, right? The goal is to reduce the fixed cost and ceremony of deployment to almost nothing, by automating not only the deployment process, but also the processes that protect us from our own mistakes.

Patterns and Antipatterns

A rich vein to mine from software development is the notion of patterns and antipatterns (which pay tribute to Christopher Alexander's notion of practical architectural patterns). Patterns describe solutions to common problems and antipatterns are commonly implemented bad solutions. Pattern languages are useful because they also provide for more compact communication encapsulating intent, motive, solution, and consequences. Antipatterns are often amusing labels for problems we hopefully don't have. (See also the Google-able terms *resign patterns* and *code smells* for inspiration.) I believe these patterns and antipatterns exist in systems work as much as they do in development. We just haven't done as much to recognize and develop the language.

Pairing

Pair programming is controversial. I was once told by a really good programmer that pair programming was the idea that you could get one good programmer from having two mediocre programmers sit together. I reject that idea, but I do think pairing is a skill and recognize that it makes people uncomfortable. I've also heard really good programmers claim that pairing makes them two to five times more productive. Research and my experience say that in general the average team will get about as much work done in the same amount of total time spent, but the quality of the work will be significantly higher. Furthermore, productivity is only part of the story. My colleague, who rejected the idea of pairing, while highly productive was essentially a silo unto himself, which made working on his code very difficult for other people on the team.

A team of specialists is a team of single points of failure. I've seen engineers who would rather spend hours wrestling with a problem than admit they don't know something or ask the team member who knows that domain for help. Talk about a waste of resources! I contend that an undeniable benefit of pairing, and in particular, promiscuous pairing (which just means that pairs switch partners frequently), is the osmotic learning about the systems and each other's expertise. The problem solving tends to be better, everyone's work is continuously reviewed, and pairs generally make better choices than either would individually. The buddy system is also useful in firefighting situations, which is why real firefighters use it. Someone sitting next to you and checking what you are about to do to production systems can save everyone a lot of heartache. The minutes in "overhead" can save you hours of cleanup and apologies. Get each other's backs…

Managing flow

There are lots of "Agile" methods for planning, estimating, and prioritizing the work to be done. I won't explain them all here, but they all have some utility, and if you happen to find one that is particularly suited to how your organization works, by all means try it as an experiment and get your own data. My strong recommendation is that ops teams (and dev teams, for that matter) research and adopt a Kanban approach to task management. The basic idea is all tasks (or stories) are represented by physical cards on a Kanban board. The cards are prioritized in a queue and they move across the board in various stages. The key to Kanban is to limit the work in progress in each stage, creating a pull-based progression as work is completed; there is no set way to identify those stages, but something similar to "Backlog," "Developing," "Testing," and "Deployed" for the columns and maybe some different rows for the teams could be one way to go (see Figure 16-3). Ideally, the Kanban board is shared with the dev team. For ops, I like to have red cards that represent an escalation that interrupts work in progress; the cards are pulled off the board and the root cause with the time spent is recorded on the card when the escalation is over. Keeping these red cards together with the other accomplished tasks gives the team and management a real sense of how much time they spend firefighting and avoids situations where people wonder why other tasks aren't being completed. The board also acts as a physical information radiator which makes obvious what everyone is working on, what is done, what is waiting, and what will be worked on next. If your ops team is large or distributed or if there are organizational impediments to sharing a board with the developers, do your best to make your Kanban flow as accessible to everyone as possible.

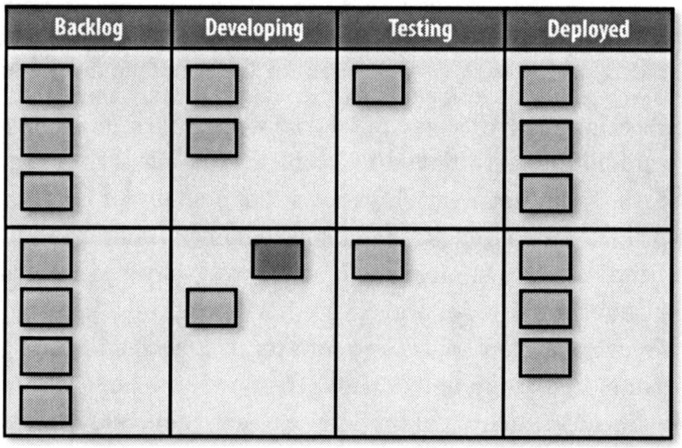

Figure 16-3. *Do you Kanban?*

Each of these ideas could probably be expanded into a full chapter with examples, some of which are covered by other authors in this book. This list is not finished, but I suggest that you start with version control and configuration management and work toward continuous deployment when you have rock-solid monitoring that you can make sense of and consistently use to detect issues. You can't think about continuous deployment until every single deployment is effortless. "Effortless" may take quite a bit of work.

Communities of Interest and Practice

Operations should be a community of practice. Blogs, conferences, and books such as this one help to build the community. As people share their experiences, approaches, and solutions with each other, a community of practice grows a vocabulary and ethos. As jargon develops, people in the community use it to both communicate more effectively and identify each other.

Development is another community, as are sales, marketing, testing, and design, each with their own jargon and ethos. Each group speaks a different language and values different things. Some organizations have "walls of confusion" between each of these communities of practice, potentially starting with the executives. These walls create turbulence as each group tries to protect its interests from the perceived interests of the others.

I recently had a conversation with an executive consultant who believed it was critical for a CTO to have some background in marketing and sales so that she could understand the needs of the business. After further discussion, I concluded that the ability to communicate with all the personas in their own language was the difference maker. (Perhaps sales and marketing at a tech company need a background in technology? Hmm?) The consultant's key point was that sorting out perspective and vocabulary in every communication is expensive and potentially problematic, whereas the solution is an overlap in understanding and language to bridge the communities.

What can developers and sys admins do to work through the differences in worldview and language? A good first step would be to recognize that everyone is part of a community of interest: the interests of an organization. No group can effectively do that alone.

Trading Zones and Apologies

Developers, sys admins, network engineers, and database administrators are all "technologists" with different expertise, and these coarse distinctions could be subdivided further. Building and maintaining a massive web application (remember, the infrastructure is the application) requires input and optimizations from all these perspectives.

"Trading zones" is a metaphor credited to Peter Galison's explanation of physics and engineering disciplines working together to produce particle detectors and radar:

Two groups can agree on rules of exchange even if they ascribe utterly different significance to the objects being exchanged; they may even disagree on the meaning of the exchange process itself. Nonetheless, the trading partners can hammer out a local coordination, despite vast global differences. In an even more sophisticated way, cultures in interaction frequently establish contact languages, systems of discourse that can vary from the most function-specific jargons, through semispecific pidgins, to full-fledged creoles rich enough to support activities as complex as poetry and metalinguistic reflection. (Galison, P. [1997]. *Image & Logic: A Material Culture of Microphysics*. Chicago: The University of Chicago Press, p. 783.)

When disparate groups have a common interest in an exchange for mutual benefit, the language they need to work together emerges from working together. Of course, this emergence can be a clumsy and painful process, but a facilitator conversant in both disciplines mitigates the problems.

An institutionalized wall of confusion prevents the exchange. Ideally, everyone adds expertise and value, and this is true in a high-functioning organization, especially when the team is small. Sadly, from my experience, this is often not the case. I've had more than one conversation with members of an operations team who described problems working with the developers and vice versa. On several occasions, after hearing about the problems, people balked at what I thought were quite simple solutions involving a combination of conversations and technology. Suggestions to implement a versioned, package-based deploy process were "never going to happen," and often the nonstarter was just having a conversation to bring it up with members of the other team who ostensibly worked on delivering value for the same business. The "other" group would never understand. "They" aren't like "us"; "they" are different.

Narcissism of Small Differences

Sigmund Freud coined the phrase "narcissism of small differences" to describe the situation where negative feelings are sometimes directed at people who we closely resemble, while we focus on and take pride in the "small differences" that distinguish us.

The time and pain caused by working around and talking past each other was obvious, at least to the operations team, but taking the first step toward making things better required courage that some people couldn't find on their own. The root cause, in my opinion, is a "deficit of trust."

I started by saying all your problems are people problems. The obstacles to clear before an organization can progress are not technology issues. Installing a better tool can never solve them. The best hammer is only as good as the arm that swings it. Often, the answer is simple, but simple isn't always easy. In reading this book, if you are being honest you probably see things that could be better in your organization. Precisely because you are reading this, I suspect you might have already made efforts to improve things. Trust isn't just blind faith that someone will do the right thing. Trust also implies that everyone can propose improvements in good faith. This doesn't mean everyone needs to agree on everything. As I said, conflicts are opportunities to optimize. High-functioning teams with highly talented people don't always agree. High-functioning teams respectfully balance out the concerns that cause the disagreements. Not-so-high-functioning teams hide information from each other, disregard each other's concerns, and push the distrust envelope as far as possible. Most teams are somewhere in the middle.

Trust debt is at least as hard to pay off as technical or credit debt, requiring awareness, discipline, and courage to overcome inertia and entropy. The best strategy is not to acquire the deficit and to create boundary objects to facilitate communication and coordination. Shared information, shared version control, shared metrics, shared goals, and shared space can solve a lot of problems before they exist. Everyone can see that is happening. No one changes things in secret, but people also aren't required to waste time with high-process ceremony, especially for routine low-risk changes (which are of course fully tested). Not only can we start to see the work of others, but we can also get insight into how our decisions impact their work. When you make mistakes take responsibility; when someone else makes mistakes take responsibility. If the collective culture encourages everyone to minimize surprise and apologize, trust should grow with compounding interest.

What to Do?

Every human action begins with a thought. Agile operations is about a mindset as much as any technology. Ironically, the most Agile teams never really trumpet that fact and teams that decree Agile loudly are rarely Agile.

Cargo Cults

Cargo cults often appear when isolated people covet another foreign group's resources and advanced technology but are unable to understand or obtain it easily through trade or their established traditions. Cargo cults conduct rituals imitating the outward and observable behavior of those possessing the desired wealth. Well-known cargo cult rituals include building mock airstrips, constructing nonfunctioning radios with coconuts, and holding daily standup meetings. In the proper form, these things are all potentially useful, but without understanding they just seem incredibly wasteful, although the rituals seem vital to the believer. Sometimes Agile adoptions are like a cargo cult: a collection of misunderstood practices with few or no results.

The key to really making progress is honest assessment and reflective improvement, realizing you are on a path with direction but without a destination. Start with the circumstances and resources you have and make changes. Some of those changes might be obvious and the results might be measurable, and sometimes the best ideas are going to come from a gut feeling and will be qualitative. All things being equal, I prefer a team feeling better about how they perform over contrived, unactionable metrics.

Bruce Lee said, "Absorb what is useful, discard what is useless." This is likely the most misinterpreted quote of modern times, typically used to justify focusing on what someone already prefers over things he doesn't understand. "Discard what you don't understand" just doesn't have the same ring to it. Sometimes the effort to learn something new is a high barrier and you need an external motive to gain understanding. This is especially true when you are the "expert" and have been for years. The best teams, who from my observations tend to also be the happiest teams, cultivate a learning culture. They reflect on their own understanding, but they also look outside themselves. They know other people have answers they don't have...yet!

Don't start out thinking you have to do everything perfectly, because you never will. Start simple, get version control, try talking to each other and the other teams, and then reflect on the results. Pick something to work on—configuration management, automated provisioning, monitoring, and trending—and then reflect on the progress. Don't get distracted with meta-on-meta navel gazing, but stop long enough to get perspective, and collectively focus on creating forward pressure toward results.

Conclusion

"Agile" has often been misunderstood and misapplied. If you have been the victim of developers "delivering working software every two weeks," please accept my sincere apology. They really didn't understand the full consequences of their actions. I assure you they meant well. Don't judge them, help them. Help them help you. You need each other.

The infrastructure renaissance is being driven by the lessons learned in web operations. Cloud computing is predicated on web operations, whether leveraging clouds or building them. Abstractions exposed through APIs driving every aspect of the infrastructure make operations work start to have a lot in common with software development. The infrastructure is an application. Embrace the future by learning lessons from the communities of practice that have been building software for decades.

"Agile" is one such community, a great resource for both technical and social techniques worth studying. The community is filled with colorful and knowledgeable characters, most of whom love to share their ideas and experiences.

Don't forget where you came from. Operations isn't going away; it is becoming more important and powerful. System administration is also a rich domain, with plenty of skilled and brilliant people. Introduce yourself to the community of practice. Help that community grow by adding your experience and voice.

Don't limit ideas to any one mindset or perspective. The best ideas often come when two cultures collide. Steal every good idea you can find; make good use of what you understand and give back when you can.

Don't worry about being "Agile"; aim to be "Awesome."

People are the solution to all your technical problems.

Be good to each other.

## CHAPTER SEVENTEEN

Things That Go Bump in the Night (and How to Sleep Through Them)

Mike Christian

SEVEN YEARS AGO, YAHOO! HIRED ME to co-develop a Business Continuity Planning program. With my set-top-box programming background and supercomputer-video-server parenting experience, I was well prepared to immediately step in and say, "Um, what the heck is BCP?" It sounded so formal and businesslike; where was the technology vector here? I was more than a little concerned about the job I had just accepted, until I suddenly realized: "Wait, we have how many hundreds of millions of customers???" (My previous company had all of three clients.) I thought about all of the websites I use every day and wondered what life would be like without them. At that point, though still fairly early in the life of the Web, I was no longer capable of living a normal life without it. Something as simple as checking out a new restaurant downtown would be impossible without an online map product. I communicated with friends and family mainly through email and instant messaging; I didn't even have many of their phone numbers anymore. All of my financial planning and stock price ogling was done online. If the Web went down, my daily life patterns would be in disarray. Multiply this pain by a few hundred million, and I suddenly understood the meaning and importance of my new job. I had to keep the Web running, or at least my part of it.

One fine morning, soon after I started, a friend and coworker of mine got paged by a mail farm throwing alerts. Thinking it was probably a server or filer crash, he quickly started poking around the relevant systems to see what needed to be kicked. He was horrified to find that an entire filer volume, containing a few hundred thousand email accounts, was *gone*. It wasn't broken, it wasn't offline, and it didn't have disk failures; it no longer existed. Within minutes, a second alert went off; another volume had blinked out of existence, and a few hundred thousand more people lost years of saved conversations, contact information, and their ability to communicate with friends and loved ones. He logged in to the system console in time to see a third volume unceremoniously deleted. Now armed with the guilty party's user ID, he rushed into the next cube over, blocked the keyboard, and asked a question not fit for print. The response: "I was practicing the vol destroy command!" On a live farm??? "Oh, I thought it was the new one..." Backup tapes saved us that day.

BCP means a lot of things to a lot of different people. For many in the years following 2001, it evoked visions of airplanes flying into buildings, hurricanes, or firestorms. BCP was expensive and difficult insurance against highly unlikely events. To me, however, it was protection against the day-to-day missteps and accidents that kept our pagers sounding off. It was protection against practicing vol destroy, flaky routers, and leaky datacenter roofs. It wasn't insurance; it was a valuable tool that let me sleep at night while the gremlins prowled.

At its simplest BCP is "two of everything." But the more you dig in, the more difficult it gets: two servers, two switches, two uplinks, two power distribution units, two routers, two completely independent network planes touching all points? Of course, failover between each set of two needs to be completely automated, because human response time is glacially slow in Internet terms. As you start adding more and more redundancy and more and more automation, complexity goes up. At some point, the system is so complex that you just end up *adding* more points of failure. It's not just about diminishing returns as you scale up your plan; you eventually hit the point of negative return on your investment.

The answer to this dilemma is found at the macro level. You have to plan for disasters that affect regional services—earthquakes, hurricanes, and the like. So, you need to distribute your services across widely separated geographical areas. It's vital to have an automated way to shift your traffic to the East Coast when the next major earthquake takes out all of your Silicon Valley datacenters. Once you've solved that problem, all of the little things become less important. If a power distribution unit, a router, or a switch fails in one datacenter, your traffic will automatically move to the other metro. Obviously, *some* level of local redundancy is required to prevent traffic from flip-flopping across the country, but you no longer need to take it to the point of diminishing or negative returns.

Contrary to popular belief, datacenters do go down, sometimes for the oddest reasons. One day I was attending a conference when I received a call from our operations center informing me of a major datacenter outage. Worried that this event was about to ruin the conference for me while we cleaned up the mess, I immediately phoned one of my coworkers to understand the extent of the impact. To my relief, she let me know that all of our properties had already failed out of that location, shifting traffic to other datacenters, and that she was looking forward to roasted squirrel for dinner. Turns out the little bugger had crawled into an electrical box and chewed through a major power distribution cable. The squirrel did not survive that day, but we came through without a scratch.

Definitions

As I previously mentioned, BCP means different things to different people. Let's take a look at those definitions and what they mean to your site. To start, I'd like to discard a large portion of the definition—people and places. An important part of a comprehensive BCP plan is managing the workforce; if your office building burns down, where are all those people going to work? I'm an engineer, and that's not my area, so I'll just focus on the High Availability (HA) portion of BCP: keeping the site up. Even within HA, there are a variety of techniques, ranging from Hot/Hot to Hot/Warm to Hot/Cold to Disaster Recovery.

Hot/Hot is the ultimate in HA. Your users can use the full range of the application from any datacenter. Both reads and writes can happen anywhere. This makes it extremely simple to automate failover. But it's not a panacea. You'll have to do some serious thinking about handling data consistency issues. If a piece of data is written in two locations at the same time, there will be collisions during replication. Which write is the correct one? The Internet is such a dynamic medium that in many cases it doesn't matter. Just make sure you plan for it.

Hot/Warm is a great way to go if you can't tolerate data inconsistency. Many applications are very read heavy, with just the occasional (but important) write. In this case, it makes sense to handle the two operations differently. Keep your reads Hot/Hot, available from any datacenter, with swift automated failover; this keeps the bulk of your app very highly available. But write to only one datacenter at a time; this keeps your data consistent, at a cost of slower failover times for a small portion of your app. However, assuming you want decent site performance, you're not going to use synchronous data replication. When a write occurs, you'll make a best effort to get it to all other locations as soon as you can, but with no guarantees. Replication lag can range from seconds to minutes to hours in some cases. So, what happens when a write occurs in one location followed by an immediate read in another location? The update may not have arrived yet, and you can get stale data. We call these *critical reads*. You need to identify and mitigate critical reads, through either error handling or proxying the read back to the original site.

Hot/Cold scares me. This architecture sends both read and write traffic to a single location, with another identical deployment sitting idle somewhere over the horizon. It's easy to set up, but very low in value. When disaster strikes, you'll start to question the sanity of your plan. Will it really work? Are the software versions up-to-date? When was the last time you logged in to the cold site? Often, the cold site will sit idle and unused for a year or more. By the time you need it, it may be woefully out of date. Fear, uncertainty, and doubt inevitably lead to extended downtime. I've seen countless incidents where the cold site was so untrusted that we just took hours of downtime rather than try to fail over. If you can't use your cold site in an emergency, what's the point?

Disaster Recovery is the worst technique, and is essentially vaporware. It's not intended to protect you against common occurrences, just to give you some option to rebuild in case of a major disaster. One company we acquired had a Disaster Recovery plan which involved paying a monthly "insurance" fee to a third party who maintained a large datacenter footprint full of idle servers and storage. If our datacenter failed, we could just use theirs. Of course, if there were a large-scale disaster, we would be competing with every other one of their customers for resources. There was no real plan, and nothing had ever been tested. As we started to explore what an actual failover would look like, we found some pretty astounding issues. It turns out that they had different departments for servers and storage; the servers were in one building and the storage was in the other. There was a gigabit Ethernet link between buildings. Clearly that wouldn't work. They offered to hook up a second gigE link, at which point we just decided to do it ourselves.

How Many 9s?

Ask any executive how much downtime is acceptable, and you will get the same answer: "None." Tell the executive how much that will cost and the performance impact, and he might answer differently. Five 9s is the gold standard for availability, championed mainly by telcos, but that's primarily due to lifeline requirements. Most Internet applications haven't yet reached life-or-death availability requirements. Five 9s remains a worthwhile goal for web operators, and critical parts of the infrastructure can (and should) be architected to those levels, but for individual applications it may be overkill. The computers that end users constantly fight with, Internet connections, and cheap, at-home NATs don't come anywhere close, so a few minutes of server disruption here or there often goes unnoticed.

Instead of focusing on 9s, it's beneficial to analyze your recovery-time objective (RTO) and recovery-point objective (RPO). RTO is how long it takes you to get the site back up after an outage. RPO is how much data you are willing to lose. Often, the two goals are in competition. If you have a zero RPO and your replication lags by a few minutes, you make choose to take a multihour outage while you get the primary back up, rather than lose those few minutes of data by failing over. On the other hand, if you have a zero RTO, you may decide to fail over immediately, willing to take the loss of a few in-flight transactions. The only way to get both is to sacrifice performance by using true synchronous replication. Have you ever noticed how long it takes to withdraw money from an ATM? This is due to the extremely tight RTO and zero RPO of the backend systems. It's quite simply unacceptable to drop an ATM transaction, and financially disastrous if the entire system goes down for any length of time. So, anytime you withdraw money, you have to sit and listen to the machine whir, while it writes, replicates, and commits your transaction to multiple sites around the world. If you are not a bank, you need to be realistic about RTO and RPO. A rare minute of downtime or the loss of a comment on a popular message board may be a fair trade for consistent high performance in the steady state.

Impact Duration Versus Incident Duration

May 31, 2008, at 5:00 p.m. local time, high-voltage lines in the main electrical room of a datacenter in Houston owned by hosting provider The Planet shorted. The resultant explosion was large enough to knock down three walls. Due to fire safety concerns the backup generators were taken offline as well. Power was able to be restored to portions of the datacenter after a few days. But for thousands of servers, failover in this case involved physically transporting the boxes to another datacenter.

When disaster strikes, all you need to worry about is getting your user traffic away from the problem as quickly as possible. You need to mitigate against impact, *now*. Don't overly worry about fixing the original problem; once you've stopped the impact, you have plenty of time to remediate the incident. Some rare accidents, such as the explosion mentioned in the preceding paragraph, may take many weeks to repair. But as datacenters get larger, even the more common incidents such as brief power loss can take days to recover from. It takes a *long* time to bring up a datacenter containing a hundred thousand servers. Focus your architecture on minimizing impact duration, rather than incident duration (which is often out of your hands, anyway).

So, how do you get your user traffic away from the problem site? The usual solution is to use a Global Server Load Balancing (GSLB) platform. This is essentially a dynamic authoritative DNS server that can hand out different IP addresses for the same domain name lookup, depending on a number of factors. The most common of these factors are proximity and availability. Let's assume you have two servers, one on the West Coast and one on the East Coast, each with a different IP. When a browser in San Francisco looks up your domain name, the GSLB will usually return the IP address of your West Coast server, because that is closest to the user and will result in the best performance. However, if a moose eats your West Coast server, the GSLB, having detected that it's no longer responding, won't hand out that IP anymore. The next time the browser looks up your domain, the GSLB will instead give out the IP of your East Coast server. It may be a bit farther away, but hey, at least it's working.

In reality, GSLB is not quite that simple or perfect; it suffers from two main problems. First, the browser never actually asks the GSLB anything directly. Instead, it talks to a local caching recursive DNS server. Not to be confused with an authoritative DNS server (like your GSLB), the local recursor is there to do most of the work for a whole bunch of users, caching the results to significantly decrease DNS traffic to the auths while improving performance for end users. It's the recursor that actually talks to your GSLB auth. So, your platform can only determine proximity based on the location of that recursor; it has no idea which browser made the original request or where that browser is. In most cases, the ISP provides the recursors, and they sit fairly close to the end users. So, routing based on recursor proximity is generally close enough. There are certainly cases, however, where someone is using a recursor halfway across the planet from her computer, which will lead to incorrect proximity routing and a slower Internet experience in general.

The second problem involves caching. Each DNS answer is cached at various points along the way. The local recursor caches it, and the browser caches it. If your GSLB decides to suddenly start handing back a different IP, it will take awhile for the old address to expire from the caches so that the new one can get through. Most people use a Time to Live (TTL) of one to five minutes on their GSLB entries, so you can expect your traffic shifts during failover to take at least that long (and usually a bit longer). Note that some recursors, browsers, and other devices don't respect the TTL for various reasons. They may just hang on to that old moose-eaten IP address forever, despite the fact that it's expired and no longer working. As a result, some small percentage of your users will not shift to the new datacenter anytime soon. It's a very trivial amount, however. Because of these issues, some people consider GSLB abusing the DNS system; I just call it mostly functional.

Datacenter Footprint

We know that datacenters do fail, so you're going to need at least two of them. But is that enough? Would three or more be better? That depends on three factors: cost, complexity, and performance. Ironically, availability isn't a factor; once you have at least two datacenters in widely disparate regions, the chances of losing both at the same time are strikingly low.

In a two-datacenter model, you need to provide enough capacity in each datacenter to handle 100% of the load, in case the other one dies during peak traffic. So, in total, you're going to have to purchase twice as much server gear as you would with a single-datacenter solution. That's a 200% increase in CapEx; ouch. If you instead move to a three-datacenter model, those numbers start to go down. Now you need to build capacity for only 50% of the load in each datacenter. Assuming one goes down, you can just split your traffic evenly between the remaining two datacenters to handle 100% of your traffic. Add those three datacenters up, and you have a 150% increase in CapEx. Better! On the other hand, the additional infrastructure, rent, and staffing required to build out the third datacenter may eat up that savings, and more.

A three-or-more-datacenter solution also adds complexity and additional risk. It's difficult to guarantee that, having lost one datacenter, the remaining traffic will split perfectly evenly across the remaining two. Without that guarantee, you may be subject to cascade failure. Let's say you have three datacenters: one West, one Central, and one East. Under normal conditions, they each have 50% capacity, and take 33% of the load. If your East datacenter fails, the traffic it was handling will likely all go to the next closest datacenter, Central. Suddenly, Central is getting hammered with 66% of the load, when it has capacity for only 50%. Overloaded servers have a tendency to melt down quickly, as accept queues fill and connections start dropping. The overload can quite easily take out Central, and your GSLB will try to help by shifting that traffic to West. Now West has 100% of the traffic, with 50% capacity. It's easy to see how quickly your entire global infrastructure can come crashing down in a cascade failure.

There are many GSLB tricks and techniques to mitigate cascades, such as real-time load feedback or static fallback configurations, but these again add complexity and risk. The two-datacenter model quite simply does not have this problem. Any failure is predictable and easily handled, because both datacenters have full capacity available.

The real reason for moving to a three-or-more-datacenter solution is performance. The closer you get your servers to your users, the faster your pages will load. Bits can't traverse the Internet faster than the speed of light, and every millisecond counts. An 80 millisecond round-trip time across the United States may not seem like much, but if you have 100 items on your page, that can add up to many seconds of additional load time. Deploying a large number of widely dispersed datacenters will get your content closer to your users and really speed up your website.

> When I first started using proximity GSLB routing, I expected to see most of the traffic hitting the West Coast. After all, this is home to Silicon Valley, right? It turns out that, in general, around 66% of traffic hits the East Coast, with only 33% going to the West Coast. There are, quite simply, more people on the East Coast; hence the disparity. It gets even more interesting, however, when you look at the diurnal patterns of traffic. On the East Coast, there is a huge peak in traffic during the daytime, then a very low trough after work and at night. West Coast traffic, meanwhile, stays fairly constant throughout the day. I assume this to mean that people on the East Coast have real lives, go out to dinner after work, and sleep at night. We westerners, however, just sit in front of our computers day and night. This is Silicon Valley, after all!

Keeping all of this in mind, the best strategy is a mixed one. Run your most complex backend applications and data stores out of two datacenters, and distribute the simpler user-facing frontends as widely as you can.

Gradual Failures

When replicating extremely large data stores between two quite distant locations, it may become infeasible to achieve real-time or even near-real-time replication delays. A write which hits one datacenter may take up to several hours to be copied to the other, along with all the other simultaneous writes carpooling along in the replication stream. This can make it quite difficult to achieve a tight RPO. If one site were to suddenly fall into the ocean, you would lose several hours' worth of data! Fortunately, datacenters don't fall into oceans very often. Sudden outages generally occur only when a utility power failure combines with a UPS or generator failure (with the odd explosion from time to time). However, there are plenty of other ways for datacenters to fail, and a surprising number of them happen slowly. If you detect the problem and react quickly, this can give you precious time to sync up your replication stream and save the data.

> A few years back, we had an HVAC failure in one of our datacenters (an HVAC is basically an air conditioner the size of a Mack truck). This caused the temperature to start rising in one part of the facility. It shouldn't have been that big a deal; the datacenter was designed to be able to lose an HVAC and still keep the ambient temperature at a reasonable level with the remaining units. Unfortunately, there was a fire sensor in the

area that was getting hot. It sent a false positive, trigging the alarm. Now, the first thing you do in a datacenter fire (besides dumping Halon, which didn't happen in this case) is to shut off the flow of fresh oxygen to the area. The fancy automated system happily complied by shutting off *all the remaining HVAC units*. Linux servers are *hot*. Multiply hot by fifty thousand or so, and a datacenter with no HVAC will become dangerously hot within minutes. But, while the servers were still running, all was not lost. We were able to swiftly flush our replication data and start clean shutdowns. The inside air was so fiery, we had to send in our site operations people in five-minute shifts, to shut down as many machines as they could before they needed to evacuate.

There are a number of ways in which datacenters fail slowly. Leaky roofs, bad HVACs, and flaky networks all give you time to fail out cleanly. When there appears to be a partial problem in a datacenter, don't wait for it to be fixed and hope you don't have to fail out. Flush the replication data immediately!

Trust Nobody

Just as the most reliable datacenters go down from time to time, you can expect even the best third-party vendors to have issues now and then.

In 2006, a company by the name of Blue Security came up with an innovative way to fight spammers. By installing the Blue Frog client on your computer, every spam message you got would result in a polite request emailed to the spammer, asking him to stop. The hope was that the spammers, to avoid being overwhelmed by the flood of messages from half a million Blue Frog clients, would simply exclude those recipients from future spam campaigns. Instead, the spammers chose to fight back. A war of escalation ensued. In the end, the spammers fired off a massive DDoS attack against Blue's DNS provider, UltraDNS. By taking out UltraDNS, they took out Blue Security. Blue gave up the fight at this point, and folded. Unfortunately, that's not the whole story. Because UltraDNS hosts a large number of high-profile customers, the battle resulted in significant collateral damage. Innocent bystanders such as Tucows and Six Apart were taken offline in the process, through no fault of their own. Incidents such as this continue to happen, including several massive attacks in 2009 that caused secondary outages to companies such as Amazon and Salesforce.com.

The short story is that you can't put all your faith in a single vendor, especially if the vendor is hosting multiple companies. Someone else might get attacked, and through no fault of your own, your site goes down. The solution is to always maintain multi-vendor solutions, particularly when they rely on shared resources. Go in with the assumption that at some point, one of the vendors will suffer an outage, and you can just switch to the other.

Failover Testing

BCP plans are just that. They are plans. To turn your failover plans into reality, you need to actually execute them. A full peak-traffic failover can be a daunting task. So daunting, in fact, that I have seen many websites take hours of downtime, hoping the affected datacenter would magically come back, so that they don't have to go through a failover process that *might or might not* work. It's much better to test your procedures when you're not in an emergency situation so that if something goes wrong, you can fall back. By testing early and often, you'll gain the comfort and experience to swiftly do the right thing when disaster strikes.

Not only is regular failover testing an essential part of disaster preparedness, but it can also be a valuable tool in the day-to-day operations of your website. How many times have you pushed a new code release, only to find it breaks the site? A much better release mechanism is to fail traffic out of one datacenter, upgrade the software in the cold site, QA it appropriately, and only then fail traffic back in. Repeat with your other datacenter. This way, if something goes wrong during the upgrade, your users won't be affected. It also makes sense to implement failover to avoid risk because of standard maintenance. Need to swap out one of your redundant routers? Fail out of the datacenter, in case the other router goes bad. Testing your UPS? Fail out, lest things go wrong. The more you use your BCP plan, the better it will become. Your failovers will be comfortable and lightning fast, so when the day comes that you really need it, failing over will be a nonevent. A major datacenter disaster now becomes a brief blip in your daily workload.

Monitoring and History of Patterns

In the middle of the night, late 2008, we were migrating a huge number of websites from one GSLB platform to another. We'd done plenty of due diligence ahead of time, to ensure that the change in proximity routing algorithms wouldn't significantly affect the traffic flows. Mid-migration, the owners of one site suddenly panicked; they saw a significant spike in traffic on their East Coast site! Was the new GSLB configuration wrong, or was something broken? We spent more than 30 minutes debugging the problem, but everything we looked at told us the platform was functioning correctly. Eventually, somebody thought to look at a weeklong traffic pattern history, instead of just the last few hours most of us were monitoring. As it turned out, that site had a traffic spike of identical size on the East Coast every day at the same time. It was just a search engine doing its daily site scrape, not at all related to the migration. We'd blown 30 minutes of many engineers' sleep time chasing nothing but normal. If the site owner had been aware of his normal traffic patterns, it would have saved everyone much grief.

The moral of this story is to know your daily, weekly, and monthly patterns. If you are aware of the oddities of your normal traffic flows, you won't be surprised during failovers, migrations, or upgrades. Make sure your monitoring includes week-on-week graphs and trending, which includes not just aggregate traffic levels but also what goes where when proximity routing.

You should also recognize the evolutionary nature of monitoring. It's not something you can set up just once and then ignore until it pages you. Proper application-level monitoring is an ongoing process of adjusting the signal-to-noise ratio. Too many unimportant pages and your on-calls will start sleeping through them. Dial down too much signal and you may miss something important. Document every page received, and use that data to continually adjust your alerting thresholds so that you're not waking people up for things that don't really need immediate attention. Done right, you should be able to reduce the pager workload to a few alerts a week, even with a platform that runs on hundreds of servers in tens of datacenters.

> In the early years at my current position, we set up additional monitoring systems in our datacenters, intended to mimic real user traffic, measure speed and availability, and alert on thresholds. One day, a developer looked at his traffic graphs and saw zero traffic. This seemed odd, because the site was working fine for him. The in-datacenter monitors were happily replicating a trickle of real traffic, and all indications were green. Not a single page had been sent, but suddenly, we had no users. What happened? As it turns out, there was a bad configuration push to our edge routers that blocked all port 80 (HTTP) traffic to that datacenter from the outside. Everything looked fine from our monitoring systems, because they were inside the datacenter. We were blind to our actual users' experience.

It's not enough to monitor from within your own datacenters; that won't adequately tell you what your end users are seeing. If you have enough global footprint you can monitor cross-colo, but for most people it makes sense to seek help from third-party monitoring services such as Gomez or Keynote.

Getting a Good Night's Sleep

BCP is not about planning for unforeseen disasters; it's about preparing for the day-to-day, week-to-week, or even year-to-year random blowups that make the lives of web ops engineers hectic. If you can plan ahead, solve for the big problems, and exercise your failovers regularly as part of your day job, any failure in any part of your platform will become an easily handled event, rather than a crisis.

> Remember the story I told at the beginning of the chapter, about volumes on live mail farms being deleted, because some yahoo was practicing vol destroy? Well, just a few months back, I received the following page (paraphrased): "Sev 1 outage: 5 Flickr Photo volumes accidentally destroyed." Hmm, "accidentally destroyed"; that sounds familiar, I thought. This time it was our top storage expert, trying to repurpose an old retired filer, instead of a newbie practicing on live farms. The cause was the same, however: issuing the right command on the wrong machine. By this point, we had a solid BCP plan, and the data was already mirrored across the country. We just flipped a switch in DNS, millions of users' photos magically reappeared, and we went back to work.

Mistakes happen, both to new employees and to the most seasoned. Expect these mistakes, and plan for them; we are all human, after all. By planning for human error, machine error, and infrastructure error, you can recover from pretty much anything.

If you are going to treat BCP as a once-in-a-blue-moon occurrence, it's guaranteed to be fairly useless. So, don't bother spending the time or money; you'll just end up taking the outages and associated revenue and reputation loss anyway. On the other hand, by looking at outages as daily possibilities, and by treating failovers as risk mitigation strategies rather than disaster recovery insurance, your site can achieve an extraordinarily high level of availability, even in the face of the worst of luck.

Do it right, and the next time you get paged at 3:00 a.m. during a major datacenter failure, you can glance at a traffic graph, verify that your users have automatically shifted away from the problem site, roll over, and go back to sleep. Ah, now that's a job well done.

Contributors

John Allspaw has worked in systems operations for over 14 years in biotech, government, and online media. He started out tuning parallel clusters running vehicle crash simulations for the U.S. government, and then moved on to the Internet in 1997. He built the backing infrastructures at Salon, InfoWorld, Friendster, and Flickr. He is now VP of Tech Operations at Etsy, and is the author of *The Art of Capacity Planning* (O'Reilly).

Heather Champ (hchamp.com), formerly Director of Community at Flickr, has joined with her husband, Derek Powazek, to create Fertile Medium (fertilemedium.com), an online community consultancy. She never leaves home without a camera or three.

Mike Christian, Director of Infrastructure Resiliency, Yahoo!, has spent the last seven years building highly available systems for Yahoo!, from global replication of petabyte data sets, to massively distributed CDN and traffic routing mechanisms dispersed to points throughout the world. Prior to that, he spent nine years building interactive television systems at Oracle and Thirdspace, wrestling bus-sized parallel supercomputing systems, and building fast lightweight DVR client applications. He particularly enjoys solving unsolvable problems.

Dr. Richard Cook is a physician, educator, and researcher at the University of Chicago. His current research interests include the study of human error, the role of technology in human expert performance, and patient safety.

Richard graduated with honors from Lawrence University in Appleton, Wisconsin, where he was a Scholar of the University. He worked in the computer industry in supercomputer system design and engineering applications. He received his MD from the University of Cincinnati in 1986, where he was a General Surgery intern. Between 1987 and 1991, he was a researcher on expert human performance in Anesthesiology and Industrial and Systems Engineering at The Ohio State University. He completed an Anesthesiology residency at Ohio State in 1994. Since November 1994, he has been faculty in the Department of Anesthesia and Intensive Care of the University of Chicago. His is an Associate Director for the GAPS (Getting At Patient Safety) project sponsored by the Veterans Health Administration.

Richard was a member of the Board of the National Patient Safety Foundation from its inception until 2007. He is internationally recognized as a leading expert on medical accidents, complex system failures, and human performance at the sharp end of these systems. He has investigated a variety of problems in such diverse areas as urban mass transportation, semiconductor manufacturing, and military software systems. He is often a consultant for non-profit organizations, government agencies, and academic groups. He does not do any expert witness testimony for litigation.

His most often cited publications are "Gaps in the continuity of patient care and progress in patient safety," "Operating at the Sharp End: The complexity of human error," "Adapting to New Technology in the Operating Room," and the report "A Tale of Two Stories: Contrasting Views of Patient Safety."

Alistair Croll is a principal at the analyst firm Bitcurrent, the founder of start-up accelerator Rednod, and a frequent contributor and author online. Prior to Bitcurrent, Alistair cofounded Coradiant, a leader in online user monitoring, as well as research firm Networkshop and Human 2.0, which focuses on the convergence of humans and technology. He has held product management positions with 3Com Corporation, Primary Access, and Eicon Technology.

Alistair has coordinated and spoken at a wide range of industry events, including Interop, Cloud Connect, Enterprise 2.0, Structure, eMetrics, Bitnorth, Ignite, and Web2Expo.

He also serves as an advisor to several technology venture firms and is a partner with Year One Labs, a start-up incubator. He is the author of numerous articles on Internet performance and security; a coauthor (with Eric Packman) of *Managing Bandwidth: Deploying QOS in Enterprise Applications* (Prentice-Hall) and a coauthor (with Sean Power) of *Complete Web Monitoring* (O'Reilly.)

Patrick Debois, in order to understand current IT organizations, has a habit of changing both his consultancy role and the domain within which he works: sometimes as a developer, manager, sysadmin, tester, and even the customer.

If there is one thing that annoys him the most, it is the great divide between all these groups. But times are changing now: being a player on the market requires you to get these "battles" under control between these silos.

He first presented concepts on Agile Infrastructure at Agile 2008 in Toronto, and in 2009, he organized the first devopsdays. Since then, he has been promoting the notion of "devops" to exchange ideas between these groups and show how they can help one another to achieve better results in business.

Eric Florenzano is a software developer currently living in San Francisco and working at Mochi Media. He's also the cohost of Django Dose, a podcast about all things Django. He likes to use Python to sling his HTML, NoSQL when it makes sense, and blogs occasionally at *http://www.eflorenzano.com/*.

Paul Hammond makes things on the Internet. He's currently working on Typekit, a cloud-based font subscription service for web designers. Previously, he led a group of hard-working supernerds at Flickr. He was involved in early versions of Yahoo! Fire Eagle and Yahoo! Pipes, and has helped build infrastructure for the BBC, Yahoo! Bookmarks, and Delicious.

Paul has spoken at conferences on subjects ranging from the future of broadcasting to how to win *Monopoly*. He lives in San Francisco with 2 kids and no dog, and keeps an irregularly updated technical weblog at paulhammond.org.

Justin Huff is a small-company veteran, who started his career building embedded systems ranging from imaging sonar to home automation. Then, he jumped head first into web operations by building the backend infrastructure for Picnik.com. He is currently a software engineer in Google's Seattle office.

Adam Jacob is a 12-year system operations veteran. He is the CTO of Opscode, whose mission is to bring "Infrastructure Automation to the Masses." He is the primary author of Chef.

Jake Loomis is currently Vice President of Service Engineering at Yahoo!, where he pioneered Yahoo!'s efforts to be consistently reliable in a fast growing, rapidly changing environment. At Yahoo!, he developed and implemented a service engineering discipline across widely varied applications, including Yahoo! Mail, Yahoo! Messenger, Flickr, Yahoo! Answers, Yahoo! Groups, and numerous backend platforms. The service engineering discipline leverages best practices for operational tools, process, and people who can dramatically improve the effectiveness of web operations teams.

Before Yahoo!, Jake graduated from MIT with a degree in Brain and Cognitive Sciences and then went on to work as an engineer and manager at multiple companies, including Sapient, Embark.com, and FactSet Research Systems. His true passion at Yahoo! is working on systems that regularly handle hundreds of millions of users and providing each one with the most reliable experience possible.

Matt Massie has been working in scientific computing and system operations since 1993. He started his career writing software and building systems employed in neuro-science research at Purdue University and then later at Washington University in St. Louis. In 1999, he conceived and implemented the Ganglia cluster and Grid monitor-ing system while doing research at the University of California, Berkeley. Today, Matt is a member of the technical staff at Cloudera and serves as the VP for the Apache Avro project.

Brian Moon has been working with the LAMP platform since before it was called LAMP. He is the Senior Web Engineer for dealnews.com. He has made a few small contributions to the PHP project and been a casual participant in discussions on the PHP internals list. He is the founder and lead developer of the Phorum project, the first PHP/MySQL message board ever created.

Anoop Nagwani loves solving very large-scale storage and data management prob-lems with robust, scalable, and intelligent solutions. He has designed and managed the global storage infrastructures for Facebook, Zynga, Flickr, HotJobs, and Yahoo!. He has a Bachelor's degree in computer science from Columbia University. Prior to entering the Internet space, Anoop was an EMT and the Director of Operations for Columbia University Emergency Medical Service in Manhattan. He is currently the manager of storage engineering at Zynga.

Sean Power is a consultant, analyst, author, and speaker. He is the cofounder of Watching Websites, a boutique consulting firm focusing on early stage start-ups, products and non-profits as they emerge and mature in their niches. He has built professional services organizations and traveled across North America deliver-ing engagements to Fortune 1000 companies. He helps executives understand their competitive landscape and the future of their industry. He did the technical edition of *Troubleshooting Linux Firewall* (Addison-Wesley) and coauthored (with Alistair Croll) *Complete Web Monitoring* (O'Reilly).

Eric Ries is the creator of the Lean Startup methodology and the author of the popu-lar entrepreneurship blog Startup Lessons Learned. He previously cofounded and served as chief technology officer of IMVU. In 2007, *BusinessWeek* named Ries one of the Best Young Entrepreneurs of Tech and in 2009 he was honored with a TechFellow award in the category of Engineering Leadership. He serves on the advisory board of a number of technology start-ups, and has worked as a consultant to a number of start-ups, companies, and venture capital firms.

He is the coauthor of several books including *The Black Art of Java Game Programming* (Waite Group Press). While an undergraduate at Yale Unviersity, he cofounded Catalyst Recruiting. Although Catalyst folded with the dot-com crash, Ries continued his entrepreneurial career as a senior software engineer at There.com, leading efforts in agile software development and user-generated content.

Andrew Clay Shafer has experience in high-performance computing, computational science, embedded development, web applications, and Agile methodologies. He cofounded Reductive Labs, where he evangelized building computational infrastructure using Puppet and other modern tools. Andrew's formal education is in mathematics, but finds people's interactions with tools, process, and one another fascinating. His hope is to make practical positive contributions to the practice of deliberately creating value and likes to believe that Agile Infrastructure and DevOps will in that regard.

Theo Schlossnagle is a founder and CEO at OmniTI, where he designs and implements scalable solutions for highly trafficked sites and other clients in need of sound, scalable architectural engineering. In his role at OmniTI, he has founded several successful start-ups, including Message Systems and Circonus. Theo is a participant in various open source communities, including OpenSolaris, Reconnoiter, Apache, PostgreSQL, perl, and many others. He is a published author in the area of scalability and distributed systems, as well as a veteran speaker in the open source conference circuit.

Baron Schwartz, a.k.a. "Xaprb," is a MySQL expert and consultant, who lives in Charlottesville, Virginia. He's the lead author of *High Performance MySQL* (O'Reilly), creator of the open source Maatkit toolkit for MySQL administration, and an internationally sought-after speaker.

Baron is Vice President of Consulting at Percona, a firm that provides consulting, support, and training for MySQL users."

Index

R

Rails, 192

randomness, 43

RCA (root-cause analysis), 3, 59, 109–111, 155, 221–218

RDS (Amazon), 20, 205

reactive caching system, 128

real-time alerting, 58

real user monitoring (RUM), 168–171, 177

real-world metrics, 63

recency effect, 223

recovery-point objectives (RPOs), 229, 288

recovery-time objectives (RTOs), 229, 288 (see also MTTR (Mean Time to Repair/ Resolve))

recursors, 289

Redis, 249, 260

redundancy mechanisms, 89–93, 101, 224

reflective process improvement, 274

reinstallation, automating, 105

relational database architecture (see databases, web)

releases
  and customer relations, 60
  management strategy for, 140, 225, 245
  marketing vs. engineering, 54, 61

remediation stage, 223

rendering, 12, 16–18

repeatability, 72

replica pair strategy, 259

replication delay, 197, 204, 211

replication slaves, 194–197, 207, 212–214, 259

"Report Abuse" queues, 118

responsiveness
  application, 161
  what makes a site slow, 163–165

RFCs, 5

Richardson, Michael, 259

Rich Internet Applications (RIAs), 181

ring replication, 211

Robbins, Jesse, 3

rollouts, gradual, 61

root-cause analysis (RCA), 3, 60, 109–111, 155, 221–224

Round Robin Database (RRD), 22, 159, 215

RPOs (recovery-point objectives), 229, 288

RSS feeds, 181

RTOs (recovery-time objectives), 229, 288 (see also MTTR (Mean Time to Repair/ Resolve))

Ruby on Rails, 151

RUM (real user monitoring), 168–171, 177

S

S3 (Amazon), 12–15

SaaS sites, 174

safety in complex systems, 112

Saint Exupéry, Antoine Jean-Baptiste Marie Roger de, 264

sandboxes, 51

Sanfilippo, Salvatore, 260

satellite phone "expected latency," 3

ScaleDB, 205

schema changes, 191, 214

seasonal usage levels, measuring, 23, 25

security group, 88

senior operations, 8

separation of concerns, 276

serial dependencies, 90

ServerManager, 16–20

server-sent events, 183

server-side RUM, 170

service-centric architectures, 181

service-level agreements (SLAs), 139, 171–173, 229

service-oriented architecture (SOA), 67

Colophon

The cover fonts are Akzidenz Grotesk and Orator. The text font is Adobe's Meridien; the heading font is Akzidenz Grotesk; and the code font is LucasFont's TheSansMonoCondensed.

CPSIA information can be obtained at www.ICGtesting.com
Printed in the USA
LVOW11s1547210813

349008LV00020B/842/P

9 781449 377441